RISING ABOVE
THE
MADNESS

Profiles of the Greatest NCAA
Basketball Coaches of All Time

LAURA AMATO

Ulysses Press

Published in the US by:
Ulysses Press
P.O. Box 3440
Berkeley, CA 94703
www.ulyssespress.com

ISBN: 978-1-61243-893-1
Library of Congress Control Number: 2018967984

Printed in Canada by Marquis Book Printing
10 9 8 7 6 5 4 3 2 1

Acquisitions editor: Casie Vogel
Managing editor: Claire Chun
Project editor: Claire Sielaff
Editor: Renee Rutledge
Proofreader: Shayna Keyles
Cover design: Rebecca Lown
Cover artwork: © Oleksii Sidorov/shutterstock.com
Interior artwork: © GoTaR/shutterstock

Distributed by Publishers Group West

CONTENTS

INTRODUCTION

February 9, 1895, Saint Paul, Minnesota. The teams were Hamline University and the Minnesota State School of Agriculture. The game was basketball and it was the first time two college teams squared off on the hardwood. It was history in the making, the start of something that would go on to shape the American athletic world for years to come.

That very first game, reportedly organized by Hamline athletic director Ray Kaighn, was different from the sport we know now. Under the rules set by James Naismith, who invented the sport four years earlier, each team fielded nine players on the court and shot at peach baskets. Minnesota won the game 9–3, not exactly the high-octane, high-energy sport basketball fans have come to know and love.

In those early days of college basketball, most games were scheduled against local YMCA teams, but the game between Hamline and the Minnesota State School of Agriculture marked the first time two collegiate programs had ever faced off. A year later, the University of Iowa and the University of Chicago became the first teams to play with five-man lineups.[1]

The game has, of course, evolved from there. The peach baskets are gone, the scores are substantially higher, and the National Collegiate Athletic Association (NCAA) Tournament, better known as March Madness, has become one of the world's most exciting sporting events each year. The Tournament is an emotional roller coaster, able to inspire and elate casual and die-hard viewers alike. There have been players and moments, games that took fans' breath away and seemed to pause time itself, matchups that have cemented themselves in history and, through it all, coaches pacing the sideline and shouting at referees, the spark that makes their teams go.

Every coach brings something to the game. They inspire and frustrate their teams in equal measure, are lauded by fans and jeered by those who are certain they could do a better job. Every single one of their decisions is questioned and highlighted and, more recently, dissected in detail on late-night sports programming and social media. It's not an easy job—particularly when that job ensures coaches never set a foot on the court or, really, partake in the game at all. But coaches still have as much impact on the game as anyone.

Coaches aren't taking the final-seconds shots, but they draw up those plays. They aren't locking in on defense, but they watch hours of film to fine-tune that defensive approach. They study the game and live the game, hold their breath on every buzzer-beater, and scream as loudly as some of the fans when things don't play out perfectly. Coaches don't pack their own personal stat sheets, but they help shape the game and, sometimes, have such an impact on the game that their names and successes are synonymous with the sport itself. The ten men featured in this anthology are those types of coaches:

---

1 Courtney Martinez, "The First Intercollegiate Basketball Game Was Played on Feb. 8, 1895," NCAA (February 2017), https://www.ncaa.com/news/basketball-men/article/2016-02-09/possible-first-intercollegiate-basketball-game-was-played-feb.

- John Wooden (University of California, Los Angeles)

- Phog Allen (University of Kansas)

- Adolph Rupp (University of Kentucky)

- Dean Smith (University of North Carolina)

- Mike Krzyzewski (Duke University and Army West Point)

- Bobby Knight (Indiana University, Texas Tech, and Army West Point)

- Jerry Tarkanian (University of Nevada, Las Vegas, and Long Beach State)

- Jim Boeheim (Syracuse University)

- Lou Carnesecca (St. John's University)

- Jim Calhoun (University of Connecticut)

These ten coaches didn't just influence the game of college basketball; they changed it, altered the course of it, and made sure that the very first matchup between collegiate teams wasn't some kind of athletic fluke. They helped bring college basketball to the forefront of the sports world, a game that has occasionally been called madness and deserved the title. These men didn't all coach at the same time, but there are connections between them, coaching trees and relationships, and, at the very core, a deep-rooted desire to win.

Even in that very first college basketball game, the coaches of those two teams desperately wanted to win. It's more fun that way. The ten men featured in this anthology went about it differently, each one bringing their own approach and mindset to the hardwood, and their success is unprecedented. They are the best of the best, a marker for other coaches and names even the most casual sports fan is aware of.

CHAPTER ONE

JOHN WOODEN
The Wizard of Westwood

"In the end, it's about the teaching, and what I always loved about coaching was the practices. Not the games, not the tournaments, not the alumni stuff. But teaching the players during practice was what coaching was all about to me."

–JOHN WOODEN

There are great coaches. There are coaches who have won national and conference championships, and mentored some of the most talented players to ever sink a jump shot. There are coaches who have embraced the spotlight and some who have shunned it altogether. And then there is John Wooden.

To say that John Wooden was successful would be a disservice to the word. He was more than that. He was more than the plays he drew up or even the championships he won. Of course, the former UCLA coach won plenty of championships; ten in twelve years, in fact, a mark that still remains one of the most dominant performances by any team in any sport at any time.

Of those ten national championships he won with the UCLA Bruins, seven came in consecutive seasons from 1967 to 1973, and his teams made nine straight Final Four appearances. Wooden also won eighty-eight consecutive games during the 1971, 1972, and 1973 seasons and recorded four perfect records (1964, 1967, 1972, and 1973) as well as eight undefeated conference seasons in the Pac-8. He won just over eighty percent of the games his teams played in over forty years of competition. Wooden was a basketball coach of the highest order. He led his teams to the kind of success that in today's world of one-and-done stars most coaches can only dream about achieving.

Wooden is college basketball. The John R. Wooden award is presented annually to the most outstanding men's and women's college basketball players, and while Wooden hasn't patrolled a sideline in decades, the weight his name carries remains the same. Wooden's legacy and his impact on the sport as a whole are undeniable. He is still regarded as the marker that all other coaches measure themselves against. His accolades are touted throughout the season, highlighted every time the UCLA men's basketball team takes the court because, even after all these years, it's difficult to disassociate Wooden from the program. Wooden's legacy, however, does not merely lie in his victories or his winning percentage.

It's bigger than banners or championship rings or even records that, very likely, will never be broken. Wooden's impact is on the profession itself, a style of coaching that was bigger than directing players or running drills at practice.

Wooden never considered himself simply a coach. He was a teacher and a leader. To understand that kind of coaching mindset, it's important to understand where Wooden came from and, especially, whom he learned everything from.

SMALL-TOWN START

The second son of Hugh Joshua and Roxie Anna Wooden, the eventual Hall of Famer was born in Hall, Indiana, on October 14, 1910. The Wooden family welcomed two more sons in the next four years, moving from small town to small town across the state before finally settling in Martinsville, Indiana. The town boasted a population of fewer than 5,000 people. Wooden's father worked at the local sanitarium to support his family.[2]

It was in Martinsville that everything changed for Wooden. There he met his future wife Nellie, and he started playing basketball. Wooden thrived on the hardwood, learned the ins and outs of the game, and thrilled at the energy from the crowd. It was never big because Martinsville was never big, but the enthusiasm and the sounds were, according to Wooden, more than "anything he experienced at the college level as a coach."[3]

It didn't take long for Wooden to settle into a leadership role with his high school squad. He was named team captain in 1928 but suffered one of the most crushing blows of his early career when his final-second shot attempt in the Indiana state high school championship missed the hoop. Rival school Muncie went on to win the game 13–12, and Wooden never forgot that moment. It was a feeling he despised and one that helped shape his winning mentality for the next fifty years.

Wooden didn't like to lose. He detested the feeling, hated the jeers and the disappointment that came when the final buzzer sounded and his team wasn't on top. Losing didn't often happen for Wooden; he recorded just one such season as a coach when his Dayton Green Devils, a Dayton, Kentucky, high school team, finished 6–11 in 1932, but even the thought of coming up short in the biggest moment was enough to shake him to his core.

---

2 "The Journey," John Wooden, Accessed November 2018, http://www.coachwooden.com/the-journey.

3 "The Journey."

Losing did not make sense to John Wooden. It did, however, make sense to his father.

A FATHER'S ADVICE

Hugh Joshua Wooden grew up poor, without indoor plumbing or electricity. He grew up working, taking odd jobs to help his family and, as far as Wooden knew, never complaining once. That was life, and Joshua Wooden was ready and willing to work.

Wooden described his father's work ethic in 2006, telling *The Los Angeles Times*: "My dad was a gentle man. I never heard him use a word of profanity. I never heard him say an ill word about anybody else. He tried to teach us the farm, and he read scriptures and poetry to us every night by coal lamp."[4]

Joshua Wooden was a simple man. He had simple ideals and believed simple truths, and he was determined to pass them on to his children, including the son who would eventually go on to change the game of basketball.

The story goes like this: When Wooden graduated from eighth grade in 1924, his father handed him a two-dollar bill and a card. On one side of the card, he'd written a poem by Henry Van Dyke, and on the other side of the card, he'd written a list of seven things that, supposedly, had defined his life and would eventually shape Wooden's entire career, both on and off the court.

The list read:

1. Be true to yourself.

2. Help others.

3. Make each day your masterpiece.

---

4 Sam Farmer, "It's No Surprise Where the Legendary UCLA Coach Picked Up His Wholesome Values," *Los Angeles Times,* (June 2006), http://articles.latimes.com/2006/jun/18/sports/sp-wooden18.

4. Drink deeply from good books, especially the Bible.

5. Make friendship a fine art.

6. Build a shelter against a rainy day.

7. Pray for guidance, and count and give thanks for your blessings every day.

The moment changed Wooden's life, and while he never enjoyed losing, his father's list helped him understand and appreciate the lessons that losing provided. Everything was a challenge. Everything was an opportunity to better himself, the people around him, and, as Wooden rose through the coaching ranks over the course of his life, the players who depended on him every time the whistle blew. Wooden described the moment in his autobiography, *My Personal Best: Life Lessons from an All-American Journey*: "I turned the little white card over and saw that Dad had also written down the creed he so often shared with my brothers and me: seven simple rules to follow in life," he wrote. "As I began to read it, he said, 'Johnny, try and live up to these and you'll do all right.'"[5]

The Seven Point Creed was featured in *Guideposts*, a monthly religious magazine with more than one million readers in 1967. At the time, the list was published as an excerpt under the title "The Creed I Try to Live By."

It didn't take long for the message, and Wooden's father, to become as much a part of the coach's story as anything else. Wooden discussed the card and the moment hundreds of times throughout his career, referring to it as the "Seven Point Creed." Joshua Wooden grew into an almost mythical figure, a man wise beyond his years who believed every word he said and wanted to keep his son on the best path. He was a homegrown figure, if not a little old-fashioned, and a reminder of a more optimistic mindset.

"He was a tremendous influence on me, more so than anyone else," Wooden told *The Los Angeles Times*.

---

5 John Wooden and Steve Jamison, *My Personal Best: Life Lessons from an All-American Journey*, (New York: McGraw-Hill Education, 2004).

THE PYRAMID

The Seven Point Creed took on a life of its own throughout Wooden's coaching career, documented in published works and articles, and served as the basis for Wooden's personal philosophy, the Pyramid of Success.

The pyramid, as the name implies, is a set of rules that, if followed, will lead a person to success. It starts off with broad, general ideas for what makes a good person, which include industriousness and enthusiasm, the two cornerstones of the pyramid; as well as friendship, loyalty, and cooperation. A person then works their way up, bolstered by their faith and patience, reaching a different plateau and, along the way, learning different values. The second level of the pyramid includes self-control, alertness, initiative, and intentness, while the third focuses on condition, skill, and team spirit. The fourth adds poise and confidence before an individual reaches the apex and achieves "competitive greatness."

According to Wooden in his book *Wooden on Leadership*, competitive greatness was "having a real love for the hard battle knowing it offers the opportunity to be at your best when your best is required..." Wooden believed a true leader must be a vocal, commanding presence who could inspire those around him with only a few words. The test of a leader was their ability to embrace challenges and rise above them while maintaining a focus on the ultimate goal. Wooden didn't believe leadership automatically led to success, but true leaders persevered through obstacles and continued to put forth their best effort no matter what. That, he believed, would make all the difference.

Wooden's competitive drive was evident every time he stepped onto the court. It grew out of his childhood and the ideals his father set forth, evolving at Martinsville High School and coaching jobs across the country. He found success by approaching the game differently, highlighting the rule of threes: Wooden's game was based on playing with a forward, guard, and center, all of them working together to drive, pass, and shoot the ball. He also highlighted conditioning, skill, and teamwork.[6]

UCLA's play style was revolutionary at the time of Wooden's coaching, focused on ball movement and quick passes that kept opposing defenses from settling into any specific scheme. Wooden preached conditioning to his players. He cared about what his players could control, not what they walked into the gym with. Wooden couldn't make his teams taller, but he could get them to work, and his practices were notorious for running his players ragged.

It was that physicality, however, that led Wooden to trust his players implicitly once they took the court. He couldn't actually play the game, but Wooden's up-tempo style of coaching gave his players the chance to make their own decisions. UCLA rarely ran set plays. The Bruins moved too quickly for that and the team's collective basketball IQ didn't require it. They knew how to pass, so they knew how to get the ball to the hoop and, more importantly, get it through the hoop.

Wooden's coaching style with UCLA didn't undergo many changes during his career, but the Pyramid of Success did not happen overnight, and it saw a handful of changes over the years. It began when he was a student and player at Purdue, while he was studying the pyramids of Giza. Wooden realized that the pyramids needed a strong base and sturdy supporting cornerstones to stand tall. His philosophy included different blocks to represent the ideals he deemed crucial to obtaining success.

Wooden tested several different versions of the pyramid over the years, looking to find the perfect combination of ideals. The only elements that were kept from the original draft were the cornerstones of industriousness and enthusiasm, as well as the use of faith and patience to move up the pyramid. Wooden's effect on college basketball continued even after his coaching career ended, thanks in large part to his

---

6 "John Wooden," Basketball Hall of Fame, accessed November 2018, http://www.hoophall .com/hall-of-famers/john-wooden1.

philosophies. He wrote books, toured the country, and spoke publicly about the positive impact of the pyramid.

To this day, other big names in athletics continue to credit Wooden's philosophy for their own success, including his former player and current ESPN broadcaster Bill Walton, former New York Yankees manager Joe Torre, and the legendary Dick Vitale. The Wooden Effect (#thewoodeneffect) even made its way to Twitter in November 2016 as thousands of people, both in the sports world and out of it, detailed the way the former coach influenced their lives.

Wooden, at his core, wanted to be the best, and part of that determination was born because he wanted to live up to the marker his father set for him. He wanted to make his parents proud. He wanted to make his hometown proud. It worked. He did just that and, even now, continues to be one of the most inspirational names in any sport, at any level. It was also based, at least, partially, on a lie.

A CHANCE FINDING

Paul Putz wasn't looking for information about John Wooden. A PhD candidate at Baylor University, Putz's dissertation focuses on the blending of athletics and religion, detailing the cross-section of the two and how, more often than not, the lines between what most would consider vastly different things tend to blur together. He'd heard of Wooden, of course, particularly during his own high school basketball career when his coach would reference stories of the legendary Hall of Famer before games or during practices. It was that familiarity, however, that led Putz to find something he never expected to find.

Putz was flipping through issues of *The American Magazine*, a publication that, at its height in the 1920s and '30s, was read by nearly two million people across the country. He was reading what he thought was a run-of-the-mill issue when he came across a January 1931 article titled "Help Yourself to Happiness," based on an interview with John H. Clarke, a former Supreme Court Justice who resigned from his position in 1922. Originally not thinking much of the story, Putz traced over words and paragraphs, then realized something. The words sounded very familiar. In fact, they were almost identical to John Wooden's Seven Point Creed, the same mantra Putz's high school basketball coach had quoted more than once.

Clarke's advice for happiness was an almost word for word copy of Wooden's famous creed, with one glaring difference. The list published in *The American Magazine* was only six points, condensed by writer Merle Crowell, who introduced them as "a few simple rules...that any one of us can follow with profit." It was a jarring discovery for Putz who, like most sports fans, believed that Wooden's Seven Point Creed was created and passed on to him by his father, Joshua.

"I considered Wooden sort of a hero of mine," Putz said. "I was familiar with [the Creed] and then I saw this [article]. And when I looked at it and read it, I noticed right away that it was basically the exact same list that I had learned for John Wooden's Seven Point Creed."

Clarke was just one of the many men profiled in *The American Magazine* over the course of its publication. He was, at the time, a picture of success, the kind of man whom the general populace would look to and seek to emulate. In fact, *The American Magazine* regularly prided itself on its ability to highlight "traditional nineteenth-century values alongside the more modern precepts of teamwork, cooperation, and open-mindedness." This was not a periodical that focused on material gain, but rather social and ethical constructs, homespun values that resonated with Middle America and a society that was hoping to find a light at the end of the tunnel during the Great Depression.[7]

The six-point list inspired by Clarke and detailed by Crowell wasn't groundbreaking advice. It was simple words and simple thoughts meant for an audience seeking entertainment and guidance when the rest of the world appeared to be falling apart around them. At the time,

---

7 Paul Putz, "John Wooden's Homespun Creed Was Not So Homespun," *Slate,* (May 2017), https://slate.com/culture/2017/05/john-woodens-seven-point-creed-came-from-a-1931-magazine-article.html.

the United States was facing an unemployment rate of 15.9 percent, the drought in the South continued and, just a few weeks after Clarke's advice was published, food riots broke out as people desperately tried to keep their families fed.[8]

Clarke's advice was easy. It was uplifting. It was hopeful. Work hard and good things will happen. But its existence means that Wooden's father was not the folk hero he's grown into over the last few decades. He was, much like the rest of the country, a man who read a magazine and saw a list he agreed with. But the question remains, when did that list become Wooden's Seven Point Creed, and how did the legend grow into something high school basketball players still learn about to this day?

"It's all incredibly interesting," Putz said. "Somewhere along the line, something got translated and copied, and it's grown into this thing that is only associated with Wooden."

PARENTAL CONTROL

The first time Wooden spoke about the Seven Point Creed was for a 1956 article in *The Los Angeles Times*. He was quoted saying that he told his players at UCLA about his father's advice and "an adopted creed, which I have always carried in my wallet," and that he used the words to help focus on character and strong life values. At that time, Wooden listed the same six points that appeared in *The American Magazine* twenty-five years before. He didn't mention the seventh point, nor did he add "especially the Bible" after the fourth point. Wooden also never mentioned that his father was the one to come up with the life-changing advice.

Joshua Wooden did not write his son's Seven Point Creed, nor did he come up with the six pieces of advice detailed in a popular periodical. It's also safe to assume that Joshua Wooden did not, as the story now goes, give his son the advice when he graduated from middle school.

---

8 Kimberly Amadeo, "Great Depression Timeline," *The Balance,* (April 2018), https://www .thebalance.com/great-depression-timeline-1929-1941-4048064.

The list was published in 1931, while Wooden was enrolled at Purdue University. But it clearly resonated with Joshua, and Putz believes that Wooden kept the card in his wallet throughout his coaching career.

Wooden respected his father. He trusted his father and valued the same values his father did, and widely discussed the impact his father had on his life and his career, but Joshua Wooden was not a great mind nor remotely philosophical. He was a man who wanted to help his son, who read something, believed it, and thought it may be useful. So he copied it. That doesn't mean, however, that he did it with anything except the best intentions.

"I don't think there's anything…devious about what he did, at all," Putz said. "Wooden would talk about his father often and in other stories, he often talked about the wisdom he received from his father."

Even if the specifics of the story have grown hazy over the years, Wooden's father wasn't doing anything out of the ordinary for a man of his time. Clarke's list was meant to be seen and meant to influence. It was, in all likelihood, even meant to be copied, the advice applied practically to everyday life in an America that was desperately looking for something to believe in. Joshua Wooden believed in the list and, as of 1956, so did John Wooden. There was nothing backhanded about any of it, but at some point, Clarke's list became Wooden's Seven Point Creed, and the legendary coach's story started changing a bit.

GETTING THE DETAILS RIGHT

Wooden's depiction of his father began to change around 1966 when the creed was discussed in an article for the book *Courage to Conquer: America's Athletes Speak Their Faith*. That book didn't reach a large audience, and the crossover between those readers and people who may have seen Clarke's list in *The American Magazine* were few and far between, but there was certainly an interest regarding Wooden's father and the advice he passed on. The coach spoke about his father with pride, referred to him in his autobiography and, in 1968, a revised version of the creed was syndicated and sent to newspapers across the United States as part of a "Lenten Guideposts" series. Wooden's Seven Point Creed had suddenly reached a national audience, and it wasn't the same set of rules he'd detailed in *The Los Angeles Times*. This version included the story that Wooden received the list from his father when he graduated middle school, and that Joshua had come up with the ideals himself, naming it "Seven Things to Do." The revised creed also added the seventh point, which included a focus on religion that Judge Clarke did not allude to in *The American Magazine*.

It was after that publication that Wooden's mythos started to take off, and, again, the state of the country at the time may have played a large part in the public's initial response. The United States was at war in 1968, fighting in Vietnam while protests raged across college campuses and cities. At the same time, the Civil Rights Movement was in full swing, with students speaking out against racism, sexual and societal traditions, and most authority figures. Whether it was intentional or not, Wooden, in the midst of his legendary national championship run, became a symbol of Middle America, a success story borne from the purest of ideals. People began to flock to that.

"I think there is something about him that people connect to," Putz said. "I think, sort of the cult surrounding Wooden since he retired, is driven by this deeply held belief in the mythology. They're the kids of small-town America. The idea that anyone can be successful in life if they practice and follow these basic, common rules for life."

Wooden's homespun wisdom, and the ideal of his father as an everyman who worked as hard as he could and did his best to provide for his children, grew throughout the late '60s and even into the early '70s. Putz suggests that it was likely a direct response to the culture and climate of the era, an homage to simpler times, in the same way that Clarke's original list was in the 1930s. But it also may not have been Wooden's idea to spin the narrative in that direction.

"The idea that this all originated from the common man, folky Midwesterner, that really gets played up in the '60s," Putz said. "That might have been the *Guideposts* editors who thought it would resonate with Middle Americans who were pining for the nostalgia and simpler times."

Putz adds that despite the nostalgia associated with him, the legend of Wooden always begins with his coaching tenure. At the time when the creed was published in 1968, Wooden was winning basketball games, garnering headlines, and sparking an interest in college basketball that had never been seen before. He was a celebrity in his own right, a name that people knew whether they understood or were even interested in the game. Wooden won in a way that may never be duplicated, but after he walked away from the game, it was his belief system that was most inspiring to people. No one was ever going to be a coach like Wooden, but, maybe, if they followed his rules for life—the Seven Point Creed or the Pyramid of Success—they'd be able to find success in their own field. That's the draw of Wooden today. It's why so many people still regard him as one of the most prominent names in any field, at any level, and why he continues to be discussed even years after he left UCLA. He's a goal as much as a person, a standard by which to measure oneself and one's own work ethic.

Wooden's success has always been marketable, first when he was a coach and filling seats at basketball games, but then in print. There have been dozens of stories and books detailing every aspect of his life. That, of course, includes the creed and the ever-growing legacy of Joshua Wooden. The facts have changed, but the message has mostly stayed the same, and it's a message that resonates just as strongly now as it did in the Great Depression and the 1960s.

KEEPING THE LEGACY ALIVE

Pat Williams wrote a book about Wooden in 2011, *Coach Wooden: The 7 Principles That Shaped His Life and Will Change Yours*, and in it he asked some of the coach's former players what they remembered most about the Seven Point Creed. Most of them didn't remember the specifics. They said they didn't speak much about it while they were playing, and while Wooden's advice was certainly important throughout their lives, those seven bullet points didn't have any seriously lasting impact on the way they presented themselves to the rest of the world. The same can't be said, however, for the hundreds of thousands of people who still revere Wooden.

The basketball world regards him as one of the best to ever play or coach, but there's also a group, one that Putz refers to as "the cult of Wooden," who view his messages off the court as even more important. They aren't athletes. They're businessmen and associates, professionals, and the furthest thing from Middle America as anyone could imagine. It's almost ironic, after the transition the creed went through, but the message first published for Middle America in *The American Magazine* still rings true for these career-oriented people nearly eighty years later.

"The people who love Wooden now, they're extremely successful and clearly in tune with modern capitalism," Putz said. "They also, I think, find in Wooden a way to justify their own success or connect their success in modern life with the values they lived with as kids. It's an essence of America they imagine themselves to be connected to."

Wooden's impact on the American culture, not just basketball, is obvious. He believed in things and helped spark that same belief in generations, even after his retirement and death. Wooden's old-fashioned convictions are comforting. They're a reminder of a simpler time and an easy way of life, the certainty that hard work leads to positive outcomes simply because that's the way the universe should respond.

But Wooden was more than that. His success on the basketball court cannot be overstated. Wooden won more awards and more honors than there is room for in any book. He was enshrined in nearly a dozen different Halls of Fame at a variety of levels and, in 2006, on his ninety-sixth birthday, a post office in Reseda, California, was renamed the Coach John Wooden Post Office. That is the kind of influence he had. His impact on the game and the names we now consider legendary is apparent every time a new college basketball season starts. Kareem Abdul-Jabbar's legacy began at UCLA, working with Wooden and forming a relationship he chronicled in his book *Coach Wooden and Me: Our 50-Year Friendship On and Off the Court*. Bill Walton, now known for his enthusiastic commentary during college basketball season, also played under Wooden before being selected first overall in the 1974 NBA Draft. Meanwhile, Walton's son, Luke, is now the head coach of the Los Angeles Lakers.

Wooden's legacy is apparent on other NBA teams as well, including the Golden State Warriors. Bob Meyers, the Warriors' general manager, played at UCLA in the late '90s, long after Wooden coached, but said he was still inspired by the coach. He told CBS Sports his favorite Wooden quote has resonated with him throughout Golden State's run, saying, "'It's amazing what you can accomplish when no one cares who gets the credit.' And I think that epitomizes our group."[9]

When Wooden passed away in 2010, many of his former players were unable to bring themselves to speak publicly, too overcome with emotion at the loss of a man who helped shape their lives on and off the court. He instructed his players on how to carry themselves long after the game ended, and while some couldn't quote the Seven Point Creed or the Pyramid of Success, the memories of those lessons lingered decades after they were first spoken.

"He rarely talked about basketball, but generally about life," Walton said in a release from UCLA after Wooden's death. "He never talked about strategy, statistics, or plays, but rather about people and character. Coach Wooden never tired of telling us that once you become a

---

9 Zach Harper, "Warriors' Bob Myers Patiently Built the Next Influential Team Model," CBS Sports (June 2015), https://www.cbssports.com/nba/news/warriors-bob-myers-patiently-built -the-next-influential-team-model.

good person, then you have a chance of becoming a good basketball player."[10]

Wooden's nostalgic way of looking at the world may not be entirely accurate, and his father's advice may not have been much more than a magazine clipping. Joshua Wooden was only a father trying to do his best, the card may or may not have stayed in Wooden's wallet for his entire coaching career, and the reasons why any of it changed may never be truly known or understood. It really doesn't matter. Wooden's victories and his approach to the world as a whole are what have stood the test of time.

Wooden never wanted his career to be just about basketball, and it's not. It's about work and responsibility and, at its core, being good. The values are still there, just as relevant as ever no matter the journey they took to get to this point. Should that journey change the way we look at Wooden? Maybe. Maybe not. This was a man who inspired players and fans alike, whose philosophies are still driving trends on social media, and no matter what, those national championship banners at UCLA are going to remain a marker of the lasting influence Wooden will have.

It was never about wins or losses, but they're still pretty darn impressive.

● ● ● ● ●

BREAKING DOWN THE PYRAMID

The story behind Wooden's Seven Point Creed has become a convoluted one over the years, but the origins of his Pyramid of Success have been well-documented since he first started detailing its specifics. Wooden initially toyed with the idea of the pyramid while he was still playing college basketball at Purdue University. The then-teenaged Wooden had watched his parents work as hard as possible to take care of their family, taking odd jobs and putting their, quite literal, blood, sweat, and tears into the work. It was a

10 Office of Media Relations, "John Wooden's Former Players React to the Death of Their Coach," UCLA Athletics Newsroom (June 2010), http://newsroom.ucla.edu/stories/ john-wooden-s-former-players-react-159695.

mindset that influenced Wooden throughout his own career, and one that he realized required a certain personal fortitude.

Wooden's pyramid went through a handful of revisions throughout his years in college and even through his early coaching positions, but the general idea of it was always the same. Work hard, respect others, and then, for good measure, work a little harder again. The pyramid itself isn't easy to ascend. It begins with vague ideas about what makes a person good and the sort of ideals that help a person find happiness, generic beliefs that range from loyalty to friendship and cooperation. Wooden was always focused on individual success, but he was a coach and he understood better than anyone the importance of teamwork and understanding. The first level of the pyramid shows that. No one is an island and, according to Wooden, finding and building those bonds with whatever type of team may be around you is crucial to jumpstarting any sort of victory.

After understanding the first five blocks of the pyramid, an individual was able to move to the next level, buoyed by the use of faith and patience. Wooden honored those values, perhaps, more than anything else, and frequently spoke about his own belief system throughout the course of his career.

The use of faith and a belief in a power bigger than the self was critical in achieving any kind of success in Wooden's eyes. His pyramid never required a specific religion or a specific god, but understanding that there was more to the world than simply physical achievements remained at the crux of Wooden's teachings.

He was a devout Christian, reportedly read the Bible daily, and frequently said he hoped his faith helped inspired others. Wooden even went so far as to say in *Wooden: A Lifetime of Observations and Reflections On and Off the Court* that if he were to ever face religious persecution, he hoped there was simply "enough evidence to convict" him. Wooden also said that despite the numerous honors he racked up throughout his career, being named "Outstanding

Basketball Coach of the US" in 1969 by the Christian Church in America was the most important.[11]

Each level of the pyramid continued to focus on different aspects of a person's self-worth, relying on the ever-growing faith and patience to hone each skill. It's interesting to point out, however, that things like skill and confidence don't appear on the pyramid until the upper levels. Natural skill wasn't important to Wooden. He appreciated it, of course, loved when a player could sink a basket with ease or settle into a defensive scheme without much prompting from the sidelines, but it wasn't the key to success. Wooden's pyramid, instead, focused on hard work and a determination to be better every single day.

"If you make the effort to do the best of which you're capable, try to improve the situation that exists for you, I think that's success," Wooden said during a 2009 TED Talk.

The apex of Wooden's pyramid is competitive greatness, an ideal that at first glance is more than a little confusing because none of Wooden's pyramid is explicitly about winning. This is not a basketball play. It's not the blueprint for a buzzer-beater shot. It's far bigger than that. Wooden defined competitive greatness as "be at your best when your best is needed. Enjoyment of a difficult challenge."

Wooden didn't care if anyone won, whether it was at basketball or a job promotion or getting through dinner without setting the smoke alarm off. He wanted to win, that much is obvious in his basketball career, but if Wooden had never won the championships, never hung the banners or been enshrined in the Naismith Memorial Basketball Hall of Fame, he still would have been content with his career as long as one thing was true—he tried. Competitive greatness does not require a 100 percent win rate. That's unreasonable. It does require an attempt. You've got to turn the oven on to make the dinner, or lace up your sneakers and, at least, stand on the basketball court. There has to be a goal and it has to be worked for. If

---

11 "Coach John Wooden—Biography," UCLA Bruins, accessed November 2018, https://uclabruins.com/sports/2013/4/17/208274589.aspx.

there's an attempt—a real, honest attempt and a work ethic—then, as far as Wooden was concerned, the person was successful.[12]

The Pyramid of Success is far from perfect. It's not an exact set of rules for every person in every situation, but the message behind it has resonated with generations long after Wooden walked away from college basketball in 1975. This is his legacy.

"My players will tell you that I never mentioned winning," Wooden said in 2009. "I just wanted them to be able to hold their head up after a game. That's what really matters."

Wooden coached college basketball for twenty-nine years. He spent twenty-seven of those years at UCLA. He died in 2010. But Wooden's approach to life and his determination, even obsession, with being the best version of himself no matter the circumstances continues to be the driving force behind his reputation. He toured the country long after he stopped coaching, discussing the levels of the pyramid and the meaning behind each one. Wooden inspired the people who listened to him and continues to do the same for the people who learn about him and the pyramid, as hopeful as ever that hard work will lead to greatness.

● ● ● ● ●

Wooden's Best Games

The First Championship

When UCLA hired John Wooden in 1948, the idea of a national title run was almost laughable. The players, pieces, and culture for that kind of success simply didn't exist. Wooden, naturally, balked at that idea. It took some time, but the Bruins captured a national championship in the 1963–64 season, defeating Duke in historic fashion.

It was UCLA's first title appearance and the squad's recently acquired fast-paced approach to the game that helped notch a 98–83 victory

---

12 "Pyramid of Success," John Wooden, accessed November 2018, http://www.coach wooden.com/pyramid-of-success.

over the Blue Devils. The Bruins had to play quickly—they didn't boast a single player over six foot five.

Some of the names from UCLA's first championship roster still hold weight in the college basketball world and, interestingly enough, the business world. Jack Hirsch, who only agreed to attend UCLA if his father quit smoking, left basketball after graduating, joining both of his family's businesses: bowling alleys and pornography. Buzzy Harrison walked away from the game despite a fantastic jump shot and became a doctor twice over, earning degrees in divinity and medicine. Walt Hazzard was the top pick in the 1964 NBA Draft, and while he never became a star at the pro level, he never left the game either and returned to coach at UCLA in 1984. Keith Erickson, whom Wooden regarded as one of the best athletes he ever coached, went to the 1964 Olympics as a volleyball player before competing in the NBA for a decade.[13]

The Last Championship

The cliché is a cliché for a reason—save the best for last. Wooden won his tenth and final championship in 1975, leading UCLA to a victory over Kentucky, but it was the game before, a dramatic OT showing against Louisville, that brought more drama than any screenwriter in Los Angeles could dream of.

Louisville star Terry Howard hadn't missed a free throw in his twenty-eight attempts all season, but with a 74–73 lead over the Bruins and twenty seconds left in OT, his attempt rang off the front end of the hoop. It was the loudest sound in the arena, at least until UCLA hauled in the rebound, got the ball across half-court, and called timeout with thirteen seconds left on the clock.

Wooden drew up the play. His players believed it would win them the game. Andre McCarter caught the inbound, passed it to Marques Johnson who, in turn, saw Richard Washington cutting toward the block. He passed the ball and an entire arena held its breath. Washington

---

13 Reeves Wiedeman, "Catching Up with the Players from the 1964 NCAA Championship Game," *New York Magazine* (March 2014), http://nymag.com/intelligencer/2014/03/march-madness-memories-1964-championship.html.

turned, hit the eight-foot jumper, and gave the Bruins a lead they'd never surrender, keeping the season alive and adding one more notch on Wooden's ever-growing legacy.

Wooden captured his tenth national title two days later on March 31, 1975, but the emotions from the Final Four and the legendary coach's announcement that he was retiring afterward set the win over Louisville apart from all the others. It was special. It was the end. And it was just as sweet as it had always been.[14]

---

14 Gerard Gilberto, "#Flashback Friday: March 29, 1975 -March 31, 1975," NCAA (February 2015) https://amp.ncaa.com/news/basketball-men/flashback-friday/2015-02-13/going-out-style.

CHAPTER TWO

PHOG ALLEN
The Father of Basketball Coaching

"The story of basketball is Naismith inventing it and Phog Allen popularizing it. The two of them worked together at Kansas."

—DAVID BOOTH

There is a street in Lawrence, Kansas, called Naismith Drive, a half-mile away from where the University of Kansas basketball team plays. It's not an unusual street, nothing particularly notable about it except its name. Naismith, after all, refers to James Naismith, the inventor of basketball and a man who helped shape one of the most storied programs in college history simply by teaching his game to another man—Phog Allen.

Allen didn't invent basketball; he didn't even help come up with the idea, but he did help perfect it, and he did that at Kansas. Allen's relationship with Naismith, a mentorship that defined his career and the careers of so many others, has become the stuff of basketball legend and the subject of dozens of stories, documentaries, and discussions. It was also valued at $4.3 million. That's the price David Booth paid for two worn, typewritten pages on which Naismith wrote down his original thirteen rules of basketball, the same rules he taught Allen in Lawrence, Kansas.[15]

It was, at the time of its sale in December 2010, the most anyone had ever paid for a piece of sports memorabilia, far surpassing the $3 million spent for Mark McGwire's seventieth home run ball in 1998.

Bidding on the rules originally began at $1.4 million, but Booth refused to back down even as the price continued to climb. This was a piece of Americana, an artifact that not only changed the way the country views sports, but also changed Allen's life and set the entire state of Kansas on a path that it's still walking to this day, one of basketball dominance and influence, and a coaching tree that is, unquestionably, one of the most impressive in any sport.

The history of college basketball begins at the University of Kansas, with Allen reading those pages and learning a game that would influence the athletic world more than a century after its original inception. The pages are still housed at the school, and Booth has spent years working with the University to build a facility focused specifically on showcasing the rules.

There is no game without those rules, but there is no basketball culture, no widespread fandom or kids who grow up wanting to be coaches, without Allen. He learned at the feet of Naismith, memorized all thirteen rules, and brought basketball to the forefront of American athletic culture.

A FOOT IN THE DOOR

Forrest "Phog" Allen arrived on the Kansas campus in 1905 with sky-high expectations and a reputation that grew every time he stepped onto a basketball court. He was one of the first recruits in Jayhawks' history, a name spoken in whisper and excitement, in discussions of

15 Richard Sandomir, "Naismith's Papers Fetch Record $4.3 Million," *New York Times* (December 2010), https://www.nytimes.com/2010/12/11/sports/ncaabasketball/11naismith .html.

his talent and what he could do to help the team win. Allen was going to put Kansas on the basketball map, an admittedly young one, but as the game grew in popularity, so did the hype surrounding it. And there was plenty of hype surrounding Allen.

It started two years before, when Allen competed for the Kansas City Athletic Club (KCAC). He was regarded as one of the best players on the roster and, in February 1904, was elected as the team's captain, leading the squad to a 27–10 victory over the University of Kansas. The entire state sat up and took notice. Allen didn't slow down, nor did he stop putting the ball in the hoop.

In 1904, at the first-ever national Amateur Athletic Union (AAU) tournament, the Germans, a team from Buffalo, New York, breezed by the competition. They started to call themselves national champions, but Allen, then just nineteen years old, didn't take kindly to the self-imposed title. He sent a telegram to the team, inviting them to Kansas City for a three-game series. Allen even offered to pay for the team to get there. The Germans accepted, a move not many except Allen expected, including his own team. He'd mentioned neither his invitation to the Germans nor the now-planned basketball series.

Allen didn't miss a beat, or a basket. He found investors for the series, booked the 5,000-seat Convention Hall in Kansas City for the games, and sparked enough interest that the *Kansas City Star* reported on the upcoming event. *The Star* interviewed then-Kansas basketball coach and inventor of the sport James Naismith about the games, as well as his clear interest in the young upstart Allen. Naismith gave the edge to the Germans, but added that if "Kansas City's teamwork [was] on par with its individual players..." then the "Buffalo men ... will have their work cut out for them."

Kansas City turned out in droves for the games, which drew nearly 10,000 spectators over the course of three days in March 1905. The teams split the first two games, but neither side trusted the officiators for the rubber match and, at the request of the Germans, Naismith stepped in to referee his own sport. Allen impressed the coach, connecting on seventeen free throws and leading KCAC to a 45–15 victory over the AAU champions.

The event made Allen a local legend and basketball hero, and his performance piqued Naismith's interest in him. It was the start of a relationship that would alter both men's careers, and when Allen arrived on the University of Kansas campus, the school paper celebrated him as "the best goal thrower in the world."

In his first-ever game for the Jayhawks, Allen scored twenty-three of his team's thirty-seven points, leading Kansas to a victory over Nebraska, and in his final game that season, he scored twenty-six of his team's sixty points. The performance was a record-setting one for Kansas, a scoring mark that stood for nearly a decade, and Allen led the Jayhawks to their most successful record under Naismith that year. But lightning, as they say, can't strike twice, and despite a dominant freshman season, Allen's playing career would never be the same.[16]

SIDELINE STORY

Allen was elected team captain after his freshman season at Kansas and, as far as anyone on the team knew, was ready and willing to return to the hardwood in late 1906. Money, however, was an issue. Allen didn't have much. There's no concrete record of where Allen was actually born; some records list his hometown as Jameson, Missouri, some list it as Jamison, but the most common story was that he was born in Jamesport on November 18, 1885. It doesn't matter what the name of the town was, the only thing that mattered was that it was small. It was rural. It was Middle America before Middle America was a term. Even today, the area is home to historic Mormon religious sites and Amish and Mennonite farmers still work the land, doing their best to provide for their families. Not much has changed in the last hundred years.

---

16 Mark D. Hersey, "Phog's First Farewell," KU History (March 2018), http://kuhistory.com/articles/phogs-first-farewell.

Allen's father served as the Jamesport town clerk, collector, and constable, and the family struggled more often than not. Allen saw basketball not just as a game but a means to an end, a chance to better his station in life and fuel that competitive edge that had been growing in him from the time he was born—wherever that might have been. So, despite being elected team captain and being a bona fide basketball star, Allen left Kansas after his freshman season to pursue other, more lucrative, opportunities and a chance to influence the game the way he wanted.[17]

"[Dr. Naismith] was more interested in the game as a way to provide exercise and develop character," said Curtis N. Marsh, the director of the DeBruce Center at University of Kansas. "He was not very intrigued with the notion of coaching it, so when he had Phog Allen on his team [Allen] told the coach, you know, I think we can do some things as a team that will enhance our chances of winning a few more games. He left KU to get that started."

Allen was offered a coaching position at Baker University, a school just thirty minutes away from Lawrence. He wanted to come back to the University of Kansas, to compete again and possibly break a few of his own records, but the Baker deal came with a stipend as well as room and board, and the chance was too good to pass up.

There are multiple reports of what happened next. Some documents claim Allen continued to play while also coaching at Baker, some say he didn't, while others say that the future Hall of Famer was a three-time letter-winner at Kansas. The one thing, however, that remains true is that Allen caught the coaching bug as soon as he stepped onto the campus at Baker, and while his playing career may have never taken off the way he originally intended, he still found his calling and maintained his love of the game.

Allen squared off against his mentor in 1907 as Baker defeated Kansas 39–24, and, once again, Naismith's interest was piqued. Naismith

---

17 Clinton Thomas, "The Man Behind March Madness," *News Press Now* (March 2009), http://www.newspressnow.com/news/the-man-behind-march-madness/article_eaa2fef0-85ed-530d-b526-9663e9447682.html.

stepped away from coaching in 1907, and it didn't take long for Allen to assume the position. As far as Naismith was concerned, there was no other man for the job at Kansas, and the school, the state, and its fans were thrilled by the return of their prodigal basketball son. Kansas captured its first Missouri Valley Conference championship under Allen, posting an 18–4 record in his first season on the sidelines.

Once again, however, Allen's interests strayed away from the game. He left Kansas in 1909, this time to enroll at Central College of Osteopathy. That's right, the kid from a hometown no one is entirely sure of, whose name is synonymous with coaching dominance, was also a doctor.

Allen suffered from back problems throughout his playing and early coaching days and, after he was displeased with the care he received from area physicians, decided to do something about it himself. It was the same drive that led him to take on the Germans and enroll at Kansas, and Allen met every medical school challenge head on. Not one to shy away from anything, Allen embraced medicine like he'd done everything else, in perfect stride.

Although he didn't stay in school long, graduating from Central College in 1912, Allen never left the medical profession, even once he started coaching again. He returned to Kansas in 1919, after stops at Haskell Institute and Central (Missouri) State Teachers College, and continued to treat players across the sports world for the rest of his career. The Kansas City Athletic Club, the same team Allen played for from 1903 to 1905, sent players to visit him throughout his time coaching at KU, and Johnny Mize, a standout with the New York Yankees, hit twenty-five home runs in the final ninety games of the 1950 season after receiving treatment from Allen.[18]

Allen's players never called him coach. They called him "Doc," and for the nearly fifty years he spent patrolling the Kansas sidelines, Allen was just that. He was a doctor and a fixer and a coach, a father figure to an

18 Blair Kerkhoff, "Phog Allen: Remembered as a Jayhawk but His Greatness Began in Jackson County," Jackson County Historical Society Journal (2014), www.jchs.org.

entire generation of basketball talent that learned the ins and outs of the game from a man who'd gotten it straight from the source.

The entire Kansas campus revered Allen, but not just for his successes on the hardwood. There were plenty of those, of course, but Allen's influence didn't begin or end at practice. It lasted a lifetime, on and off the court, in doctor's appointments and one-on-one meetings, in explanations of game plans and road trips. Allen was the kind of man who spent hours in the gym, but also refused to close his private osteo-pathic practice. His son Bob, who played for him at Kansas in the early 1940s, kept the family's medical tradition alive, working as a doctor at St. Luke's Hospital in Kansas City, Missouri, where he also served as chairman of the department of surgery and president of the surgical staff.[19]

Allen never let expectations get in the way of what he wanted. He wanted to challenge the Germans to a basketball game, so he planned a tournament. He wanted a medical degree and some extra income for his family while he was coaching, so he got one and kept his practice open for decades. He wanted to up the tempo of basketball, to bring in star recruits and lift Kansas to the pinnacle of the sport. So that's exactly what he did. Allen wasn't only a basketball coach, he was an innovator, and throughout his career with the Jayhawks, he sparked a wave of change that still has ripple effects on the game today.

GETTING LOUD

When Naismith invented basketball at a YMCA in 1891, he did so with one intention: to allow gentleman to exercise and burn off extra energy indoors when they couldn't play soccer outside in the winter. It was a slow sport, methodical and low-scoring. It was, at times, incredi-bly boring. Allen played the sport that way originally, thriving under Naismith's system while he was at Kansas, but that competitive streak

---

19 Mike Belt, "Kansas Basketball Family Mourns Allen's Death," KU Sports (April 2003), http://www2.kusports.com/news/2003/apr/06/kansas_basketball_family.

was still a mile wide, and when he took over his own team in Lawrence, he wanted to change the game.

Allen believed in rivalries. He believed in high-scoring contests and quick-moving plays that would excite a jam-packed crowd. He didn't simply want a friendly contest between a few sporting chaps. Allen wanted games and feeling and noise. He wanted excitement. He wanted to get loud.

His players called him "Doc," but Allen was also known as "Phog" throughout his career, a nickname he picked up while umpiring baseball games. As the story goes, his voice was something akin to a fog horn, the same sound that helps ships make their way through choppy waters and dangerous shores, finding a harbor before a storm descends on them. It might not have been the most complimentary of nicknames, but it was accurate, and Allen's association with the sound was also synonymous with the way he coached.

Allen's enthusiastic approach to the game changed the way it was viewed across the country. His 1922 and 1923 teams captured the Helms Foundation National Championship, a title later regarded as the earliest incarnation of the NCAA title. His 1940 and 1953 teams won the NCAA Western Championships before losing in the national finals, but it was Allen's 1952 squad at Kansas that truly changed everything.

This was still in the early days of the NCAA Tournament, with a field of only sixteen teams, but the Jayhawks were brimming with confidence after a regular season that saw them post a 28–3 record and an 11–1 showing in the Big Seven conference. This was a team that lost back-to-back games just once all season and racked up thirteen straight victories with its eyes on a national championship and Allen's voice ringing in its collective ears. According to Bill Mayer, who chronicled Kansas's run for the *Lawrence Journal-World* that season, it was those back-to-back losses that made the biggest difference for the Jayhawks.

Mayer claimed that Allen pulled then-assistant coach Dick Harp aside after Kansas' second loss at Oklahoma State, demanding a change.

Allen told him, "I don't know what you're going to do, Dick, but get something done. Do something." Harp and Allen worked closely together during their time in Lawrence, and the assistant had been toying with the idea of changing the defense that season.

He suggested the shift to Allen, who responded in kind, implementing a man-to-man press that was unlike anything the college basketball world had seen at that point. The press, a defensive scheme that brings pressure before the opposing team has crossed half-court, was more aggressive than anything Allen had devised before. The Jayhawks moved quickly, swarming to the ball with the deft-footed backcourt of Dean Kelley and Bill Hougland. The defense changed Kansas for the better that season, making the Jayhawks a force to be reckoned with, and other teams simply could not keep up. The press forced opposing teams to play at the Jayhawks' tempo and rushed the otherwise slow-moving offenses. Kansas attacked from every angle, getting out in transition and racking up points as the ball moved from the backcourt to the frontcourt and a massive target underneath the hoop. It was, after all, difficult to miss Clyde Lovellette.[20]

An imposing figure at five foot nine and 234 pounds, Lovellette was known as "the Great White Whale" during his time at Kansas. He earned first-team All-American honors and was the kind of player that Allen had been waiting for, one that would help change the game and usher in a new era of big men on the block. Lovellette took up space, an undeniably strong presence under the hoop with an athleticism that, occasionally, intimidated opposing defenders. He was talented as well as tall, averaging twenty-five points per game throughout the course of his career in a Jayhawks uniform. His senior season in 1952 was one of the best by any Kansas player in program history.

Allen trusted Lovellette, both on and off the court. He consistently told his other players to "get the ball to Clyde," certain that any open look

20 Jesse Newell, "Jayhawk Flashback: Video of 1952 NCAA Championship Game," KU Sports (May 2010), http://www2.kusports.com/news/2010/may/28/jayhawk-flashback-video -1952-ncaa-championship-gam.

he had at the basket would end with points, but the pair were also close even after the final whistle blew. Allen, who was notoriously nervous on planes, was jittery on the team's flight to Seattle for the 1952 championship game, and Lovellette was always quick with a joke and a smile. "Relax, Doc," Lovellette said. "If we pile in, you're dressed for the funeral." It was enough to calm Allen down and, per Mayer, help ease any anxious energy the team was feeling ahead of its final game because, as far as the Jayhawks were concerned, if Lovellette was ready to go, so were they.

Lovellette was the foundation upon which the Jayhawks' entire 1951–52 season was built. He averaged 28.4 points and 12.8 rebounds per game and didn't miss a beat in the NCAA Tournament, scoring thirty-one points in Kansas' opening-round victory over Texas Christian University. He added a forty-four-point performance, going twelve of fourteen from the free throw line against St. Louis, and poured in thirty-three points against Santa Clara in the national semifinal.

Kansas squared off against an underdog St. John's team in the national championship, but the Jayhawks hardly flinched en route to an 80–63 victory. Lovellette, again, dominated on both sides of the ball, finishing his final college game with thirty-three points and seventeen rebounds. It was the first national championship for Kansas in the modern era, and the success of that season shaped the program for the next seventy years.[21]

Allen wasn't the first coach to recruit big men or institute set plays, but he was one of the first coaches to be dominant at it. He didn't just want players who would jog up and down the court. He wanted physical, competitive athletes who listened and understood every scheme he drew up, including a defensive approach that would shape the game in coming years.[22]

21 Braden Shaw, "1952: Kansas' First NCAA National Championship," *The University Daily Kansan* (February 2018), http://www.kansan.com/special_issues/2018_120_years/kansas-first-ncaa-national-championship/article_4f66bad0-15f1-11e8-a2a3-836c44e4ab96.html.

22 Larry Schwartz, "Basketball Pioneer Phog Allen Dies at 88," ESPN Classic (September 1974), http://www.espn.com/classic/s/moment010916-phog-allen.html.

The 1951–52 season was a defining year in Allen's career, not just for the championship, but for the reaction it sparked from the entire Lawrence community. Mayer said the team was greeted by nearly 15,000 fans when the Jayhawks returned from Seattle, a crowd that, at the time, "was an incredible turnout." There were fire trucks and crowds, noise, and celebration, and today, anyone who walks into Allen Fieldhouse where the Jayhawks now play can still see a photograph of Lovellette sporting a Lawrence Fire Department hat on the mural inside. It was exactly the kind of moment Allen hoped for when he first started coaching, a love of the game that fueled him throughout five decades pacing the sidelines and, for a few days, made Kansas the center of the basketball world.

GOING FOR GOLD

Allen always had a vision for the future of basketball. He wanted to grow the sport, provide opportunities for athletes across the country and, eventually, around the world. He helped make sure that happened in 1936, working to get basketball officially recognized as an Olympic sport when the Games were played in Berlin.

Basketball had been part of the Olympic program prior to its inclusion in Berlin, but only five teams participated in the 1904 Games in St. Louis, and all of them hailed from the United States. It wasn't exactly an international event at the time. Allen, however, helped change that. He'd already been coaching at Kansas for over two decades, and his name pulled plenty of weight with the athletic community, particularly with the Olympic committee. The challenge, however, was fielding a team. Allen got basketball on the Olympic docket, but the United States still needed to get players overseas.

Eight teams arrived in New York City in April, 1936, facing off at Madison Square Garden following a qualifying tournament earlier in the year. There were five college teams, one YMCA team, and two Amateur Athletic Union (AAU) squads, both of which had to pay their own way into the competition. In the end, though, the two AAU teams faced off in the finals with the Universals defeating the Oilers 44–43. The winning team filled out half the United States roster, while the Oilers added six players of their own, with James Needles serving as head coach. Allen didn't travel with the team to Berlin, but James Naismith, his former coach at Kansas, did, set to be honored for inventing the game nearly fifty years earlier.

There was a nervous energy ahead of the games, even for Allen. This was a world that, in just five years, would see the attacks on Pearl Harbor; a world that was already teetering on the edge of war, and an Olympic Games that would earn notoriety as Jesse Owens won four gold medals while Nazi Germany looked on. Still, the United States basketball team was hopeful heading into competition, determined to live out Allen's dream of making the sport available to an international audience.

"We had hoped to display to sports fans of other countries the skills, the science, and the speed of this native American game," Sam Balter, who competed for the United States, told *Sports Illustrated* in 1996.[23]

That, however, was easier said than done. Naismith and Team USA arrived in Berlin to find that an event actually hadn't been scheduled in his honor and, although a ceremony was eventually held, the competition at the Berlin Games was decidedly lacking. The sport was thriving in America, but it was brand new on the other side of the Atlantic and the International Basketball Federation even attempted to place height restrictions on teams ahead of the competition. The games were also played outside, with a ball that was less like a basketball and, according to players, more like "a slightly warped soccer ball." There was a downpour during the gold medal game between the United States and Canada, but the United States prevailed with a 19–8 victory.

Balter went on to call the Games "a priceless bit of Chaplinesque comedy," a series of errors and miscues that were far from what Allen

---

23 Brad Herzog, "The Dream Team of 1936 in the First Olympic Basketball Competition, the US Won the Gold Medal Easily," *Sports Illustrated* (July 1996), https://www.si.com/vault/2016/08/17/dream-team-1936-first-olympic-basketball-competition-us-won-gold-medal-easily.

had hoped when he pleaded the sport's case to the Olympic committee. But it was a start. It was the first time basketball, maybe not in its truest form, but at least a competitive one, was seen on the world stage. It was a game-changer, quite literally, for athletes and Olympians, a chance for players outside of America to suit up and take to the court and, even now, the game continues to grow across the world.

Allen did eventually find his way to the Olympics. He served as an assistant coach for the 1952 games in Helsinki, Finland, only a few months after leading Kansas to its first NCAA Championship. The United States, once again, captured gold and, once again, took on an athletic enemy that also had real-world implications. Team USA defeated the Soviet Union in the final game, notching a 36–25 victory, led by Clyde Lovellette's nine points.[24]

Olympic basketball has changed over the years. There have been Dream Teams and disappointments, professional stars and some of the world's best amateur athletes, but none of it would have been possible without Allen's determination. He always saw basketball as an avenue to success and knew it was much more than just a gentlemanly pursuit in the winter. This was a game that could change lives, and Allen, no matter where he was coaching or when, was certain he could make it do just that.

COACHING TREE

There are coaching trees and then there is Phog Allen's coaching tree. This was a man who coached for fifty seasons, who helped shape the careers of players and athletes and assistants. Allen's coaching tree is actually so massive that it's almost easy to get lost on some of the branches. This is a redwood, chock-full of Hall of Famers and record-breakers, practically bursting with championships and All-Americans. It's more than impressive; it's the root of current college

---

24 "Games of the XVth Olympiad—1952," USA Basketball (June 2010), https://www.usab .com/history/national-team-mens/games-of-the-xvth-olympiad-1952.aspx.

basketball. They call Allen "the father of basketball coaching" for a reason.

When talking about Allen's coaching legacy, it's easiest to start with some of the biggest names, men who would go on to influence the game in their own right, pacing their own sidelines with their own players for years to come. Dutch Lonborg, who played two years at Kansas, went on to win 237 games as the head coach at Northwestern University, and his 1930–31 team was retroactively named the national champions by the Helms Athletic Foundation. Ralph Miller worked as a head coach for nearly forty years, posting an overall record of 657–382 at the University of Wichita—which later became Wichita State—and the University of Iowa and Oregon State.

Then there are the even bigger names. Adolph Rupp played college hoops at Kansas from 1920–23, competing on two national championship teams before serving as head coach at Kentucky for thirty-nine years and turning the program into a national powerhouse. He retired with 876 wins, a number that, at the time, was the most in college basketball history. Dean Smith, meanwhile, topped even that. The former University of North Carolina head man, who played on Allen's 1952 title team, coached the Tar Heels from 1961 to 1997, amassing 879 victories and two national championships.

"The three programs that really, consistently, throughout the history of college basketball, that have been the most prominent have been Kentucky, Kansas, and North Carolina," Marsh said. "I can't think of any more simple proof of Phog Allen's reach than the basketball arenas for the other two schools are named after players of his. They were Jayhawk players that learned from Phog Allen and then became extraordinary influences."

There are also lesser-known students of Allen's game who are just as successful. John Bunn played at Kansas from 1918–20 and served as an assistant for the Jayhawks from 1921–30 before taking over the head coaching job at Stanford. There he coached Hank Luisetti, whose one-handed shot became one of the most dominant offensive weapons in the history of college hoops. Bunn also coached at Springfield College and Colorado State and was the first chairman of the Naismith Memorial Basketball Hall of Fame from 1949–63. He was inducted into the Hall as a major contributor in 1964, penned six books, and the Hall still hands out an award in his name, honoring an international or national figure who has contributed to the game of basketball. It's the most prestigious award the Hall gives, outside of enshrinement.[25]

Forrest "Frosty" Cox is another name that Allen helped influence. He played at Kansas from 1928–31, serving as captain while picking up All Big Six and All-America honors in '30 and '31 before taking the head job at Colorado University. Cox was methodical. His favorite saying was "a basket saved is a basket earned." He helped bring the sport to the Rocky Mountains. Cox posted a 147–89 record at Colorado, winning four league titles and earning three berths to the NCAA Tournament. He also coached Byron "Whizzer" White, a standout multi-sport athlete in the 1930s who also was a Heisman Trophy runner-up, an NFL star, a World War II veteran, and a Supreme Court justice.[26]

White's success isn't inextricably tied to Allen, but it's connected, and the basketball family tree that was planted at Kansas continues to grow to this day. Allen didn't just mentor future coaches. He helped future Hall of Famers find their on-court footing as well, names ranging from Clyde Lovellette and Paul Endacott to Bill Johnson and Wilt Chamberlain. Allen even coached former United States Senate Majority Leader Bob Dole.

The coaching tree gains even more depth when certain branches are examined at length. San Antonio Spurs coach Gregg Popovich is actually a basketball descendant of Allen. As mentioned previously, Allen coached Dean Smith, who coached Larry Brown who, in turn, cut

25 "The John W. Bunn Lifetime Achievement Award," Naismith Basketball Hall of Fame updated 2018, accessed November 2018, http://www.hoophall.com/awards/john-w-bunn -lifetime-achievement-award.

26 Bill Mayer, "Phog Allen Protege List Goes On," KU Sports (February 2010), http://www 2.kusports.com/news/2010/feb/05/phog-allen-protege-list-goes.

Popovich from the 1972 Olympic trials. There's more. Current Kentucky coach John Calipari served as an assistant on Brown's staff at Kansas while former UConn coach Kevin Ollie was the backup point guard on Brown's Philadelphia 76ers.[27]

Allen saw hundreds of players pass through the doors at Kansas, watched their victories and their defeats with equal measures of pride and frustration. He taught the game the way he thought it should be played and influenced a generation that's still writing its legacy now. Allen's name still holds clout. There's a respect that comes when mentioning his time at Kansas and the incredible coaching tree he helped create may never be matched.

PHOG'Y WITH A CHANCE OF VICTORY

Phog Allen didn't create basketball, but he helped perfect it. He shaped the game, brought in changes and big men and quick defenses, schemes that today's coaches still reference when coming up with their own plans of attack.

Allen made Kansas basketball. He coached the Jayhawks to twenty-four Missouri Valley, Big Six, and Big Seven Conference championships. He helped the game grow, whether stateside or around the world, and brought some of the country's best athletes to Lawrence, Kansas, because he knew that would make basketball more competitive. Allen loved the game with a fierceness that is sometimes overlooked by his other accomplishments.

It's a strange way to remember him, but Allen wasn't just a good coach. He was a competitor and man who wanted to be the best, no matter who he was playing, what players he was coaching, or where he had to go to do any of those things. Allen did everything in his power, throughout his career, to make basketball as competitive as it could be. He was

---

27 "Larry Brown's Coaching Tree: From Dean Smith to Gregg Popovich, Brown Has Extensive Ties," SportsDay (March 2014), https://sportsday.dallasnews.com/college-sports/smumustangs/2016/07/08/20140318-larry-brown-s-coaching-tree-from-dean-smith-to-gregg-popovich-brown-has-extensive-ties.

instrumental in creating the NCAA Tournament, serving as one of the founders of the National Association of Basketball Coaches. He was enshrined in the Naismith Memorial Basketball Hall of Fame in 1959, three years after retiring from the game as the all-time wins leader in college basketball history with a 746–264 record. Allen passed away in September 1974, but he's never really left Kansas. The Jayhawks play in an arena with his name on the side and his grave is just a short drive from campus, a tourist attraction that's as macabre as it is respectful.[28]

Allen was Kansas basketball and his influence on the game and the sport and the state itself is still felt in every single Jayhawks season. He's revered as an icon, a pioneer, and a father figure to hundreds of players who continue to shape basketball at every level.

• • • • •

PAY HEED ALL WHO ENTER

The legend of Jayhawks' arena, Allen Fieldhouse, is vast. It's loud. It's distracting. It's packed with raucous Kansas fans who make it their soul job to affect the outcome of a college basketball game by screaming at opposing teams. They don't sit down. They don't stop. They shout and stomp and break noise records.

Kansas fans at Allen Fieldhouse set the record for loudest crowd roar during an indoor sporting event on February 14, 2017, reaching a decibel level of 130.4 during the first half against West Virginia.[29] The arena, named for Phog Allen on March 1, 1955, has become a place college basketball teams dread playing. It's the kind of place Allen himself would have dreamed about playing in when he was coaching. It's the kind of arena where fans can show their love of the game and their team, and where a banner that hangs over the north end of the court has become the stuff of college hoops lore.

---

28 "Phog Allen, Basketball Coach of Kansas Jayhawks Dies at 88," *New York Times* (September 1974), https://www.nytimes.com/1974/09/17/archives/phog-allen-basketball-coach-of-kansas-jayhawks-dies-at-88.html.

29 Anthony Chiusano, "KU-WVU: Allen Fieldhouse Breaks Record for Loudest Crowd Roar," NCAA (February 2017), https://www.ncaa.com/news/basketball-men/article/2017-02-13/kansas-west-virginia-allen-fieldhouse-breaks-record-loudest.

Todd Gilmore was a student at Kansas. Sitting in class in 1988, doodling in his notebook, he came up with a phrase: Pay Heed All Who Enter, Beware of "The Phog." He showed the drawing to his friends, fellow Jayhawks basketball superfans who immediately agreed it was the perfect catchphrase. "It's ominous," Michael Gentemann told the *Kansas City Star* in 2018.

The friends decided to make a banner, one they could bring with them to Jayhawks games. The problem, however, was finding a canvas that was large enough. This had to be big. It had to be visible. It had to make the fans at Allen Fieldhouse look up and notice. They had used bedsheets for banners in the past, but this was different. This was more serious. This needed shower curtains. The group broke into one of the other dorms on campus, scaling five floors and unhooking shower curtains while avoiding being caught. They managed to get away with nine shower curtains, as well as an ever-growing audience of friends who wanted to see them actually draw on those curtains and, most importantly, express a few opinions on the design.

Gentemann drew the letters, using a charcoal pen to outline the original sketch while others followed up with paint and strict instructions to stay within the lines. The entire project only took one night, but the friends still needed a little inside help to get the banner into Allen Fieldhouse. They got it from Floyd Temple, then the assistant athletic director in charge of facilities. Temple let the banner come into the arena, and with the help of another fan, known colloquially as "The Foot" because of his heavy stomping during Jayhawks games, the friends tied one of his shoes to a rope, threw it over the catwalk, and hung the banner.

The original plan was for the banner to stay up for one game—against Duke. It was raised again for Danny Manning's Senior Night, honoring the Jayhawks standout who helped lead his team to the 1988 NCAA championship, left the program as its leading scorer, and got an unexpected endorsement from Allen's granddaughter, Judy Morris. She wanted the banner to stay up permanently and the athletic department agreed. The banner hung in the rafters until the stolen shower curtains started to break apart, replaced by a new, sturdier version, but the sentiment and the slogan remain the same. Allen Fieldhouse is a place where fandom reigns supreme. There is nothing more important than the game, the victory, and finding incredibly creative ways to insult the opposition.

"The energy and the electricity in the field house are incredible," Marsh said. "And there have been really strong efforts to keep it from feeling any different than it has since it was built. It's still the old barn."

The original group of banner-designing friends never trademarked "The Phog"; there are no royalties or extra income for their enthusiasm. They don't care because it was never about that. The nickname has taken on a life of its own, used by broadcasters and reporters and those who hardly keep track of college basketball outside of March. The arena's reputation for noise has become synonymous with Kansas basketball and Allen's legacy. Allen helped create those first few sparks of interest in Jayhawks hoops, but it's only grown from there. [30] Phog Allen was loud; that's how he got the nickname, but so is the school he left behind, and the noise is a testament to everything he accomplished.

● ● ● ● ●

Allen's Best Games

The 1940 NCAA Championship Game

Kansas lost the championship, falling to Indiana 60–42, but the appearance marked a brand-new benchmark for the Jayhawks basketball team. The postseason itself wasn't that impressive, just eight teams and two game venues, but it offered the still-rare opportunity to name a national champion.

College basketball had been steadily growing over the last few years and Allen's determination to help the game evolve was apparent on

---

30 Jesse Newell, "The Story Behind KU's 'Beware of the Phog' Banner...from the Men Who Created It," *Kansas City Star* (January 2018), https://www.kansascity.com/sports/college/big-12/university-of-kansas/article194617979.html.

the national stage. This was the first time the country was introduced to the Jayhawks—and to Allen's brand-new approach to game play. He'd sped up the game, fine-tuned his press and, suddenly, made basketball even more interesting.

Kansas didn't capture a title, that would come a few years later, but it left an impact on the athletic world, and the country started to notice Allen and his team.

The 1952 NCAA Championship Game

Welcome to the top, Kansas basketball.

It wasn't the first time they were there, but it was the first time the Jayhawks won and, most importantly, the start of something much bigger. Kansas captured its first national championship in 1952, defeating St. John's 80–63 on March 26, in Seattle. It was also the first true "Final Four" in college hoops history, with both semifinals at the same site. Clyde Lovellette stole the show, finishing a championship game record of thirty-three points.

CHAPTER THREE

ADOLPH RUPP
The Baron of Bluegrass

"He'd find a university or college that would employ somebody past seventy and start building on his record. He was that competitive. His success was that important to him."

—DAN ISSEL, AN ALL-AMERICAN AT KANSAS

In 1968, vice-presidential candidate Ed Muskie was scheduled to hold a rally and speech at Memorial Coliseum in Lexington, Kentucky, and the Secret Service had the gall to suggest that Adolph Rupp cancel basketball practice. He didn't appreciate it. In fact, according to a 1996 *Sports Illustrated* article, Rupp told the Secret Service that Muskie would "lose votes here" if he prevented the Wildcats from playing.

There was no argument. There was no back-and-forth exchange or an attempt at a compromise. The Secret Service took one look at Rupp, his schedule, and his competitive nature and walked away. Muskie postponed his speech, and practice went on, just as it always did.

Muskie also didn't become vice president. He and running mate Hubert Humphrey narrowly lost the election to Richard Nixon and Spiro Agnew, a fact that Rupp probably would have taken complete credit for if he was ever asked. The man thought he could stop basketball. He had no right to be Vice President of the United States.[31]

Rupp was known as "The Baron of Bluegrass" during his tenure on the sidelines, and anyone who knew him well enough to call him that without running the risk of being yelled at also knew him well enough to realize that nothing got in the way of his game plan. Rupp was the kind of coach who believed in order. He believed in discipline and a moment-by-moment attack that would inevitably lead to victories, national championships, and a legacy that would linger decades after he walked away from the game.

Rupp was not an easy man to play for or play with. He grew up on a basketball court, much like many of his contemporaries, but his determination and his competitive nature were unparalleled. This was not a man who was content to linger in mediocrity. He believed he was the best, he believed his team was the best, and he refused to accept the idea that either of those things were incorrect—even in the face of national security.

Rupp helped change the game while he was at Kentucky. He brought a fiery determination to the program that had never been seen before, a style of coaching that, now, is the norm, but in the late 1960s was seen as almost controversial. He was loud. He was intense. He demanded perfection. Rupp wanted to win. He wanted to set records and be better than any other team that suited up against his. He didn't leave the game willingly and, very likely, would have kept coaching for years if his health had allowed him to do so.

Rupp lived and breathed basketball, but his reputation outside the game has been twisted over the last few years. There are plenty of stories, rumors, and mutterings about what he was like away from the court; he held a set of personal beliefs that, looking back, paint him in a less-than-positive light. It's a fine line to walk, a career that was

31 Kansas Athletics, "Once a Jayhawk, Always a Jayhawk: Adolph Rupp," University of Kansas (November 2014), https://kuathletics.com/story.aspx?filename=MBB _1112145519&file_date=11/12/2014.

undeniably successful, but the question still remains: who was Adolph Rupp, really?

LEARNING CURVE

Rupp was born in September 1901 in Halstead, Kansas, a town that, as of 2010, boasted just over 2,000 people. He attended the local high school, playing basketball and learning the game, and joined the team at the University of Kansas in 1919. It was a moment Rupp had been waiting his entire life for, a chance to prove himself on a stage far bigger than anything Halstead would ever be able to provide.[32]

Rupp thrived on knowledge. He wanted to know everything about everything, and his curiosity was almost laser-focused when it came to basketball, particularly when he got to college. It didn't take long for the small-town kid to start questioning everything. He wanted to know why certain plays worked and why others didn't, why practices were run a specific way, and he seized every opportunity to pick his coach's brain. Of course, when that coach was Phog Allen and his mentor James Naismith, the inventor of basketball, Rupp was confident he was getting the best information possible.

"He actually took classes with Dr. (James) Naismith," Rupp's son Adolph Rupp Jr. told Kansas Athletics in 2014. "He took what he learned from both of those men, and then added his own innovations to it."[33]

Rupp wanted to learn, but he didn't do much on the court. He was far from the most talented player on the Kansas roster and when the team won the Helms national title in 1922 and 1923, he spent the majority of those games cooling his heels at the end of the bench. So he kept listening. He kept learning, retaining knowledge, and hanging on every word out of Allen's mouth because as far as Rupp was concerned, they were the most important words he'd ever heard.

---

32 "Adolph Rupp," Kansas Sports Hall of Fame (2013), accessed November 2018, http://www.kshof.org/component/content/article/2-kansas-sports-hall-of-fame/inductees/222-rupp-adolph.html.

33 "Once a Jayhawk, Always a Jayhawk." University of Kansas.

He knew he wasn't going to make a career out of playing basketball. There were plenty of other athletes at Kansas and around the country who were better at the game than Rupp could ever hope to be, but after spending four years with the Jayhawks, he believed he was the best man to find that talent.[34]

Rupp still wanted to win, but he knew he had to go about it a different way. He wasn't going to pack a stat sheet. He was going to take what he learned from Allen and Naismith and the entire Kansas basketball program and start his own powerhouse a few states over. Rupp got the chance in 1930, taking the head coaching job at Kentucky and laying the building blocks of a program that is still considered one of the best in the nation.

GETTING CAT'Y

Rupp might not have been the most dominant scorer on the Kansas roster or the best defender, but he never lost his confidence. There are some who might say he had too much confidence, was far too certain of his own talents even before he'd been challenged by much of anything. According to ESPN, when a twenty-nine-year-old Rupp interviewed for the head coaching job at the University of Kentucky in 1930, he was asked why he should be hired. His answer was simple. "Because I'm the best damned basketball coach in the nation," Rupp said.[35]

Rupp believed in his potential and what he could do when five guys stood on a basketball court with a ball, a hoop, and the desperate desire to win games. At his very core, that's what Rupp was. He was desperate to win and he was willing to change the fundamentals of the game to do that.

---

34 Kyle Tucker, "Forever Linked: Kentucky-Kansas Connection Goes Back to Phog Allen, Adolph Rupp," *The Atlanta Journal-Constitution* (January 2017), https://www.myajc.com/sports/college/forever-linked-kentucky-kansas-connection-goes-back-phog-allen-adolph-rupp/77m5MjXGFlZkTOFw3kCznM.

35 Bob Carter, "Rupp: Baron of Bluegrass," ESPN Classic, accessed November 2018, http://www.espn.com/classic/biography/s/Rupp_Adolph.html.

When Rupp was hired by Kentucky, basketball was slow. It was an even-paced game with tried-and-true methods that were considered correct because that was simply the way they'd been done since Naismith first tried to throw a ball through a peach basket. But Rupp had learned the game from Naismith himself, and that intimate knowledge changed the way he approached his own team. He was tired of slow and steady. Rupp wanted quick and quicker.

He first learned the concept of a three-man fast break from Allen during his days at Kansas, but Rupp was never the kind of person to be satisfied. He took it a step further. Rupp's practices, those same ones that even the Secret Service couldn't slow down, were marathons of training and conditioning, running up and down the floor and fine-tuning a transitional game that would eventually become the calling card at Kentucky.

Former Wildcats standout Cotton Nash told *Sports Illustrated* in 2012 that Rupp's teams would practice for exactly one hour and forty-five minutes every day. They never stopped moving. They ran and practiced plays and then ran some more, doing their best to out-sprint each other while Rupp paced the sidelines and shouted. Rupp wanted to change the tempo of the game. If his players could move faster than their opponents, then it only served that they'd be able to score more than their opponents, and you need to score more to win.

"We tried to exhaust the other team, and we were in better shape than most teams we played," Nash explained.[36]

While his players were working up a sweat, Rupp was coming up with offensive schemes that would keep other teams on their toes. Kentucky was going to push the game, keeping opponents off-kilter and never letting them catch their breath. The idea was easy, if not a little revolutionary, but Rupp had never been one to simply accept the way of things. He wanted to win and he was going to figure out a way to do just that.

---

36 "Once a Jayhawk, Always a Jayhawk." University of Kansas.

It worked. In his first game coaching at Kentucky, Rupp and the Wildcats rolled to a 67–19 victory over Georgetown College, and it only got better from there. His career would become the stuff of Kentucky legend.

FINDING A RHYTHM

Rupp wasn't content with his first victory at Kentucky. There were more plays to draw up, players to find, and expectations to blow past. His offense didn't slow down and neither did Rupp. He settled into a pattern of success at Kentucky that most modern coaches can only gape at. Rupp went 30–5 in his first two seasons, before the program joined the Southeastern Conference (SEC), and Kentucky won its first conference title in 1933, just three seasons after hiring its young, upstart coach with a considerable amount of confidence.[37]

Kentucky quickly became the team to beat in the SEC, capturing victories and titles as other teams struggled to keep up with the Wildcats on and off the court. Rupp didn't have to look far for talent. He recruited nearly eighty percent of his players from the state of Kentucky, but was notoriously picky when it came to who got playing time. Rupp wanted talent, but he also wanted a specific type of athlete, one who would fit into his game plan because he certainly wasn't going to change that plan for a player. He believed he knew the game as well as, if not better, than anyone, and his approach was not to be questioned.[38]

Rupp was a stern taskmaster, a devoted schedule-keeper, and a stickler for the rules, but only when he came up with them. He wasn't easy to listen to or play for, but the players who wore Kentucky jerseys in those early days of the program's success could never imagine competing for anyone else. Rupp didn't consider himself a pseudo-father for his players. The team was just that, not a substitute family or anything except a group of men who wanted to notch another tally in the win column every time they stepped on the court. Rupp's cool demeanor toward

---

37 Carter, "Rupp: Baron of Bluegrass."

38 "Adolph F. Rupp," Naismith Basketball Hall of Fame, accessed November 2018, http://www.hoophall.com/hall-of-famers/adolph-rupp.

his team after practices and games were over is still muttered about in Kentucky basketball lore. If they weren't competing, Rupp didn't really acknowledge his players. It wasn't an insult. It was just his personality. Rupp's players respected him, but they didn't always like him.

"A lot of people think we run a Marine Corps outfit," Rupp reportedly said. "Fine, if they think that, that's fine. I knew when I came here that the only way I could be successful would be to go out and win these basketball games."[39]

Rupp's attention to detail may have, at times, frustrated his team, but it also helped keep that same team winning. The Wildcats won a whopping twenty-seven Southeastern Conference titles, a National Invitation Tournament (NIT) championship, and four NCAA championships (1948, 1949, 1951, and 1958), and Rupp coached twenty-five All-Americans throughout the course of his career. That 1948 championship, however, would set the stage for the rest of Rupp's time in Lexington and may be the most important of them all.

Kentucky boasted one of the strongest starting lineups in the country that season, bolstered by the group known as the Fabulous Five; Ralph Beard, Wallace "Wah Wah" Jones, Alex Groza, Kenny Rollins, and Cliff Barker. The group opened up the season with seven straight victories and despite falling to Temple on a buzzer-beater, went on to win twenty-seven of its next twenty-eight games. They beat Temple the second time around, and all five Wildcats starters earned postseason accolades from the SEC.

Kentucky breezed through the SEC Tournament, winning four games by 111 points. There were a few tense moments in the title tilt against Georgia Tech, but the Wildcats pulled off the 54–53 victory and built on that success throughout their NCAA Tournament run. Kentucky topped Columbia and Holy Cross en route to a national championship berth against Baylor.

---

39 Sam Goldaper, "Adolph F. Rupp Dies: Tribute for Renowned Coach Scheduled for Tonight," *New York Times* (December 1977), https://www.nytimes.com/1977/12/12/archives/adolph-f-rupp-dies-tribute-for-renowned-coach-scheduled-tonight.html.

It was the national stage Rupp had been waiting for since arriving at Kentucky eighteen years earlier, and his players didn't disappoint. The Wildcats' defense held Baylor to just sixteen points in the first half, out-pacing the Bears, and Rupp's fast-paced approach to the game looked all but genius. Kentucky captured its first-ever NCAA championship with a 58–42 victory, becoming just the second team in the history of college hoops to win both the NIT and NCAA title. It also put Rupp, and his program, on the map.[40]

WIN, WIN, WIN

The Wildcats kept winning. Rupp wouldn't accept anything less, and after that initial taste of championship glory and national accolades, the coach who was never known for his outspoken demeanor found himself at the center of a historic run.

Kentucky won a basketball game, as it was apt to do, on its home court on January 2, 1943. Then the Wildcats kept winning basketball games—for years. Kentucky didn't lose a single home game for the next twelve years. That's 129 consecutive games. Think about that for a moment. That's more than a decade of winning, a decade of complete and utter dominance, national championships, and perfect seasons. The undefeated run included three NCAA titles (1948, 1949, and 1951) and a 1954 team that posted a 25–0 record and a No. 1 ranking by the Associated Press. The United States had three different presidents over the course of Kentucky's run. Other teams have come close to duplicating that kind of success. John Wooden and UCLA won eighty-eight consecutive games, home or away, and St. Bonaventure won ninety-nine straight home games from 1948 to 1961, but Rupp's record at Kentucky still causes basketball fans to sit up and take notice.

The end of that streak, however, was a point of contention throughout the rest of Rupp's career. He didn't like losing, especially when the eyes

---

40 Kentucky Athletics Department, "1948 Men's Basketball National Champions," University of Kentucky, accessed November 2018, https://ukathletics.com/sports/2016/5/16/_13146180 9047653077.aspx.

of the entire country were watching. The streak came to an end on January 8, 1955, with a 59–58 loss to Georgia Tech. Tears were shed, fans sat in the stands stunned and a little horrified, and the silence that enveloped Lexington's Memorial Coliseum that night continued to give Georgia Tech coach John Hyder chills years later.

"A lot of people in the crowd that night had never seen Kentucky lose," he told *Sports Illustrated*.[41]

Georgia Tech came into the matchup with a 2–4 record, including a loss in its last game and, as the years went by, Kentucky players admitted they were looking past the Yellow Jackets. This wasn't a team they felt threatened by, particularly not when national powerhouse DePaul University was on the schedule two days later.

Kentucky trailed by as many as eight points in the second half, but held a one-point lead with less than a minute on the clock. The Wildcats thought they had the game in the bag, but then Billy Evans, the Kentucky captain, turned the ball over.

Georgia Tech's Joe Helms, a five-foot-nine guard and by far the smallest player on the court, grabbed the ball, sprinted down the court, and sank a twelve-foot jumpshot to beat the Wildcats at their own game. Kentucky had two chances to reclaim the lead in the waning moments, but neither team found the hoop and as the final horn sounded, no one could believe what they'd just witnessed. History had ended.

John Brewer, a Kentucky reserve, told *Sports Illustrated* in 1994 that Rupp didn't yell when the Wildcats got back into the locker room. There was no sense of anger, but a clear sense of disappointment and the weight of carrying that loss with them for the rest of their careers.

Georgia Tech continued to be a thorn in the Wildcats' side for the rest of Rupp's career. Hyder posted a 9–16 record against Rupp before the

---

41 William F. Reed, "A Dark Night in Kentucky," *Sports Illustrated* (February 1994), https://www.si.com/vault/1994/02/21/130514/a-dark-night-in-kentucky-in-1955-georgia-tech-ended-the-wildcats-129-game-home-winning-streak.

Yellow Jackets left the SEC, a showing that was as good as any other coach when stacking up against the legend.

Kentucky blew out DePaul two days after the history-shattering loss, but the previous game remained a mark on Rupp's personal record. Much like Hyder, he never forgot the silence that had followed.

Rupp did his best to make sure the losses never stacked up. He believed in rules, regulations, a defined system that would lead to national championships, and a clear line between coach and player. A 1957 *Sports Illustrated* article likened his practices to a "drill session at the Marine boot camp on Parris Island."[42] At the time, freshmen on the Kentucky basketball team were taught the Rupp system by his assistant, Harry Lancaster. The deal was simple: listen, no joking, speak when spoken to, and don't bother asking if you can bring a visitor to practice.

Any player whose attention was remotely wandering during practice faced a variety of punishments that ranged from colorful curses to running sprints to even being barred from the gym for any length of time. Rupp graded his teams after each practice. The details of every Wildcats season were passed on from recruiting class to recruiting class. It was a rite of passage, learning the ins and outs of Rupp's beliefs and making sure not a single toe or shoelace was out of line.

Vernon Hatton, part of the Wildcats' 1958 NCAA championship team, told ESPN that it took "six or eight years to get over playing for Coach Rupp," but after that "you get to like him."[43]

Rupp thrived on order and believed in consistency. He made sure he got both in every facet of his life, including the smallest parts of his coaching routine. He had a strict set of pre-game rituals before every Kentucky basketball game. He drove the same route to each game, parked in the same spot, and reportedly tried to find four-leaf covers and hairpins before games, believing they'd both make him that much

42 Jeremiah Tax, "Big Week for the Man in Brown," *Sports Illustrated* (December 1957), https://www.si.com/vault/1957/12/16/605646/big-week-for-the-man-in-brown.

43 Carter, "Rupp: Baron of Bluegrass."

luckier. His most obvious ritual, however, was the brown suit he wore for every game. Rupp never changed, not once in forty-two years, and, much like with every other coaching decision he made, there was a reason for it.

It all began when he took his first coaching job at a high school in Freeport, Illinois. Rupp bought a new blue suit and then promptly lost his first game. He decided then and there to never wear a blue suit again and instead turned to the other brown suit in his closet. Rupp won his next few games and boasted an eighty percent win total at the high school level. He wore the same color for the rest of his coaching career.

"He had his ways where he felt it was important for these things to happen in order to have the games to turn out the way he wanted them to," Rupp Jr. told Kansas Athletics.[44]

It was strange. It was superstitious. It was Rupp. His players were likely confused by it, although unwilling to voice their opinions out loud for fear of more sprints during practice. Rupp believed in his system and its ability to win national championships.

Rupp wanted to change the game of basketball. He wanted it to go faster, with quicker players and even quicker shots. He thrived on the kind of suffocating defense that completely shut down an opposing team. He liked change, but only in that regard. At his heart, Rupp was a stickler for the rules and his own set of beliefs for what quantified success. Rupp was obsessed with winning, and he wasn't above doing whatever he could to make sure he did. That, however, was where his problems began.

A DENT IN THE LEGACY

Rupp retired from coaching in 1972 at the age of seventy, boasting one of the most dominant careers in college basketball. He left the game as the winningest coach in college hoops history, but Rupp was

---

44 "Once a Jayhawk, Always a Jayhawk," University of Kansas.

not without his miscues or controversy. Kentucky was at the center of a national betting scandal in 1951 and while Rupp famously boasted "they couldn't reach my boys with a ten-foot pole," it eventually became clear Wildcats players were involved. Five Kentucky players were found to have accepted a $500 bribe and shaved points during a 1948 game against Loyola of Chicago, and the investigation had immediate impacts on the college basketball world.

The NCAA suspended Kentucky for the 1952–53 season, one of the first punishments of its kind handed down from the athletic organization. Rupp didn't take kindly to the punishment or the limelight. In the Wildcats' first year back, a team that compiled a 25–0 record, Rupp and his squad turned down a postseason invitation after the NCAA found that three of Kentucky's players were ineligible.

Rupp shook off the cloud cast by the scandal, capturing the NCAA championship in 1958 with his "Fiddlin' Five," a team he said "fiddled around enough to drive me crazy."[45]

Kentucky returned to the championship game in 1966, but the headlines in that matchup were more concerned with what was going on off the court than on it. The Wildcats, a team with five white starters, were slated to take on Texas Western, a team with an all African-American starting lineup. It was the first game of its kind and a major marker in the Civil Rights Movement that was spreading across the country. The 1966 NCAA title game was a defining moment in a time of social and cultural turmoil in America. It was a step forward while the past was desperately trying to cling on, and Texas Western's 72–65 victory has become the stuff of sports drama lore, the kind of underdog victory that is the perfect fodder for movies.

It was also the kind of moment that has left some questioning Rupp's legacy and the way he approached the game itself, sparking rumors of racism in the Kentucky locker room. *Sports Illustrated* reporter Frank Deford was allowed to be in the room with the team during halftime and

---

45 Carter, "Rupp: Baron of Bluegrass."

witnessed Rupp's outburst regarding his team's play and the opposing squad. He told the *Chicago Tribune* in 1997 that he was "stunned" and added that Rupp used several racist terms when discussing defensive schemes with his players.

"A chill went through me," Deford said. "I was standing in the back of the room, and I looked around at the players. They all kind of ducked their heads. They were embarrassed. This was clearly the type of thing that went over the line."[46]

Rupp's view of the team on the other side of the court remains a hotly contested topic to this day. This was a man who, in his prime, was regarded as the face of SEC athletics, a man who retreated to his ranch during the off-season and held onto his rules because he believed they would lead to the victories he valued above all else. Rupp wanted to change things in the way he saw fit. He didn't believe in changing because he was told to and, in the late '60s, that's reportedly exactly what happened. University of Kentucky president John W. Oswald and Kentucky governor Ned Breathitt both urged the athletic department to start recruiting more African-American players, particularly basketball players, but Rupp was reportedly cool to the idea. He did try to recruit two players, Butch Beard and Wes Unseld, who went on to become stars at the University of Louisville, but his pursuit of both athletes was tepid at best. He never visited their homes, didn't meet with them personally, and Kentucky didn't play its first African-American recruit, Tom Payne, until 1971.[47]

The situation, however, isn't perfectly black and white. Defenders of Rupp will be quick to point out that he coached an African-American player on his Freeport, Illinois, high school team in 1927, and that he spoke at the Kentucky Negro Educational Association convention in 1938. Kentucky also regularly traveled across the country, playing

46 Rick Morrissey, "Past Imperfect; Future Intense" *Chicago Tribune* (November 1997), https://www.chicagotribune.com/news/ct-xpm-1997-11-30-9712020327-story.html.

47 Bill Livingston, "Re-examining Kentucky's Reputation for Racism as the 2015 NCAA Tournament Starts," Cleveland.com (March 2015), https://www.cleveland.com/livingston/index.ssf/2015/03/long_the_bastion_of_the_basket.html.

whatever team it could, regardless of the color of players' skin. Butch Beard, who was recruited in the mid '60s, even suggested that the SEC wanted Kentucky "to be the first to integrate. They said if Adolph did it, everybody would."[48]

But the man who demanded speed and quickness from his players, the one who would run a drill twenty times until it was executed to perfection, continued to drag his feet on the issue. Rupp was part of the old and part of the new, a coach who so desperately wanted to win, but was also incredibly aware of the mantle he wore, intrinsically tied to a culture that was quickly fading with the times.

Rupp's approach to integration remains a mystery. Elmore Stephens, a former football player who jumped at the chance to also play basketball for the Wildcats, said Rupp wasn't a racist, but simply a coach who treated all his players the same. There are also stories of Rupp recommending other African-American players to coaches whose teams were already integrated. Julius Berry, who went on to serve as an aide to Lexington's mayor, said Rupp helped get him a scholarship at Dayton.

"He said to me that they'd love to have me but that colored boys couldn't play in the SEC. He sounded genuine when he said it," Berry said. "When I chose Dayton, [coach Tom Blackburn] there said to me that Rupp had told him that if he didn't recruit me, he was crazy."[49]

Rupp's story is confusing. It's a constant contradiction of quick and slow, of forward and backward, a man who wanted to help foster talent but couldn't bring himself to let that talent grow in Kentucky.

It's a shadow on a career that others will try to emulate for years to come but sparks as many questions as it answers. Was Rupp simply a man of his time? Was he actually racist? Or was he just not willing to rock the boat of 1960s America? Rupp, at his center, was a coach with

---

48 Darrell Bird, "Adolph Rupp's Legendary Career Was Not Without Its Challenges," 247Sports (December 2017), https://247sports.com/college/kentucky/Article/Gambling -scandal-alleged-racism-make-41-year-career-of-UK-coach-Adolph-Rupp-all-the-more- fascinating-112057946.

49 Morrissey, "Past Imperfect; Future Intense."

an obsession for winning, but his actions on and off the court, in rumor and fact, will be dissected for years to come—because he kept on winning. It might not be fair, but it's the price of a legacy.

STILL REIGNING

The Kentucky basketball gymnasium was renamed Rupp Arena on December 11, 1976. The 23,000-seat space was dedicated on the same night that the Wildcats hosted Kansas, a matchup that was at the heart of Rupp's basketball career and a moment that solidified his place in the history of both programs.

Rupp was never a dominant basketball player, but he helped create dominance and inspire a whole generation of athletes to try and be good enough that they could play for him. On the night of the arena opening, Rupp quipped, "I hope they give me a parking pass for it," as if he hadn't brought Kentucky to the forefront of the game and turned the program into a juggernaut. Kentucky did one better. There was a parking pass and a blue velvet chair in the stands whenever Rupp attended a game.[50]

He didn't get to sit in it often. Rupp died 364 days after the arena was renamed in his honor. A notoriously private man away from the game, Rupp kept his deteriorating health out of the spotlight. He passed away from complications from cancer at his home in Lexington, and the news of his death sent a shockwave through the basketball community.

Rupp's impact was felt everywhere, from the Kentucky campus to Madison Square Garden and the West Coast. His fellow college coaches released statements lauding his success and his victories, detailing how committed he was to winning and the competitive fire that became his calling card in more than four decades on the sidelines.

Rupp only ever wanted to coach. It was his lifeblood, a passion as much as a job, and when he fought the Kentucky rule that required him

---

50 Goldaper, "Adolph F. Rupp Dies."

to retire at seventy, he said, "If they don't let me coach, they might as well take me to the Lexington cemetery."

His death was a day of mourning, not just in college basketball, but the state of Kentucky where he was considered a hero and a legend and a baron. Kentucky governor Julian Carroll ordered flags to be flown at half-staff the day after Rupp died, and the arena that bore his name was filled to capacity when a memorial service was held on campus.

Rupp, who was inducted into the Naismith Memorial Basketball Hall of Fame in 1969, was not a simple man. He was controversial, sometimes difficult to understand, and as loud as anyone when his players did something he didn't approve of. His legacy cannot be discussed without also mentioning the controversy that followed, but his success is unquestioned. He shaped Kentucky into the program it is now, a consistent champion and a team that still draws some of the top talent in the country.

Rupp built Kentucky basketball and college basketball, but at the end of it all, what mattered to him was winning. Anything else was unacceptable because, as he said, "If winning isn't so important, why do you keep score?"

● ● ● ● ●
A YEAR TO REMEMBER

Rupp led Kentucky to four national titles during his time with the Wildcats, but his first, in 1948, was with one of the most dominant teams at any level, at any time. The 1948 Wildcats squad had barely caught its breath after topping Baylor in the NCAA championship before it was taking on the world in the London Olympic Games and, once again, Rupp was pacing the sidelines.

The United States was not a basketball powerhouse at the time. Basketball was only just picking up popularity on the world stage and as the US Olympic committee pondered how it would field a team for the 1948 Summer Olympics, officially known as the XIV

Olympiad, a decision was made. The team would be made up of players from some of the best competitive leagues in the country, including AAU and the YMCA, and teams that competed in the NCAA, NIT, and National Association of Intercollegiate Basketball (NAIB) tournaments. An elimination tournament was held at Madison Square Garden, pitting those teams against each other, and the Olympic committee chose its fourteen players from the winning team's rosters.

Kentucky's players, once again, stood out amongst the crowd. Ralph Beard, Alex Groza, Cliff Barker, Ken Rollins, and Wah Wah Jones were chosen to represent their country, while Rupp was named an associate head coach. After the final selection, the team was split down the middle, training in Oklahoma and Kentucky before squaring off in three intrasquad games prior to the event in London. The games were, initially, designed to help players fine-tune their skills and get used to playing together, but also served as a fundraiser of sorts for the Olympic team. The hope was that the games would attract a small crowd, but no one could have been prepared for what eventually happened.

The games weren't just well attended; they were enthusiastically cheered for. Rupp's side, the one that trained in Lexington and was mostly made up of the reigning national champions, defeated Omar Browning's team 70–69 in the third game, a final-second victory that sparked as much interest in basketball as anything that had happened during the college season.

The United States team raised nearly $75,000 during the pre-Games events and left for London on the SS America on July 14. It didn't take long for the group to prove its talent against international competition and, much like it had stateside, the world took notice. The United States didn't allow more than thirty-three points in its first four games, cruising to victories over Uruguay and Mexico in the elimination rounds before defeating France 65–21 in the final.

Rupp's players stole the show in the final game. The group, which had started the game against Mexico, took the court in the second half against France and quickly showed what a well-oiled basketball machine looked like. Beard, Barker, and Rollins all notched double-digit scoring performances, while Groza finished the tournament as the team's leading scorer.

It was a whirlwind offseason for the Wildcats, who started training for the Olympics less than seventy-two hours after capturing an NCAA crown, but it was also a string of games that helped change the course of basketball's history and the game's popularity across the world. The United States showed a brand of basketball the likes of which had never been seen before, partially because of Kentucky. These were athletes who had spent seasons under Rupp's tutelage, sprinting to the sound of whistles and running plays until they were perfect. They didn't slow down on the other side of the Atlantic, as obsessed with winning as their coach was. It was a matter of pride, particularly with a different set of letters emblazoned on their chest.

The United States, which had won Olympic gold in basketball before, successfully defended its title in London, but there was something different about this trip. The team visited Scotland before the Games and met with locals in London throughout the event, discussing basketball and culture and sparking an interest in the sport that wasn't there before.

"This trip probably made more friends for basketball than they realized," *Louisville Courier-Journal* reporter Earl Ruby wrote in his account of the 1948 Games. "[The team] deserves more credit for stimulating interest in the game among other nations than for defeating those countries in the Olympics."

This was a world that was still reeling from the effects of war, only three years removed from VE day. Europe was still picking up the pieces of World War II, coming to grips with the Soviet Union's presence and control, as well as the repercussions of years of fighting. The United States Olympic basketball team didn't change that, but it offered an outlet, a clear burst of talent and competition that the whole globe could root for.

Ruby was quick to point out that "basketball made far more headway in America than it had in any other nation" during the war years, but the United States' talent was not something the European spectators resented. They were fascinated by it, intrigued by the play and the analysis US coaches were only too happy to provide if asked.

These were some of the best athletes the United States had to offer, and Kentucky's impact on the sports scene across continents is undeniable. International basketball didn't begin in 1948, but it certainly received a boost and Rupp's "Fabulous Five" are forever connected to the game and the current interest across borders.[51]

● ● ● ● ●

Rupp's Best Games

The 1948 NCAA Championship Game

They called them the Fabulous Five for a reason. Ralph Beard, Wah Wah Jones, Alex Groza, Kenny Rollins, and Cliff Barker were nothing short of dominant during the 1947–48 season for Kentucky, breezing through the SEC Tournament and winning all four games by a total of 111 points. The national championship game, however, cemented the group in hoops lore. Groza and Beard combined for twenty-six points, while the Wildcats' suffocating defense held Baylor to just sixteen points in the first half. It was Kentucky's first NCAA title, the start of a run that would cement the Wildcats as one of the top programs in the country and marked the second time a team had won both NCAA and NIT championships.

The game also introduced the country to Alex Groza. The Kentucky star was named the championship MVP, but hoops fans may know him better for his miscues than his memorable moments. Groza was drafted in the first round of the 1949 NBA Draft by the Indianapolis Olympians, but was eventually involved in a point-shaving scandal—the point shaving allegedly occurred while he was at Kentucky. Groza, whose number hangs in the rafters at Kentucky, was banned for life from the NBA.

---

51 "The Little-Known Story of the 1948 Kentucky Wildcats That Started It All," Team USA (March 2015), https://www.teamusa.org/News/2015/March/26/From-Madness-to-Medals.

The 1966 NCAA Championship Game

Kentucky lost this game. That wasn't supposed to happen. The top-ranked team in the country, better known as "Rupp's Runts" for its distinct lack of size but furious physicality, fell 72–65 to Texas Western.

It marked the first time a team starting five black players won a title and also marked the start of racist rumblings regarding Rupp's coaching techniques. This was also the only Rupp-coached team to reach a final and lose, a disappointing finish for a team that, if they'd won, would probably be regarded as one of the best ever. A loss of that magnitude was so historic, movies have been about the matchup. For a coach who has become more and more controversial with every passing year, the matchup is inextricably linked to his legacy.

CHAPTER FOUR

DEAN SMITH
The Quiet Revolutionary

"The most important thing in good leadership is truly caring. The best leaders in any profession care about the people they lead, and the people who are being led know when the caring is genuine and when it's faked or not there at all."

—HALL OF FAME COACH DEAN SMITH

Dean Smith never wanted the accolades. He didn't want the headlines or the glory or the pomp and circumstance. He certainly didn't want the basketball arena at the University of North Carolina named after him. Smith even reportedly told UNC officials to find someone else to name the space after, was desperate to shun that spotlight at all costs, particularly while he was still coaching. It was only after school administrators told him it would be impossible to fundraise for the space without his name attached to it that Smith agreed.[52]

That was the kind of coach Smith was. He wanted his players to have the best so they could be the best and, despite his aversion to fame,

---

52 David Halberstam, *Playing for Keeps: Michael Jordan and the World He Made* (New York: Random House, 1999).

Smith constantly did everything in his power to lift his teams to the next level. He did the same thing off the court as well. Smith wasn't just a basketball coach; he was the face of UNC athletics for decades. Even now, the Dean E. Smith Student Activities Center, better known by hoops fans as "The Dean Dome," is one of the loudest, most raucous facilities in all of college sports. It's the kind of place where any color except Carolina blue is shunned. In fact, while it was being built, workers were banned from wearing Duke or NC State apparel.[53]

The Tar Heels won their first game at The Dean Dome on January 18, 1986, defeating archrival Duke 95–92, and Smith spent eleven years patrolling the sidelines of the facility named after him. He led teams to emotional victories and lopsided victories and victories that inspired cheers from fans wearing that very specific shade of blue. Smith cemented his legacy on the cement that bore his name, but he was more than just the game. Smith's teams didn't just affect college basketball or even sports in general; his teams changed the way the country watched sports, how we cheered and felt and believed in the power of athletics to affect real, true change.

Smith changed the game, of course; brought his own spin and plays and little things fans take for granted. He's credited with coming up for the universal "tired signal," as well as players congregating at the free throw line before a shot and playing all of his seniors on the final home game of the regular season. But he also was a vocal activist, speaking out against segregation and the Vietnam War, and supporting a world-wide freeze on the use of nuclear weapons.

His success as a coach gave Smith a platform, and North Carolina Democrats even suggested he run for United State Senate, transferring his popularity in basketball to pull in Washington. Smith declined. He didn't want the spotlight; he wanted to do the right thing. He wanted his players to do the same, was notorious for preaching athletic and academic success in tandem. Smith's win record is one for the history

---

53 Jan Bolick, "Great Expectations at the Dean Dome," 97.9 The Hill: WCHL (August 2012), https://chapelboro.com/uncategorized/great-expectations-at-the-dean-dome-2.

books, but it's his ability to mesh that on-court approach with his own humanity and humility that led him to become one of the most respected coaches of all time and, effectively, change North Carolina from the ground up.

CHANGE AT HOME

Smith was born in Emporia, Kansas, in February 1931. It was a small city, midway between Topeka and Wichita, and Smith's family was at the heart of everything in Emporia. Both of his parents worked as teachers at the area high school, and were devout Baptists and friendly faces that people stopped on the street to wave hello to. Alfred and Vesta Smith did their best at a time when America seemed to be crumbling under the growing weight of the Great Depression and the looming threat of world war.

Emporia was a good place, a safe place, but it also was a segregated place. That was, until Smith's father did something about it. Alfred Smith knew he was never going to change the world, but he was more than willing to try, coaching the high school basketball team in Emporia and working the help integrate the team. In 1934, the Spartans won the Kansas state basketball tournament with an African-American player on the roster. It was the first time anything like that had happened in the history of the state, and it set his son Dean on a path he'd continue to walk for the rest of his life.

Smith started playing sports when he was young, a way to pass the time when there wasn't much else to do, but he was always drawn to leadership positions, no matter what game he played. He was the high school quarterback, the catcher on the baseball team, and the point guard on the basketball court. Smith liked to direct and help other teammates find their potential and, most importantly, a way to win.

Smith was a talented athlete, but he was also a dedicated student. It was impossible to be anything else with his parents keeping watch, and Smith's innate curiosity was one of his most defining characteristics when he was a child. He wanted to know everything; who and why and what, question after question, constantly trying to find the reason behind anything. Smith's older sister Joan Smith Ewing told *Sports Illustrated* of a time when he was just ten years old and went down a manhole at the end of their street with friends, simply because he wanted to know what the sewers looked like. Their mother used to refer to him as Christopher Columbus because he was always exploring, looking for the explanation and the reason, and working to find a way to change it if he didn't agree with it.

Smith continued to play sports throughout his high school career, earning a scholarship to the University of Kansas. It wasn't, however, an athletic scholarship. Smith joined the Jayhawks on his academic merit and while he was part of the 1952 NCAA championship squad under Phog Allen, Smith didn't see much playing time. It didn't matter. Smith's curiosity was piqued as soon as he walked on campus in Lawrence, and he became a student of the game during his college career, taking his place in one of the most expansive coaching trees in college basketball history.

He never met James Naismith, the inventor of basketball who taught Allen at Kansas, but Smith began to carry on his legacy before he even graduated college. During games, there was an order to the seating arrangements on the Kansas bench. According to Richard Clarkson, a sports writer and photographer for the *The Lawrence Daily Journal-World* in the 1950s, the team trainer sat at the head of the bench; then Phog Allen; Allen's assistant, Dick Harp; the team's first sub; and so on down the line. Smith generally sat toward the end of the bench. As the game went on, however, and players checked in and out, spots would open on the bench and Smith quite often found himself toward the head, sitting next to Harp and Allen. The three discussed on-court options and play calls, and while Smith wasn't yet the Hall of Fame coach he'd eventually become, his opinion became something the Kansas staff relied on during games.

Smith wasn't the most dominant athlete in Jayhawks history, but he was always trying to better his understanding of the game, that same curiosity his mother saw in him when he was a child flaring to life as soon as the first whistle sounded. It was that mindset, as well as the values his parents instilled in Emporia, that would go on to define Smith for the rest of his career.[54]

LEARNING ON THE FLY

Smith's playing days ended as soon as he graduated from Kansas. He wasn't all that upset about it; most everyone who watched Smith in a Jayhawks uniform knew he wasn't cut out for on-court stardom but was absolutely destined to help others. Smith briefly stayed at Kansas after graduating, serving as an assistant coach during the 1953–54 season, but found his wings, quite literally, when he joined the Air Force in the late 1950s.

Smith was a lieutenant in the Air Force and served a tour in Germany before taking a job as an assistant coach on Maj. Bob Spear's coaching staff at the Academy. It wasn't Smith's team, not yet, but his influence was obvious. He helped keep the shot charts during practice, tracking where players would attempt to score from and what they needed to work on, and also ran Spear's warm-up drills. There were also a few hints of the four corners offense Smith would eventually implement at North Carolina on old Air Force tape. The Falcons were far from a basketball powerhouse, but with Smith's help, Air Force took its first step toward becoming a competitive program.

"There was no question there was a certain aura about Dean," Lt. Gen. Robert Beckel, who played for Air Force from 1956 to 1959, told *Airman*

---

54 Alexander Wolff, "Dean Smith: 1997 Sportsman of the Year," *Sports Illustrated* (December 1997), https://www.si.com/vault/1997/12/22/236257/fanfare-for-an-uncommon-man-he -became-the-winningest-college-basketball-coach-of-all-time-and-capped-an-exemplary- career-with-a-graceful-retirement-for-all-of-that-we-honor-north-carolinas-dean-smith.

Magazine in 2015. "He was a perfectionist and totally committed to basketball."[55]

Smith left Air Force in 1958, joining Frank McGuire's staff at UNC and, quite suddenly, the game of college basketball was forever altered. McGuire moved onto the NBA in 1961, and the University turned to the then thirty-year-old Smith to take over the reins of the Tar Heels program. They never regretted it.

McGuire had done his best to make North Carolina a competitive force in the college hoops world, but he'd done it by breaking a few rules. His recruiting schemes brought big names and big-city talent to Chapel Hill, but they often weren't in accordance with NCAA regulations. When he left, partially at the insistence of UNC administration, McGuire also left behind a mess, including rumors of a point-shaving scandal that Smith was forced to contend with. Smith immediately did his best to start changing the perception of the program in Chapel Hill. He focused on running a clean team, less concerned with racking up victories than he was with bringing in good players who wanted to graduate with a degree and build something for future athletes. The victories, however, came anyway.

Smith brought his own spin to the Tar Heels game and it didn't take long for UNC to fine-tune the four corners approach Smith had started at Air Force. The schemes inspired faith on the UNC roster, bolstered by an unexpected victory over Kentucky in Smith's second season, but the fans in Chapel Hill were less quick to believe. This was, after all, a coach who upon taking the top job at UNC immediately started working with his local pastor to help integrate an area restaurant.

Smith was different. He was everything McGuire wasn't: quiet, a little reserved, focused on the good in people rather than the wins on the scoresheet. It took some time for the rest of North Carolina to realize that, but the team refused to take any insults lying down. Smith inspired

---

55 Airman Magazine Staff, "Coaching Giant," *Airman Magazine* (February 2015), http://airman.dodlive.mil/2015/02/18/coaching-giant.

dedication from his players, a father-like role that he took as seriously as anything else he did and, despite whatever happened on the court, his teams were ready and willing to defend him with everything they had.

In January 1965, his fourth season with UNC, after losing on the road to Wake Forest, the team returned to campus to find an effigy of Smith hanging from a nearby tree. Then-center Billy Cunningham barely waited for the bus to stop before yanking the likeness down, angered by the impatience of the Tar Heels fans. He knew what Smith could do and what the team would, eventually, do, and believed the criticism of his coach was nothing short of unacceptable. Smith didn't say anything to his players, but he was shaken by the show, worried he wouldn't be able to ever find his footing in North Carolina.

"After the Wake Forest game he called me with the score," Smith's sister told Sports Illustrated in 1997. "I remember him searching, asking himself if he was doing the right thing with his life."[56]

After that loss, UNC won nine of its next eleven games, and Smith brought in one of his first big-name recruits, a forward from Pennsylvania named Larry Miller. It was the boost Smith needed to turn the tide in Chapel Hill and, after finally moving out of McGuire's shadow and NCAA investigations, the team started to turn the metaphorical page.

This wasn't just about basketball anymore—this was about changing the culture and a society, altering traditions that, until Smith arrived on campus, were considered set in stone. His players believed in him and trusted him, and Smith made sure, first and foremost, that they never had any reason to doubt him.

MAKING THE CHANGE

Smith's start in Carolina wasn't perfect, but it only took a few seasons for him to see a shift in Chapel Hill. Winning, of course, helped, and fans began to pack the stands as the Tar Heels began to cement themselves

---

56 Wolff, "Dean Smith: 1997 Sportsman of the Year."

as consistent and legitimate contenders for the NCAA title. It wasn't just Smith's approach on the court, however, that made the difference. He hated the word "system," refusing to believe that his game plan was that stringent or concrete, and did his best to make the game function around his players instead of the other way around.

North Carolina wasn't just a team. With Smith at the helm, it was a family, and he recruited that way as well. He brought players in with a smile and the promise of a support system unlike anything else going on in college hoops at the time. There was a sense of belonging in Carolina, a unity on the roster that made it easy to win games because, as far as any of the Tar Heels were concerned, they were competing with their brothers as much as fellow athletes. It was also an approach that made it possible for Smith to bring about real, true change on campus.

Smith knew the culture he was working in. He got to Carolina in the midst of the Civil Rights Movement, facing an "us against them" mentality that didn't make much sense to him. After all, he'd watched his father work to integrate the high school basketball team in Emporia, saw his mother treat everyone with the same love and respect no matter what color their skin was, and as the wins continued to pile up and the fans continued to cheer, Smith knew he had a platform.

He could make a difference in a way that was far bigger than point totals or stat lines, and Smith found a way to do that in the form of a New York City recruit named Charles Scott. Smith had been vocal about his hopes for integration in the past. He spoke on behalf of African-American friends to help them purchase real estate in North Carolina, and had tried to bring African-American players into the Tar Heels programs for years before he discovered Scott. This was a long time coming for Smith, but meeting Scott and realizing his basketball potential was worth the wait.

Scott joined the North Carolina basketball program in 1967, the same year Thurgood Marshall was appointed to the Supreme Court and one year after the Black Panther Party was founded in Oakland, California.

The kid who got his start at the legendary Rucker Park in Harlem was, suddenly, part of the Civil Rights Movement as well, the first African-American player, in any sport, to compete under scholarship at North Carolina. It changed the game, quite literally.

"Being the first black in the South was not something I understood the importance of. Coach Smith understood its significance a lot better than I did," Scott told North Carolina athletics in November 2015. "I was blessed to play for someone like him."[57]

Scott was a two-time All-American at North Carolina, and his talent on the hardwood was unquestioned. He had attended Manhattan's Stuyvesant High School for one year, but hoped to better his chances at a basketball scholarship by transferring to a better program at Laurinburg Institute in North Carolina. Scott graduated as valedictorian, continued to dominate on the court, and suddenly, the colleges were knocking.

He was recruited by a handful of other big-name programs, all of them all-white teams, but Scott said there was something different about North Carolina as soon as he stepped on campus. It was Smith. The coach had a different air about him, an ease and comfort that Scott not only appreciated, but knew he would need if he was going to find his footing and his shot surrounded by faces that weren't only different from him, but a few that would actually hate him. Smith asked Scott to go to church with him during his visit at Chapel Hill, sparking an immediate understanding between the two men.

"That was the first time any coach asked me to go to church with him," Scott told *Newsday* in 2015. "When you do that, you're getting into a personal circumstance other than just basketball."[58]

Most of Chapel Hill was still segregated at the time, a clear line of black and white, them and us, right and wrong, but Scott felt something shift

57 Associated Press, "Charles Scott Joins College Hoops Hall of Fame," UNC Athletics (November 2015), https://goheels.com/news/2015/11/22/210521190.aspx.

58 Greg Logan, "Charles Scott Recalls His Journey with Dean Smith to Desegregate ACC," *Newsday* (February 2015), https://www.newsday.com/sports/columnists/greg-logan/charlie-scott-recalls-his-journey-with-dean-smith-to-desegregate-acc-1.9917991.

as soon as he walked into church with Smith. This was a man who simply did not care what other people thought. He wanted to do the right thing. He wanted to bring talent into the program. And he wanted to make every single one of his players feel at home in the place he'd decided to call home. It was as simple as that.

Scott said he and Smith never discussed the potential repercussions of his recruitment. There was no conversation about the challenges he might face or the whispers he might hear when he walked around campus. There was just basketball and the team and whether or not Scott saw a future with the Tar Heels. He did and, more importantly, he saw a future with Smith at the helm. He trusted his coach believed, no matter what, that this was a man who knew what he was capable of and wanted him to succeed, no matter the color of his skin.

There were moments of triumph and disappointment for Scott during his college career. He led the Tar Heels to Final Four appearances in 1968 and 1969 and averaged 27.1 points per game in his senior season. This was still America in the late '60s, however, and still the South in the late '60s, and while Scott found his place in the North Carolina locker room, there were some who saw his mere presence on the court as wrong.

He recounted a game late in his career, after a win at South Carolina, when he was accosted by a student who yelled a racial slur at him. Scott said it was one of only a few times he saw Smith react immediately and emotionally, telling *Newsday*, "It upset him that a person would have to go through the indignity that this young man was trying to put me through."[59]

The rest of the scuffle was mostly forgotten, memories and experiences that Scott regarded as part of his daily life at that point, but he never forgot the way Smith reacted, or the way he defended every one of his players, no matter what they were going through.

Smith's former players will be the first to tell anyone he was not a perfect coach. He was prone to second-guessing and worrying, believing every

---

59 Logan, "Charles Scott Recalls His Journey."

loss was his fault alone. He was critiqued and criticized for his beliefs on the court and off it, for the relationships he fostered on his roster, and even his personal life, including a rather public divorce in the early 1970s. But for all of that, Smith's players will also defend every one of his choices, even decades after they stopped wearing Carolina blue.

He wasn't perfect, but he built something and changed everything else, a determination to question the system no matter how long it had stood. Smith changed lives and, for Scott, who went on to a Hall of Fame career in both the ABA and NBA, he provided a relationship that would affect everything he did.

"While you played for him, he was your coach, your disciplinarian, your teacher," Scott said in 2015. "But more important, after we all graduated, he became a friend, a father, and a mentor, which was even better."[60]

LIKE MIKE

It would be impossible to discuss Smith's career and not mention Michael Jordan. It's like suggesting eating a cookie without milk or peanut butter without jelly—like believing that Smith, Jordan, and Carolina didn't do more for the game of college basketball than anyone.

Smith had been successful at Carolina before Jordan. The Tar Heels made three straight Final Four appearances from 1966 to 1969, and the program won the NIT in the 1970–71 season. Still, Smith knew that North Carolina could do better, and despite the consistency he was building in Chapel Hill, the coach was constantly looking for the next great talent and the one player who would help. Enter, Michael Jordan.

Jordan was a highly recruited athlete, a dominant player at Emsley A. Laney High School in Wilmington, North Carolina, who drew interest from every big-name college program in the country. He was pursued by the likes of Duke, South Carolina, Syracuse, and Virginia, but the

---

60 Logan, "Charles Scott Recalls His Journey."

North Carolina native always had a bit of a soft spot for the program in his backyard, and he met personally with Smith in 1980. The meeting resulted in one of the most famous letters in all of sports, a typewritten note from Smith to Jordan recounting the visit and reassuring the soon-to-be-star that he'd fit in perfectly at UNC.

The letter was only four paragraphs long but ended with Smith's hope that Jordan would be returning to campus sooner rather than later, writing, "Enjoyed seeing you, Michael, and hope that beginning in September 1981 I can be your coach." It worked. Jordan picked UNC and a basketball partnership was born, the likes of which would change the game and spark the career of, quite possibly, the best to ever play.[61]

Jordan's addition to the roster brought about the change North Carolina needed to reach the next level. Jordan wasted no time, arriving in 1981 and immediately settling into his role as a leader during his freshman season. He sank shot after shot, played defense as well as anyone and, when the opportunity presented itself in the 1982 NCAA championship game against Georgetown, Jordan made sure the ball went through the hoop.

Jordan wasn't the Tar Heels leading scorer in the title game against Georgetown—that was James Worthy and his twenty-eight points—but when the game was on the line, when everything mattered just a bit more, there was no other player Smith wanted holding the ball.

Smith remembered the final moments vividly, desperate to find an edge in a game that was almost perfectly matched. He called time-out with thirty-two seconds left on the clock, and as then-assistant Roy Williams recalled to *Sports Illustrated*, told his team, "We're in great shape. I'd rather be in our shoes than theirs." The team nodded, staring at Smith as he drew up the play, and when they broke the huddle, the Tar Heels believed they were going to win that game. Jordan made sure they did.

61 Sam Richmond, "Dean Smith to MJ," NCAA (August 2015), https://www.ncaa.com/news/basketball-men/article/2015-08-12/35-years-ago-dean-smith-writes-legendary-recruiting-letter.

Georgetown settled into 1-3-1 zone defense after North Carolina inbounded the ball, with Patrick Ewing standing directly in the middle of the paint. The Tar Heels swung the ball around, time ticking off the clock and anxious fans waiting for them to do something, anything, to try and get the ball inside. But Ewing was a force and this was, after all, a North Carolina program that had all but perfected the stall tactic under Smith.

The Tar Heels, facing a one-point deficit, continued to move the ball around the top of the key before Lewis Black made a move against the nearest defender, finding Jordan on the left side of the court for a perfect sixteen-foot jumper that was nothing but net. There were fifteen seconds left on the clock. Georgetown had one final chance to take back the lead, but Jordan once again made his presence known. The Hoyas' Fred Brown panicked as the North Carolina defense swarmed, passing the ball directly to Worthy by mistake and all but cementing the Tar Heels' title. It was a questionable play, one the athletic talking heads still mutter about in confused tones, but for Smith, the reason was obvious, pointing out that Jordan "got back on defense and made a play in the passing lane," forcing the miscue.[62]

North Carolina captured its first NCAA title since 1957 with the 63–62 victory, and its first championship under Smith after six previous trips to the Final Four. It was the change Smith had been waiting for, the final push and the emergence of a superstar.

"That was the birth of Michael Jordan," the eventual NBA All-Star told Turner's Craig Sager in 2016. "Before that, I was Mike Jordan. All of a sudden I make that shot and I'm Michael Jordan."[63]

Jordan, of course, went on to be Jordan. He was named Atlantic Coast Conference (ACC) Freshman of the Year in 1982, was a First

62 Dan McGrath, "Dean Smith on Jordan: 'He'd Listen Closely to What the Coaches Said and Then Go Do It,'" *Chicago Tribune* (September 2009), https://www.chicagotribune.com/sports/basketball/bulls/michaeljordan/chi-10-jordan-3-chapelhill-deanssep10-story.html.

63 Scott Rafferty, "Flashback: Michael Jordan Begins Legendary Rise with Game-Winning NCAA Championship Shot," *Rolling Stone* (March 2017), https://www.rollingstone.com/culture/culture-sports/flashback-michael-jordan-begins-legendary-rise-with-game-winning-ncaa-championship-shot-111612.

Team All-American as both a sophomore and junior, and averaged 17.7 points per game on fifty-four percent shooting during his three seasons with the Tar Heels. Jordan was drafted third overall in the 1984 NBA Draft, the start of a career that is still the marker for every professional basketball player. But he never forgot what he learned at Carolina, and the Jordan display at the Carolina Basketball Museum is a testament to everything he learned.

Smith never talked about his relationship with Jordan. It wasn't about the accolades, and while the national championship was certainly the goal every year, the true effort was to make Jordan the best player he could be. The Museum contains two letters from Smith, much like the ones he sent Jordan during his recruiting days, detailing what he should work on in the off-season. That's it, just a practice schedule and eight ways to become a better basketball player.[64]

The debate rages on about Jordan's reign as the best ever, but the discussion itself doesn't matter. Jordan's time at UNC was a defining moment in a career that was nothing short of phenomenal, and his relationship with Smith was as important as anything else in the rest of his life.

"He was more than a coach—he was my mentor, my teacher, my second father," Jordan said in a statement after Smith passed away in 2015. "Coach was always there for me whenever I needed him, and I loved him for it."[65]

ONE FOR THE HISTORY BOOKS

Smith led North Carolina to a second NCAA title in the 1992–93 season, bolstered by a squad that included George Lynch, Eric Montross, Brian Reese, Donald Williams, and Derrick Phelps. The Tar Heels rolled through most of the regular season, but the '93 title game was

---

64 McGrath, "Dean Smith on Jordan."

65 Nick Schwartz, "Michael Jordan on Dean Smith: 'He Was My Mentor, My Teacher, My Second Father'," *USA Today* (February 2015), https://ftw.usatoday.com/2015/02/michael -jordan-remembers-dean-smith.

something different altogether. North Carolina took on Michigan in a game that is still regarded as one of the biggest blunders in sports history. Michigan player Chris Webber called a timeout the Wolverines didn't have with just seconds on the clock and the Wolverines down by two.

Michigan was assessed a technical foul and North Carolina went on to capture a 77–71 victory. It was another major moment for Smith, but not the final echelon of his Hall of Fame career. That came on March 15, 1997, when Smith captured his 877th career victory, topping Colorado in the second round of the NCAA tournament and becoming the winningest coach in college basketball history.

It was a marker Smith had been inching closer to for years, bolstered by a string of remarkable successes and even better teams, but he was never striving for history. He wanted to win, naturally, but he wanted to create something more, a program that would succeed even after he walked away and an athletic culture that defied expectation. When he reached the mark, Smith was quick to deflect the glory, telling those around him, "I wasn't trying to make a legacy. I was just trying to do what I think is right."[66]

In the buildup to the record-setting victory, Smith told reporters ahead of the game, "I'm not going to talk about anything other than this team trying to win its twenty-fifth game of the season."[67]

The all-time wins record has since been broken—by Duke's Mike Krzyzewski, Syracuse's Jim Boeheim, and former Indiana coach Bobby Knight—but it never mattered much to Smith. He joked about Knight closing in on his mark while it was happening, laughing off the idea that he would be upset to be supplanted from the history books. He'd won those games and his players played in those games. The only thing he

66 Ian O'Connor, "Dean Smith Fought for Integration," ESPN (February 2015), https://abcnews.go.com/Sports/dean-smith-fought-integration/story?id=28815822.

67 Chris Dufresne, "Growing Up to Appreciate Dean Smith's Greatness," Los Angeles Times (February 2015), https://www.latimes.com/sports/la-sp-0209-dean-smith-appreciation-20150209-column.html.

cared about was whether or not they did it the right way. They were a team, first and foremost, no matter what, building each other up and making sure they all reached that metaphorical mountaintop together.

That was his approach to basketball throughout his career—pass first, find the open man, work the corners. Smith implemented the four corners offense at North Carolina, a scheme that left opposing teams frustrated, desperate to get into passing lanes and force the ball out of the Tar Heels' collective hands. It rarely worked and the play, particularly effective in late-game situations when working with a lead, was enough to force the NCAA to install a shot clock in 1985.[68] Smith coached the way he wanted his teams to play, including every man on the court, waiting for the right moment, and finding a way to win.

THE DEAN DOME

Smith never wanted the spotlight or the accolades, at least not for himself. He wanted his players to succeed, to build a program around them that fostered something bigger than basketball. When the Dean Dome was under construction, former student reporter S. L. Price, who went on to write for *Sports Illustrated*, wrote a scathing column arguing that Tar Heels athletes were getting benefits other students would never see or use. He claimed student-athletes were coddled, treated differently and better than at other athletic programs around the country.

Price said the uproar was instantaneous. There were letters and messages to the paper, and he was called into a meeting with the UNC chancellor. He also met with Smith. There was no reprimand, however. There was just a simple question; "He wanted to know what I knew, whether the system had gotten out of hand—whether there was something I could teach him that he didn't know," Price explained.[69] Smith didn't want to argue, he wanted to know what he could do better.

---

68 "Dean E. Smith," Naismith Basketball Hall of Fame (May 2007), http://www.hoophall.com/hall-of-famers/dean-smith.

69 Wolff, "Dean Smith: 1997 Sportsman of the Year."

Smith created a family at UNC and, even after he retired in 1998, maintained the relationships he'd been building for years. There were weekly phone calls with former players, updates about seemingly mundane things, and advice shared, whether it was solicited or not. Brad Daugherty and Michael Jordan told the *Charlotte News Observer* in 2013 that Smith would regularly call to check in and remind them that they didn't need multiple watches or multiple cars, since you couldn't use more than one at a time. There was a practicality to Smith, in addition to his innate curiosity and desire to inspire change. He was strict while still being caring, encouraging while still reprimanding mistakes. He was a coach. And his players never forgot that.

"The love that came from him: the caring, the advice, the education, and the persistence and determination he had in pushing all his players, not just me," Jordan said.[70]

Smith passed away at his home in North Carolina in 2015 at the age of 83. He had stepped away from the hoops world several years before, suffering from memory issues, but was still ingrained in the fabric of college basketball. His success was unparalleled, posting a .776 winning percentage, with just one losing season at UNC and thirteen ACC tournament titles. He was inducted into the Naismith Memorial Basketball Hall of Fame in 1983, was awarded the Medal of Freedom by President Barack Obama in 2013, and more than fifty of his players went on to play professionally.

North Carolina basketball took its biggest step forward under Smith, and every home game at the Dean Dome is filled to capacity because of what he started in Chapel Hill. He didn't do it for the accolades, but they came anyway because, at his core, Smith was great at what he did—coaching.

"[He] was the greatest there ever was on the court but far, far better off the court with people," current Carolina coach Roy Williams told ESPN.

---

70 Rick Bonnell, "Michael Jordan on Dean Smith: 'He Never Put One Kid Ahead of Another,'" *The News & Observer* (November 2013), https://www.newsobserver.com/sports/college/acc/unc/article10285415.html.

"Dean Smith was the perfect picture of what a college basketball coach should have been."[71]

● ● ● ● ●
OH SAY CAN YOU SEE

Dean Smith was not the first big-name college basketball coach to join the ranks of Team USA. He wasn't the first one to lead Team USA to a medal either. Team USA was expected to win the gold medal at the 1976 Olympic Games in Montreal, but while Smith's star was on the rise at UNC, he was still a bit of a gamble for the United States Olympic Committee. After all, at that point in his career, Smith was best known for losing before he could get to the big game.

Smith was fresh off a loss in the first round of the NCAA Tournament, and while his teams at North Carolina were dominant in league play, the Tar Heels struggled on the national stage. It was enough to give a few hoops fans pause when Smith earned the top job with Team USA, replacing Hank Iba, a two-time NCAA champ whose three Olympic medals included gold in 1964 and 1968. Team USA was looking for a change, however, after losing for the first time in the 1972 Games and earning silver after stumbling against Russia. Smith might have been a bit green on the international stage, but the Air Force vet had a connection to the country that few other coaches could boast.

Smith brought in Bill Guthridge and John Thompson as assistants, working with a roster that included seven ACC players and four from UNC—Walter Davis, Phil Ford, Mitch Kupchak, and Tommy LaGarde. The Tar Heels coach consistently claimed he didn't pick the team, a selection committee did, but there were murmurings when the roster looked so similar to the one Smith was used to. That didn't, however, mean the team was an automatic favorite. Team USA was the youngest in the Games and one of the smallest as well, heading to Montreal as underdogs against the reigning

---

71 C.L. Brown and the Associated Press, "Dean Smith Dies at Age of 83," ESPN (February 2015), http://www.espn.com/mens-college-basketball/story/_/id/12296176/dean-smith -former-north-carolina-tar-heels-coach-dies-age-83.

Russians. Smith still didn't change his approach. This was a group of kids that would play like a team, or they would lose like one.

"Coach Smith did not want to out-athlete the great European teams," Ford told WRAL Sports in 2015. "He wanted to out-team them."[72]

Despite the questions and the concerns ahead of the Games, Team USA opened with a dominant 106–86 victory over Italy in the first game of pool play. The squad rolled through the opening round, with just one close call against Puerto Rico, but the one-point victory in that match did more to bolster the United States' collective confidence than anything else. The game-changing moment, as it would be throughout Smith's biggest victories, occurred in the final few seconds of play. The United States, clinging to a 93–92 victory, drew a charge by Puerto Rico's Alfred Lee Jr., giving the US the ball and cementing the victory.[73] It only got better from there.

The United States topped host nation Canada 95–77 in the semifinals and breezed by Yugoslavia 95–74 in the gold medal game after the squad upset Russia in the matchup before.[74] The gold medal game wasn't ever close, a lopsided matchup that showcased US talent and Smith's coaching prowess. He wanted to build up his team, and he did, but it would be a lie to say he didn't want to win as well. This was a test of the highest international order, and coming away with anything except a gold medal was inconceivable.

"I've never been as proud as when we received our medals and heard our national anthem played," Ford said. "It was very important to basketball in America."

In six games in Montreal, the United States was held to less than 90 points only once and won games by an average of fourteen points,

72 Bob Holliday, "For Dean Smith, Team Was More Important Than Talent," WRAL Sports Fan (February 2015), https://www.wralsportsfan.com/for-dean-smith-team-was-more -important-than-talent/14462845.

73 Pat Hickey, "Montreal Olympics: Puerto Ricans pushed US Hoops team to the Brink," *Montreal Gazette* (July 2016), https://montrealgazette.com/sports/ montreal-olympics-puerto-ricans-pushed-u-s-hoops-team-to-the-brink.

74 "1976 United States Men's Olympic Basketball," Basketball Reference (August 2018), https://www.basketball-reference.com/olympics/teams/USA/1976.

a dominant showing that was sparked by Smith's coaching and practices that would go on to shape the North Carolina basketball program. It was the only time Smith coached at the Olympics. He believed most coaches couldn't duplicate that kind of success at the international level, but it was a major step in his career. The victories got Team USA back on track and gave Smith a taste of what winning in those big moments felt like. It was something he never forgot and was always trying to find again.

● ● ● ● ●

Smith's Best Games

The 1968 NCAA Championship Game

Let's get this out of the way early; UNC lost this game. That's right. The Tar Heels didn't even play very well, falling 78–55 to UCLA. This was a UCLA program at the start of its dynasty, the second of seven straight championships under John Wooden, but it was also a marker for the Tar Heels. The loss marked the first national championship appearance for Smith, and while it wasn't the performance he'd always dreamed of, it also sparked his desire to return and make sure history didn't repeat itself. That, of course, took some time, but Smith's coaching resilience and his ability to build something at UNC got its start here.

The 1982 NCAA Championship Game

It seems like an obvious choice, but UNC's final-second, 63–62 victory over Georgetown in the NCAA championship game wasn't just one of Smith's best coaching performances, it was one of the best college hoops matchups. Ever. Full stop. Consider the players in the game alone: Patrick Ewing, Sam Perkins, James Worthy, Michael Jordan. Jordan scored the game-winner on a jumper that's still regarded as one of the most important moments in athletics. It sent the man who would go on to be the best ever into the national spotlight and gave Smith the championship that had eluded him his whole career.

CHAPTER FIVE

MIKE KRZYZEWSKI
Coach K

"Your heart has to be in whatever you lead. It became
apparent that this decision was somewhat easier to make
because you have to follow your heart and lead with it
and Duke has always taken up my whole heart…"

—HALL OF FAME COACH MIKE KRZYZEWSKI

It's not pronounced the way it's spelled. Don't try pronouncing it. It's easier just to use the initial.

Mike Krzyzewski has been pacing the Duke sidelines for over thirty years, a dominant and constant presence for the Blue Devils, and part of the very fabric of the culture on and off campus. Krzyzewski isn't just a coach; he's a phenomenon, better known simply as the first letter of a last name some college basketball fans still can't pronounce. They don't have to, because Krzyzewski is more than simply any college basketball coach. He's *the* basketball coach, the one casual hoops fans and those who only tune in during March know of, the one who has become synonymous with success on the hardwood.

Krzyzewski is winning in the form of one person. He's won some of the most dramatic games in recent hoops history. Everyone remembers the shot—Hill to Laettner—and the national championship that made the Blue Devils live up to their nickname. Duke has become a championship machine under Krzyzewski, attracting some of the top recruits in the country and producing more NBA-ready talent than just about any other program. The names go on and on: JJ Redick, Kyrie Irving, Shane Battier, and, more recently, Brandon Ingram and Jahlil Okafor. They all came to Durham for one simple reason, because Krzyzewski was in Durham and they knew he could lead a team to victory. It's become as consistent as breathing for Krzyzewski.

But Krzyzewski's influence on the world hasn't been limited to the court. With a win percentage that's nothing short of impressive, he's become something bigger than basketball. Krzyzewski draws headlines every time the Blue Devils suit up, but he's also drawn storylines on a handful of TV shows, starred in commercials and, while he never actually appeared on *One Tree Hill*, was heavily featured in a season four arc on the teen drama. The characters practiced pronouncing his name after he offered one of them a scholarship to play basketball at Duke.

Krzyzewski's name has never been easy to say, or easy to spell—even former Duke star and current Boston Celtics standout Jayson Tatum had a hard time of it when asked to try his hand at spelling it in 2018. "I'm definitely going to get it wrong," Tatum said while appearing on ESPN's *Get Up!*. "K … y? K … r? I call him 'Coach K.'"[75]

That's all anyone has to do, because Krzyzewski is much more than his name. He's the championships and the influence, the face of a program that has been at the forefront of college basketball for decades. The spelling isn't important, the pronunciation isn't important. The only important thing is the results, and Krzyzewski was determined to get those as soon as he set foot at Cameron Indoor. The journey there,

75 Darren Hartwell, "Jayson Tatum's Attempt to Spell 'Krzyzewski' On Live TV Went Horribly Wrong," NESN (May 2018), https://nesn.com/2018/05/jayson-tatums-attempt-to-spell -krzyzewski-on-live-tv-went-horribly-wrong.

of course, has plenty of twists and turns, more than enough to spark a different storyline on another teen drama, but that's what makes it interesting.

The names never mattered. As far as Krzyzewski was concerned, nothing mattered except the four letters on the front of the jersey and what happened when his players put it on. It usually ended with another win.

MEETING MICKEY

Krzyzewski has been synonymous with Duke for so long, constantly winning and racking up championships and recruiting players most of the country enjoyed booing, that it's difficult to imagine that he was ever anything except the suit-sporting, perfectly coiffed head coach we've all come to know and, occasionally, resent. That usually depended on what team you were rooting for.

It's easy to imagine that Krzyzewski grew up plotting defensive schemes and rarely cracking a smile, but that's unfair to those who knew him and know him currently, because, as far as those people are concerned, the guy they know as Mickey is the same as he was sixty years ago. Krzyzewski grew up in Chicago, the son of Polish-American parents Emily and William. He regularly spent time at the White Eagle, a restaurant and banquet hall that's been a quasi watering hole for the Polish community in the city for over sixty years. Krzyzewski was a normal kid, happy and content and, according to his friends, not the unapproachable figure the college basketball word occasionally paints him as.

"He's not nearly as interesting as [the world makes] him out to be," longtime friend Dennis Wrobel told ESPN in 2015.[76]

Krzyzewski's parents were simple people—his father spent twenty-five years as an elevator operator before opening his own bar, while his mother cleaned the Chicago Athletic Club every night—and they offered him a simple childhood. He filled it with sports and often had

76 Dana O'Neil, "Do You Know Mike Krzyzewski?" ESPN (January 2015), http://www.espn.com/espn/feature/story/_/id/12161880/duke-blue-devils-coach-mike-krzyzewski-think-is.

to do it with only the support of his friends. Their area elementary school, after all, didn't have a gym, and pleas to join the local Catholic Youth Organization basketball league were quickly shot down by area administrators.

So, naturally, Krzyzewski took it upon himself to fix that. He started his own team, filling the roster with his friends, a group that had dubbed itself the Warriors, and he served as both a player and a coach. It was the start of a career that would define his entire life.

Krzyzewski, unlike the way these stories often go, was a good athlete as a kid. He loved basketball and he excelled at the game, finishing as the leading scorer in Chicago's Catholic league twice during high school. It was the thrill of competition, the chance to prove himself that drew Krzyzewski in, and he didn't stop with basketball. Sports offered Krzyzewski an escape of sorts, a chance to control things when the world didn't offer him that opportunity very much. At one point he even considered a career in professional wrestling to maintain that control, going so far as to design championship belts with his friends, but that idea didn't last long either. He was also good in school, a "brown-nose," according to his childhood friends, the kid who listened to his parents and followed the rules. He embraced the structure, thrived in the system and, eventually, left Chicago behind for West Point.

Krzyzewski's friends found this a surprising decision. This was the mid-1960s and kids didn't often leave home for college, let alone receive a scholarship at West Point and a spot on the basketball team. His parents, however, were certain. This was the chance to be better and do better, to settle onto a path that was definite. Krzyzewski wasn't quite as sure at the start—this was, still, the '60s and the Vietnam War was raging—but he, once again, found support in a close-knit group of friends and eventually packed his bags without any doubts.

Krzyzewski went to college—and kept playing well. He was captain of the basketball team his senior season, leading the team to an NIT berth in 1969 under coach Bob Knight, and finishing fourth in the tournament.

It wasn't, however, always an easy college career. This was, of course, a team coached by Knight, and Krzyzewski's success was dependent on his acceptance of his coach's game plan. During his three years on varsity, Krzyzewski played point guard and never averaged more than seven points a game. He was told, in no uncertain terms, not to shoot. His job was to distribute the ball, to set up his teammates and make sure the offense moved like a well-oiled machine. It wasn't always a role he was particularly happy with, but it was one that helped Krzyzewski learn the game from the inside out and, most importantly, one that helped spark his own approach to coaching. Krzyzewski knew basketball better than just about anyone—because he had to. Knight wouldn't have it any other way.[77]

Krzyzewski served five years as an officer in the United States Army before returning to basketball. He joined Knight's staff at Indiana as a graduate assistant for one season, from 1974–75, and took his first head coaching position at Army one year later. In five seasons with the Black Knights, Krzyzewski posted a 73–59 record and one NIT appearance in 1978. And then came the offer that changed everything.

The kid who never wanted to do anything except control everything was named the head coach of the Duke men's basketball team on May 4, 1980. It was an offer that would lift Krzyzewski to the upper echelons of coaching, a job that would make him the center of controversy and critique, of accolades and championships, but no matter what, he never did anything to change who he was. As far as his friends could tell, Krzyzewski was still Mickey. He was still from Chicago. He still refused to compete under anything except his name. It wasn't always easy—those first few seasons in Durham were dangerously close to dreadful—but Krzyzewski never doubted. He'd done that already and he wasn't particularly interested in backtracking. The future was there, waiting for him to help shape it, and he's made sure to do just that.

---

77 Seth Davis, "Coach K Passes Mentor, Colleague, Friend on Historic Night at MSG," *Sports Illustrated* (November 2011), https://www.si.com/more-sports/2011/11/16/coach-k.

GETTING CRAZY IN CAMERON INDOOR

Krzyzewski's name has been synonymous with success for so long, it seems impossible that his early teams at Duke weren't all that great. He didn't win as soon as he got to Duke. He was a young coach without much of a resume and a playing career that didn't inspire much confidence from Duke fans. In his first three seasons with the Blue Devils, Krzyzewski posted a 38–47 record, including a 13–29 conference record, and the calls for his removal were almost as loud as any cheer at Cameron Indoor.

This was Krzyzewski, though. This was the same guy from Chicago who refused to use a different last name to make sure people could pronounce it easier. He had a plan, always, and his plan at Duke was to win—he just knew it would take some time and, more importantly, the belief of his players, and a patience that would become one of Krzyzewski's most obvious coaching traits throughout his career. Krzyzewski believed he was the right man for the job, and he didn't deviate from his goal.

"I felt this was a position right for me," Krzyzewski said at the time of his hiring. "I think Duke basketball is excellent, has been excellent, and I hope to continue that tradition."[78]

It took some time, but Krzyzewski started to shape Duke, recruiting players who trusted the system and bringing in assistants that believed in the vision. The wins started to pile up from there, but it wasn't until one specific recruit and a string of victories in the late '80s that everything changed.

People hated Christian Laettner. They despised him, critiqued the way he played the game, and called him dirty and deceitful and plenty of other adjectives that wouldn't be fit for print. The legacy of Laettner has

---

78 Timothy Bella, "Mike Krzyzewski's Humble Beginnings as Duke's Basketball Coach," *The Atlantic* (November 2011), https://www.theatlantic.com/entertainment/archive/2011/11/mike-krzyzewskis-humble-beginnings-as-dukes-basketball-coach/248572.

been twisted and turned and rewritten several hundred times, but the story of how he got to Duke—and helped change the basketball culture in Durham—may be even more interesting.

Laettner was six foot seven as a freshman in high school. He was big, he was physical, and he drew defenders like bees to honey. In his first game at Nichols, a prep school north of Buffalo, New York, Laettner was elbowed in the nose. He had grown up playing pick-up games with his dad's friends and the physicality of the game was something Laettner thrived on. It was also what helped initially draw Krzyzewski's interest, along with that of nearly every other major basketball program in the country.

The first letter came midway through Laettner's freshman season, from St. Bonaventure University, and they didn't stop throughout his high school career. He grew another two inches, put on some more weight and some more muscle, and became one of the most sought-after players in the country. His mother wanted him to go to Notre Dame. Laettner didn't. He wanted to play the best basketball in the country and, as far as he was concerned, that basketball was played in the ACC. He only made three official visits: to Virginia, North Carolina, and Duke.

Krzyzewski first saw Laettner when he was a junior at Nichols, competing in the New York state tournament, and while he was impressed by his technical skills, he was even more stunned by his clear passion for the game. Krzyzewski wanted players who cared, who thrived on victory and agonized over defeat and clamored for the biggest moment. Laettner was all of that, in six feet, nine inches of pure, physical passion.

The relationship grew from there, and while Laettner visited North Carolina and Virginia, his heart was already set on Duke. It worked out well, since Duke was already set on Laettner, certain the kid from New York could help win the program's first national championship. And it wasn't lost on those who knew Krzyzewski best, that Laettner was a little similar to the Blue Devils' coach.

"I thought he was blatantly honest the way Mike had been blatantly honest back in the day," Krzyzewski's wife Mickie recalled in *The Last Great Game*. "He never tried to be charming. He never tried to flatter a person or charm a person. He just always was him."

Laettner committed to Duke in November 1987. He called the entire Duke coaching staff himself. He didn't want anyone else to speak for him because this was the most important decision, at the time, he'd ever made. And if he was going to lead the Blue Devils, and help them win a championship, Laettner needed to start things the right way.[79]

As with most things when it came to Krzyzewski, a championship was not immediate as soon as Laettner stepped onto the court at Cameron Indoor. It took some time, it took a few more players—notably future NBA star Grant Hill and current Arizona State coach Bobby Hurley—but Duke finally reached the top of the college hoops mountain in the 1990–91 season. UNLV was expected to dominate that year, coming into the NCAA Tournament with a 30–0 record and a swarming defense that was nothing short of suffocating. Duke found a way around it.

The Blue Devils topped UNLV in the 1991 Final Four, avenging a 30-point loss from the season before, as Laettner finished with twenty-eight points. Hill chipped in eleven points and Hurley dished out seven assists in that tilt, a game that almost overshadowed Duke's victory over Kansas in the national title game.

The road to championship glory always seemed to be a little more dramatic than the championship itself for Duke and, the very next season, the Blue Devils cemented themselves in college basketball lore with one play. Ask any Duke fan about "The Shot" and they'll probably duck their head and close their eyes for a moment, letting the memory rush over them. Or, if they're younger, pull their phone out to watch it one more time. Watching that play is very likely a rite of passage, a requirement to get into Cameron Indoor and refer to yourself as crazy.

---

79 Gene Wojciechowski, *The Last Great Game: Duke vs. Kentucky and the 2.1 Seconds That Changed College Basketball* (New York: Penguin, 2012).

Picture it: Duke trailing 103–102 with 2.1 seconds on the clock in the East Regional Final against Kentucky on March 28, 1992. The fans at The Spectrum in Philadelphia, Pennsylvania, were screaming themselves hoarse. No one was sitting down. There was jumping and shouting and flailing arms and the chance for one final play for the Blue Devils. They called time-out.

Krzyzewski met the team as the players were walking toward the bench, and despite the odds and the improbability of it all, he told his guys they were going to win. He kept saying it, possibly so he'd believe it too, and then he drew up a play.

"So Grant Hill...I said, 'Can you throw the ball seventy-five feet?'" Krzyzewski recounted to Bloomberg in 2017. "He said, 'Yeah, I can do that.' And I said, 'I want you to throw the ball.'"[80]

No one covered Hill on the inbound pass and that tiny little slice of space was all Duke needed. Hill found Laettner at the foul line and he didn't just throw the ball, he made the perfect pass. Laettner caught it, dribbled, spun away from the closest defender and let the shot go. It went in as the horn sounded and Duke clinched the 104–103 victory.

It wasn't the championship, but it felt that way, and Laettner's final-second shot almost overshadows what was an absolutely dominant performance throughout the rest of regulation. He was ten for ten from the field and the free throw line, finishing with thirty-one points, seven rebounds, and three assists. The only basket anyone ever seems to care about, though, is "The Shot."[81]

Duke went on to beat Indiana and Michigan, capturing its second national championship in as many seasons. There have been other championships for Krzyzewski since then, other teams and other

---

80 "Duke's Coach K Recalls Coaching 'The Shot' Moment of 1992," Bloomberg (March 2017), https://www.bloomberg.com/news/videos/2017-03-15/duke-coach-k-recalls-coaching -the-shot-moment-of-1992-video.

81 Zack Pierce, "25 Years Ago Today, Christian Laettner and Duke Broke Kentucky's Heart," FOX Sports (March 2017), https://www.foxsports.com/college-basketball/story/ christian-laettner-duke-the-shot-kentucky-25-years-ago-ncaa-tournament-032817.

players, some of whom were just as controversial as Laettner, but that team and the 1992 title run might be his most impressive. This was the team he'd been waiting for, the group that believed and trusted the system, the x's and o's Krzyzewski had been working on for over a decade.

He wasn't sure if they'd be able to beat Kentucky in that time-out, but Krzyzewski knew, as soon as Laettner let the ball go, the victory was just one second away, quite literally. After all, Laettner was the recruit that was going to help change everything and Krzyzewski knew, from there on out, Duke basketball had reached a whole new level, one he's still not ready to backtrack from.

"This team was a great team," Krzyzewski said, after the '92 championship. "It met every challenge and at the Final Four it showed its true personality by winning both games in the second half with what I like best, defense."[82]

THE WORLD'S MOST FAMOUS ARENA

Krzyzewski has won plenty of games on Duke's home court. Cameron Indoor is one of the most historic arenas in all of college basketball, a smaller-than-average gym constantly jam-packed with fans who yell and attempt to distract and earn that "crazy" label every time the Blue Devils step on the hardwood. Krzyzewski's resume since those first two national championships has only grown, and Duke's advantage in Durham is one of the most unquestionable things in any sport, at any level.

Duke has become a perennial powerhouse under Krzyzewski, recruiting some of the country's top talent and consistently contending for titles, whether those be in conference or on the national level. The court at Cameron Indoor is now named in his honor. Despite those shaky early seasons, Krzyzewski has found a way to win. In his first twenty-eight years at Duke, Krzyzewski was a twelve-time National Coach of

---

82 "Duke Basketball," Coach K, accessed November 2018, www.coachk.com.

the Year, was named "America's Best Coach" in 2001 by *Time Magazine* and CNN, and that same year, was inducted into the Naismith Memorial Basketball Hall of Fame. He's a defense-minded coach, one who thrives on bringing pressure and the right personnel for every possibility, and he's always found a way to make it work—even when it wasn't supposed to. Krzyzewski led Duke to three more national championships after those back-to-back runs, notching titles in 2001, 2010, and 2015.

Krzyzewski has made winning a habit. When Duke topped Arizona 82–72 in the 2001 national championship game, the Blue Devils finished a four-year run with a whopping 133 victories. The team lost just fifteen games during that same span, and ten of the top thirty-five four-year runs in college basketball history belong to Krzyzewski-led Duke squads. The program has become something of an enigma, always a contender, despite one-and-done stars in the current college hoops world. People hate Duke and love Duke and love to hate Duke, but no matter what kind of emotions the Blue Devils inspire, one fact still remains: Krzyzewski doesn't care. He cares about his players, and it doesn't matter what anyone else thinks.

"I thoroughly loved coaching these kids," Krzyzewski said after the 2001 championship. "Get real close to the guys on my team. That's the most rewarding thing about what I do."[83]

Krzyzewski has never worried much about the numbers surrounding his career. Unless, of course, it's the final score. He likes winning, after all.

The questions started in 2010, when those people who do care about numbers noticed Krzyzewski was closing in on one in particular: the most victories of all time by a men's college basketball coach. And in a strange twist of sports fate, Krzyzewski would have to pass his former coach and mentor Bobby Knight to achieve it. He still didn't care much about the accolades, was far more concerned with what kind of defense Duke was going to run against Michigan State on November 16, 2011, but as the seconds ticked away on a non-league, early-season game

---

83 "Duke Basketball," www.coachk.com.

at Madison Square Garden, Krzyzewski knew, eventually, he'd have to acknowledge what he accomplished. So, naturally, Krzyzewski did things a little differently.

Knight was at the game—part of the ESPN broadcast at the time—and Krzyzewski didn't hesitate before leaning over the table, wrapping an arm around his former coach, and telling him, "I know a lot of people tell you this, Coach. But I love you." It took Knight a moment to respond. He kept his head on Krzyzewski's shoulder, but according to *Sports Illustrated*, when he leaned back, the next few words out of his mouth were almost exactly what any college hoops fan would expect.

"Boy, you've done pretty good for a kid who couldn't shoot," Knight told Krzyzewski.[84]

It wasn't the only time Krzyzewski recorded a major win at Madison Square Garden. On January 25, 2015, Duke defeated St. John's 77–68, making Krzyzewski the first NCAA Division I men's basketball coach to reach 1,000 career wins. The Blue Devils weren't perfect in the non-conference matchup. Duke jumped out to an early lead before St. John's did its best to rally, leading by as many as ten points with just under eleven minutes left in the game, but the Blue Devils never wavered and Krzyzewski never worried. That particular trait has never really been part of his coaching makeup anyway.

Instead, Krzyzewski simply turned to his players and waited for them to make plays. They did. Tyus Jones notched twenty-two points, and Jahlil Okafor chipped in seventeen, and Krzyzewski credited Marshall Plumlee with taking control down the stretch. Krzyzewski can't get on the actual court, as much as he may have wanted to in games past, but he's always trusted that the players on his roster would be able to make something happen. That they were able to do it at Madison Square Garden in a game that meant as much to college basketball as Duke's overall record that day was simply a bonus.

---

84 Davis, "Coach K Passes Mentor, Colleague, Friend on Historic Night at MSG."

"Outside of Cameron, this is the best, because it's revered," Krzyzewski told *Sports Illustrated* after the win. "This is the palace. This is the best place."[85]

THE GAME PLAN

Krzyzewski's 1000th victory was a brand-new benchmark for college coaches across the country. This was uncharted territory, the kind of success other programs have only ever dreamed of. So how did Krzyzewski make it work? How, in a world where some of his best players didn't stay with the program for more than a few months, did he keep winning at that kind of pace? The answer, actually, is relatively easy: Krzyzewski stayed.

There have, of course, been other opportunities, other coaching jobs, and Krzyzewski was even forced to choose between Duke and Iowa State in 1980. The NBA has called more than once, teams looking for Krzyzewski's guidance and track record of success, but he's never felt the need to leave Durham. Krzyzewski has settled into his spot with Duke and that has allowed him to build something at Duke.

"It's one of those priceless things," Krzyzewski said. "I've never made a decision based on what will get me the most money. It was what was going to give me the most happiness, and I've been really happy and fulfilled at Duke."[86]

Krzyzewski's philosophy at Duke has been simple: next play. It's become a mantra for the last few decades—any mistake, miscue, or turnover on whatever court the Blue Devils happen to be playing on is met with the same two words. Next play. There's no point in lingering on what went wrong. The game simply won't allow it. There's another play and another chance to get better, to put the ball through the hoop

---

85 "Coach K Nabs 1000th Win as Duke Takes Down St. John's," *Sports Illustrated* (January 2015), https://www.si.com/college-basketball/2015/01/25/duke-st-johns-1000-wins-coach-k-madison-square-garden-ncaa-basketball.

86 "Duke Basketball," www.coachk.com.

or slow down an opponent. Krzyzewski has never wanted his players to linger on "what-ifs" or "could have beens."

Krzyzewski has likened the idea to a rearview mirror and regularly reminds his teams not to look in it. "They can't look back, they've got to look ahead," he told the *News-Observer* in 2016.[87] He also added that the approach grew out of his time at West Point. It was always about the next mission, the next moment; worrying too much about what had already happened would only threaten what was currently going on.

Krzyzewski's coaching style hasn't changed much since he arrived at Duke, and that carryover from team to team, from player to player, has allowed him to create the kind of program that can survive one-and-dones with relative ease. The players who suit up for the Blue Devils come into Durham knowing two things: Krzyzewski won't let them linger too much on mistakes, and he expects a lock-down defense as soon as the ball is tipped. That, however, has been a bit of a work in progress.

Duke rarely ran a zone early in Krzyzewski's tenure. The Blue Devils teams of the '80s and early '90s were fast-paced, swarming defenses that hardly ran the 1-2-2 zone Krzyzewski referred to as "12."[88] Then, the players changed and Krzyzewski had to change a bit too.

Krzyzewski still isn't all that crazy about zone defense, but he's been willing to use it during games—helped a bit by his friend, Syracuse coach Jim Boeheim—because, as he's been quick to tell his players, it's all about the next play. And if zone defense is going to help, then Krzyzewski's going to call the play.

Krzyzewski first started experimenting with zone while coaching Team USA with Boeheim. The pair implemented the defense sparingly in the early 2000s, but it wasn't until August 2010, when the United States

87 Ron Morris, "Duke's Coach K Teaches 'Next Play' to Keep Teams Looking Forward," *The News & Observer* (December 2016), https://www.newsobserver.com/sports/college/acc/duke/article123638384.html.

88 Pete Thamel, "How Three Games Made Duke Mike Krzyzewski Rethink His Defensive Philosophy," Yahoo! Sports (March 2018), https://sports.yahoo.com/three-games-made-dukes-mike-krzyzewski-rethink-defensive-philosophy-205049704.html.

barely squeaked out an 86–85 victory over Spain in an exhibition game, that Krzyzewski realized zone could work well down the stretch. Team USA had led throughout most of the game, but Spain rallied late and, as the story goes, Boeheim suggested the team go zone in an attempt to slow down the hectic pace of play in the final few seconds. Krzyzewski agreed. After all, man-to-man hadn't worked on the last play; it was on to the next one. And it worked. So Krzyzewski brought it to Duke.

It started in 2015, after Duke had been effectively picked apart by NC State and Miami. Krzyzewski was ready to try anything, and with a roster mostly composed of freshman, zone suddenly make a lot of defensive sense. It slowed down the game, allowed the Blue Devils to control tempo, and made the learning curve for a roster of first-year college players a little less extreme. The experiment was by no means perfect.

Duke alternated between zone and man-to-man throughout the season, trying to find a defensive scheme that would work. It took some time, but eventually the Blue Devils started settling into a zone more often than not and, suddenly, those points allowed per possession started to drop. To say that it took the college hoops world by surprise would be an understatement. This was not a Duke defense, at least it was not a Duke defense fans were used to. Krzyzewski did not care. If it worked, if it helped win games, then that was the defense they were going to run because he didn't have time to worry about what had happened in the past. Next play.[89]

According to Synergy Sports, in eleven games in February and March 2018, Duke played 2-3 zone on 94.4 percent of its defensive half-court possessions. There were, naturally, miscues, moments of frustration, or less-than-perfect rotations through the zone, but Duke found a way to figure it out because that's what Krzyzewski has always expected from his teams. It's a philosophy he's kept intact for over thirty years and one that's helped Duke become a national title contender every season.

---

89 Dan Greene, "How Duke Transformed Its Defense from a Susceptible Shortcoming to a Special, Stifling Zone," *Sports Illustrated* (March 2018), https://www.si.com/college-basketball /2018/03/21/duke-zone-defense-ncaa-tournament-march-madness.

POLARIZING

Krzyzewski has become one of the most interesting coaches in college basketball since he started coaching college basketball. The success is there. There are wins and championships and star players. But it's also more than that, because Krzyzewski isn't just those impressive facts and figures. He's also one of the most hated coaches of any sport at any level. There are basketball fans who hate Duke simply because Krzyzewski is pacing the sidelines or hate Krzyzewski simply because he's coaching at Duke.

Sometimes there's no rhyme or reason to the hatred. It's just there, with everything else. In fact, in 2011 *The Atlantic* published an article titled simply "Why Everybody Hates Coach K." There are opinions from a handful of panelists, all of whom regularly wrote in the sports world, and many of whom simply disliked Coach K because of who he was and the energy he and his teams gave off.

"Coach K's attitude is even worse than that—with every smirk it looks like he's saying, 'We're better than you, we know it, and you know it, but we're going to be magnanimous about it,'" wrote Jake Simpson.

The discourse, however, doesn't really matter. It'll continue as long as Duke continues to win and, as far as Krzyzewski is concerned, that's going to continue for quite some time. In 2017, Krzyzewski was voted the most powerful man in college basketball, earning 43.7 percent of the votes in a poll conducted by CBS Sports. Kentucky's Jon Calipari finished second with 20.4 percent of the votes.[90]

Krzyzewski has racked up more awards and honors than just about any other current college hoops coach. He's earned Coach of the Year from half a dozen organizations, was named *Sports Illustrated* Sportsperson of the Year in 2011, and is one of the most recognizable faces in athletics, even when people are jeering at it. Krzyzewski's connection to

---

90 Gary Parrish, "Candid Coaches: Who Is the Most Powerful Person in All of College Basketball?" CBS Sports (September 2017), https://www.cbssports.com/college-basketball/news/candid-coaches-who-is-the-most-powerful-person-in-all-of-college-basketball.

Duke runs as deep as anything, a career that's been highlighted by championships and victories, but has also left him to be despised for that same dominance. It's a fine line to walk, and for Krzyzewski, who has never made any mention of his retirement plans, even at the head of the 2018–19 season, that line has defined his coaching as much as anything.

Krzyzewski is bigger than the sport, bigger than the accolades, and even bigger than his name. He's Coach K and he's only ever cared about winning, even if it makes you hate him.

● ● ● ● ●

A KNIGHT AND A MENTOR

Krzyzewski's relationship with his college coach, Bobby Knight, was one of the most influential of his life, and also one of the most dramatic. Krzyzewski passed his mentor on the all-time wins list in 2011, but the road to those victories is one of the most interesting in the entire sports world.

"Their relationship fascinates me," Krzyzewski's wife Mickie told Sports Illustrated in 2011. "It kind of defies description."

It started at Army—a basketball team that was far from a powerhouse with a twenty-five-year-old coach who rarely took no for an answer. Krzyzewski never packed his stat line at Army, but he did his job, passed the ball, and made sure the offense moved well enough that the Black Knights made two appearances in the NIT, including a semifinal berth his senior year. That same night, just after Army lost to Boston College at Madison Square Garden, Krzyzewski's father suffered a massive brain hemorrhage. He died before Krzyzewski and Knight could get there. That's right, Knight went back to Chicago with Krzyzewski and stayed there for three days.

The relationship changed then, more father and son than coach and player, and Krzyzewski followed Knight to Indiana as a grad student. The pair stayed close even after Krzyzewski took over at

Duke—despite Knight's certainty that he'd do better at Iowa State—and Knight regularly advised his former point guard in the ways of high-stakes college basketball coaching. Then, in 1992, Knight and Krzyzewski squared off in the Final Four.

This wasn't the first time the two played each other, but it was the first time Knight entered the game as the quasi underdog. Duke was fresh off an NCAA championship, and in the days leading up to the game, the storylines continued to pile up.

When asked if he'd asked Knight on how to beat a Big Ten school earlier in the tournament, Krzyzewski responded, "No, somewhere in my seventeen years as a coach I've figured out how to scout an opponent." Knight didn't appreciate the quip and when Duke beat Indiana 81–78, the two barely exchanged more than a passing handshake. Afterward, Krzyzewski received a note from Knight that essentially ended their relationship.

The two didn't cut ties completely in the years that followed, but it was not the friendship it had been. That was until Krzyzewski was enshrined in the Naismith Hall of Fame in 2001. According to his wife, Krzyzewski said Knight was the only one who could speak at his induction, and the invitation was the metaphorical bandage on a cut that had festered between both coaches for years.

Knight's voice shook when he spoke about Krzyzewski, calling him "the best coach that I've had a team play against." They hugged. They cried. The cameras clicked. It wasn't a perfect remedy, but it was enough and, a decade later, when Krzyzewski made history at Madison Square Garden, he wanted Knight there as well, even when he was passing him.[91]

● ● ● ● ●

---

91 Davis, "Coach K Passes Colleague, Mentor, Friend on Historic Night at MSG."

Krzyzewski's Best Games

The 1984 ACC Tournament Upset

It's difficult to believe that Duke was ever really an underdog with Krzyzewski pacing the sidelines, but UNC's 1984 squad also boasted Sam Perkins, Matt Doherty, and Michael Jordan. So, beating them wasn't just a big deal, it was the biggest deal. Add into the mix that the Tar Heels came into the game undefeated in ACC play, with two wins over Duke already, and the Blue Devils' 77–75 victory suddenly becomes even more impressive. Johnny Dawkins led the way for Duke, a team that had recorded just one win against UNC and Dean Smith under Krzyzewski in his first four seasons with the squad. This game didn't win a championship, didn't start a dynasty, but it made a statement: the Blue Devils and Coach K had arrived.

The 1992 NCAA Championship Game

Everyone knows about the Kentucky game and "The Shot," but some college hoops fans forget that Duke still had another game to play after topping the Wildcats. The Blue Devils squared off against Michigan in the championship, but while the game received plenty of hype leading up to tipoff, the matchup itself was more than a little lopsided. Duke topped the Wolverines 71–51, becoming the first team to repeat as national champions since UCLA in 1973. Duke's defense led the charge, smothering Michigan from every angle. It was a dominating performance that often gets overlooked after the drama of "The Shot," but it may have been even more impressive and, most importantly, it meant another championship.

CHAPTER SIX

BOBBY KNIGHT
The General

"OK, it's true, sometimes I intimidate a kid. Usually when I first get him. That sets up the best conditions for teaching. But that's only true with basketball players, not with anyone else."

—BOBBY KNIGHT ON HIS RECRUITING PITCH

Everyone knows about the chair. It's embedded in sports history, a moment so talked about it doesn't need more adjectives. The chair was red. It matched the Indiana color scheme. It wasn't all that sturdy, just some molded plastic and four legs that might have wobbled a little when a player sat down on it. And it looked particularly violent when being thrown across the court.

Bob Knight was one of the most successful coaches in college basketball when he also became one of the most infamous coaches in college basketball, tossing the chair across the court during a February 1985 game between the Hoosiers and Purdue. Knight, whose reputation for his volatile temper on the sidelines had only grown since he first arrived in Indiana, grabbed the chair after a series of calls against his squad. He didn't agree with them. He didn't often agree with anything the referees did. This moment, however, one single decision became the defining characteristic of Knight's career.

He picked up the chair, threw it across the court, and watched as it landed underneath the basket just in front of a student section at Assembly Hall. The fans then didn't boo, except at the referees, but the trajectory of Knight's legacy changed in that moment. Indiana lost the game, one of fourteen losses the Hoosiers would suffer in a rare disappointing season under Knight, but no one remembers that. They remember the moment. They remember Knight's temper. They remember a piece of plastic flying across the court.

Knight's emotional reaction to a few calls in one game was a microcosm of how he coached. Every moment mattered. Every second mattered. Every play could change the course of a game. Knight demanded perfection, not just from the referees, but from his coaching staff and his school and every player on his roster. He was the general through and through, expecting respect and requiring results. And, for the most part, Hoosiers fans loved him for it. They didn't boo him after he threw the chair. They believed it was what the referees deserved for blowing the call. Knight was ejected after the throw, walking off the court to the sounds of his own name echoing in the arena.

"It was surreal," Charlie Miller, a former Indiana student who went on to become an editor at *The Post-Standard* in Syracuse, told *Sports Illustrated*. "But his throwing the chair was the affirmation we were seeking. See, it was a bulls--- call."[92]

This was, simply, the coach Indiana fans had come to expect. They appreciated his intensity, thrived on his shouts from the sidelines, and waited, with almost bated breath, for what Knight would do next. The rest of the country, however, was stunned, staring at TV screens with mouths open and surprise coloring their features because Knight's behavior during games was especially intense for college hoops at the

92 L. Jon Wertheim, "All the Rage: Bobby Knight's Infamous Chair Game 30 Years Later," *Sports Illustrated* (2015), https://www.si.com/longform/2015/1985/knight/index.html.

time. He was like a whirlwind as soon as he walked onto the court, unpredictable and louder with every call he disagreed with. He disagreed with most of the calls.

The chair incident is far from the only major moment in Knight's career. This is, after all, a coach who won games and set records and helped put Indiana basketball on the map, notching one of the most dominant seasons by any team in any sport ever. That success, however, makes Knight even more of an enigma. He's a winner who also managed to alienate part of the basketball world with his sideline antics and chair theatrics. He's one of the best minds in the game who has spent the last few years bad-mouthing the teams that he helped inspire. Knight's former players have spoken out against him, while others have lauded him for his contributions to the programs they suited up for and their own careers.

Knight makes sense and doesn't, all at the same time. He cared too deeply, demanded too much, and changed the game—not always for the better, but he made a difference all the same. Knight's legacy is still evolving, a string of controversies and post-coaching moves that have left even his biggest supporters scratching their heads. It wasn't always about the chair, but the chair is still a moment Knight can't shake and a perfect depiction of the fiery, passionate coach who continues to leave his mark on the game.

NOT QUITE A STAR

Knight grew up in Orrville, Ohio, a small railroad town about twenty miles away from Akron with around 5,000 people within its lines. He started playing sports young, with a determination to prove himself that only grew as he did. Knight was a sports star in Orrville, a one-man basketball powerhouse who defined himself by his success on the court and his ability to impress his father.

Knight's childhood, from the outside, wasn't all that different from that of any of the other kids in Orrville, but the future Hall of Famer was never particularly close with his parents, including his father Pat. Instead, Knight grew close to his maternal grandmother, Sarah Henthorne. She was his biggest fan, a vocal supporter of Knight's basketball career and his growing stardom in Orrville. It was a sharp difference from his parents, who, despite doing their best, never showed much interest in Knight's love of the game.

It was that disconnect that helped shape Knight's fiery competitive streak, and it only grew as he did. Knight was a star in his own back-yard, and he was certain he'd continue to be just that when he started playing at Ohio State in 1958. Things didn't pan out that way. Knight spent most of his college career with the Buckeyes on the bench, a reserve who rarely saw any playing time.

That didn't change his attitude. Knight was known as "The Dragon" to his teammates, but not because of his attitude or penchant for appearing to breathe fire. He told his teammates he was the leader of a motorcycle gang known as The Dragons. Knight wanted that respect, and maybe even wanted to be feared. The truth didn't matter as much as the impact did, and Knight made sure he left an impact wherever he went.

Knight's biggest moment came in the 1961 NCAA Championship when then-coach Fred Taylor called his name with one minute and forty-one seconds on the clock. Cincinnati was leading Ohio State 61–59, and Knight knew this was his chance. Buckeyes' assistant coach Frank Truitt told the story of how Knight practically bounded off the bench, sprinting onto the court and taking the ball. He faked a drive into the middle of the lane, crossed his defender, and drove to the basket. The ball went in the hoop and tied up the game.

"Knight ran clear across the floor like a 100-yard dash sprinter and ran right at me and said, 'See there, coach, I should have been in that game a long time ago!'" Truitt said.[93]

---

93 Steve Delsohn and Mark Heisler, *Bob Knight: The Unauthorized Biography*, (New York: Simon & Schuster, 2006).

Ohio State eventually lost the game in overtime, falling 70–65, and while Knight had been part of a title-winning team the season before, falling short that year, when he'd gotten on the court, was something he couldn't stomach. It was also another hit in a string of recent disappointments on and off the court.

Knight had returned to Orrville several times since he started college, including a visit just after Ohio State won the NCAA Tournament in 1960. He came home looking to celebrate and, perhaps, even brag a little, but, once again, the world had different ideas. His grandmother, the one who'd always supported his basketball dreams, passed away while he was home. She was still sitting in her favorite chair and some in Orrville claimed she was waiting for Knight to return, just so she could see him again.

Knight continued to play basketball, but his relationships with a variety of authority figures took a hit after his grandmother passed away. He started having trouble with Taylor at Ohio State, still not seeing the playing time he wanted, and he was never able to foster much communication with his father. Pat Knight was not much for talking anyway; he regularly turned off his hearing aid every night and read the newspaper back to front.

"My father was the most disciplined man I ever saw," Knight told *Sports Illustrated* in 1981 "Discipline: doing what you have to do, and doing it as well as you possibly can, and doing it that way all the time."[94]

Knight took all his frustration and turned it into something else—fierce determination to prove himself. He was also particular about what he did after graduating Ohio State. Knight considered a job at a high school in Celina, Ohio, taking over the top spot with the basketball team and working as an assistant with the football squad, but realized quickly he didn't want to divert his attention between two sports. It was always basketball for Knight and so he took a job as a basketball assistant in

---

94 Frank Deford, "The Rabbit Hunter: A Penetrating Profile of Bobby Knight," *Sports Illustrated* (January 1981), https://www.si.com/college-basketball/2015/01/14/rabbit -hunter-frank-deford-bobby-kight-si-60.

Cuyahoga Falls, Ohio. He broke a clipboard in his first game—coaching tenth graders.

The murmurings about Knight's enthusiasm only grew and, a year later, he took an assistant job under Tates Locke at West Point, enlisting in the Army so he was eligible. Locke left the team in 1965, and to everyone's surprise except Knight's, Knight was named head coach at West Point. He was twenty-four years old. Knight spent six seasons with the Black Knights, winning 102 games, coaching the likes of Mike Silliman and future Duke coach Mike Krzyzewski, and growing his reputation. He was never worried about the money he made while coaching, telling *Sports Illustrated* he was making $99 a month at the time. He did, however, care about winning.

Knight's temper took on a life of its own at West Point, each incident more emotional and fervent than the next. It was reported that he kicked over lockers and screamed at officials after losing to Brigham Young University (BYU) in the 1966 NIT semifinals. Knight apologized to BYU coach Stan Watts afterward, who was quoted as telling him, "You're going to be one of the bright young coaches in the country, and it's just a matter of time before you win a national championship." [95]

Knight didn't win a national championship with Army, but the kid who'd always wanted to prove himself got another chance to do just that in 1971. He was hired by Indiana University, a step up and a bigger stage, and while he still didn't care much about the money, Knight was going to make sure his teams won.

PLAYING FOR PERFECTION

Bob Knight demanded greatness from his players. This was a man who had no problem yelling at tenth graders in his first basketball game as a coach. The sky was the limit for his college teams, and even that was

---

95 Brad Rock and Lee Warnick, *Greatest Moments in BYU Sports*, (Salt Lake City: Bookcraft, 1984).

up for debate. Knight's players should have been able to get a higher jump on their vertical than just the sky.

Knight found immediate success in Indiana, winning the Big Ten in his second season with the program. The Hoosiers advanced to the Final Four, but lost to the college hoops powerhouse that was UCLA. That didn't sit well with Knight. His teams would come back, better and stronger and more talented, a well-oiled machine that, he was certain, would cement itself as a national contender every season. Indiana captured another Big Ten title in the 1973–74 season and, from 1974 to 1976, went undefeated in the regular season. The Hoosiers came up short of their ultimate goal in '75 though, stumbling against Kentucky in the NCAA Tournament after star Scott May broke his arm.

The general consensus of the college hoops world, and many in the Indiana basketball program, is that the '74–'75 team could have won it all, easily. May's injury, however, changed things, and maybe gave the Hoosiers a bit of a chip on their shoulder heading into the next season. The team knew it had been close and was all too aware of the talent on its roster, and that year, the 1975–76 team would make history.

"This team was better because they were better as players," Knight told *USA Today* in 2013. "They were older. They were a year older and they had gone through something that was very close to a tremendous success."[96]

The 1975–76 Hoosiers men's basketball team did not lose a single game. It was the kind of perfection Knight had been dreaming of since he first picked up a basketball. It was a team in the truest sense of the word, a group of athletes who complemented each other, played off each other, and consistently stunned the entire country. Indiana won thirty-two games that season, sparked by the motion offense that became Knight's calling card. The Hoosiers never stopped moving, exhausting opposing teams and keeping the ball away from any defense that tried

---

96 Bob Kravitz, "1975–76 Undefeated Indiana team Voted Best Ever," *USA Today* (April 2013), https://www.usatoday.com/story/sports/ncaab/2013/04/06/undefeated-indiana-team-voted-best-ever/2058825.

to get in their way. They set the tone from the opening whistle, found the basket, and then did it all over, every time they got the ball back.

Knight came into that season expecting an undefeated performance. It was what his teams did, and after coming up short the season before, Knight wasn't willing to accept anything except a perfect record. He told the squad winning the Big Ten or even the NCAA championship weren't enough. There needed to be a zero on that record and Knight knew his team was capable of it—if they followed his plan.

The team, which included the likes of Jim Crews, Tom Abernethy, Bobby Wilkerson, Scott May, Kent Benson, and Quinn Buckner, responded. They didn't really want to see what Knight would do if they didn't, because in the five years since taking over at Indiana, the future Hall of Fame coach had done something to the culture of Hoosiers basketball. He wanted perfect, but so did his players and, more importantly, so did their fans. There was an expectation and a level of performance that wasn't just the goal, it was the demand. Failure to reach that was, quite simply, impossible to imagine.

Knight was a taskmaster, but his players never shied away from meeting the goals he set for them. If anything, it helped bring them together on and off the court. This was a team that had to deal with the hype. There were *Sports Illustrated* covers during the season, pronouncements that they would be the best college basketball squad ever, and opponents who saw a possible victory over Indiana as important as winning the NCAA title. The Hoosiers didn't flinch in the face of any of it; they settled into their motion offense, outscored opponents by double digits, and kept winning. Because that's what Knight wanted them to do.

"He made it pretty normal for us," May said in 2016. "We just didn't feel [pressure]. We just played."[97]

97 Mike Lopresti, "40 Years Later, Remembering the Undefeated 1976 Hoosiers," NCAA (January 2016), https://www.ncaa.com/news/basketball-men/article/2016-01-06/indiana -basketball-remembering-undefeated-1976-hoosiers-40.

Indiana opened up the 1975–76 season with a challenge, one the Hoosiers embraced with open arms: squaring off against defending national champion UCLA. The Hoosiers won, 84–64, and the streak went from there. Indiana kept winning games, outscoring opponents by a cumulative total of 554 points, and while there were a few close calls, most of the Hoosiers' victories were lopsided ones.

Indiana entered the NCAA Tournament as the No. 1 ranked team, taking down St. John's by twenty points in the first round. Alabama and Marquette were the next casualties to the undefeated cause, and a rematch against UCLA in the Final Four proved little more than a warm-up exercise, another strong showing against the Bruins in the 65–51 victory. Then came Michigan. After everything, the practices and the hype and the actual, audible demands from Knight, Indiana once again took everything in stride. The team played its game, made baskets, and won a national championship in historic fashion, defeating the Wolverines 86–68 to cement the perfect season.

There's a picture of the team celebrating its victory, with May and Buckner standing near Knight; he's smiling in the photo. It didn't happen often, but the smile was genuine and emotional and even forty years later, Buckner could remember exactly what he was thinking when the photo was snapped.

"It was jubilation," he said. "It was relief. I think for all of us, the biggest part of that was to see the smile on Coach Knight's face."[98]

The '75–'76 Indiana team is the last college hoops squad to go undefeated from the first game of the season to the championship game. It's a mark that several other teams have come close to reaching— Larry Bird's Indiana State team made it to the championship game in 1979 before dropping the final game. UNLV made it to the Final Four in 1991, as did Kentucky in 2015. The record, however, still stands. The Hoosiers don't celebrate every time a previously undefeated team loses, and while they aren't sure a perfect season is possible in today's

98 Lopresti, "40 Years Later."

era of one-and-done stars, the former Indiana standouts aren't worried about their legacy being tarnished.

They know what they did and how they worked for it and what Knight expected of them every time they suited up in that red and white uniform. If another team can do it, great, but they had their moment and it's one none of them will ever forget.

"What we were able to do, we're very proud of, but we don't relish the fact that somebody hasn't had success doing what they try to do," Buckner said in 2013. "That's kind of the way Coach Knight would have us."[99]

HOOSIERS COUNTRY

Knight's success with Indiana didn't stop after the first national championship. And his coaching habits didn't change either. If anything, Knight became even more demanding after that first run at perfection, certain every new roster was another group that would, inevitably, cut down nets.

Knight won 200 games as a head coach by the time he was thirty-five. He didn't win another NCAA title in the 1970s, but the Hoosiers captured the NIT championship in 1979, defeating Purdue 53–52. Then came the '80s—and Knight's reputation in Indiana became the stuff of college hoops legend, a looming figure who was larger than life because he was louder than anyone else. The persona of Bobby Knight that even the most casual sports fan knows evolved in the '80s, settling into himself and his emotional outbursts on the sideline. Knight kept winning, and he made Indiana a powerhouse, but he also became something else in his second decade with the program.

Sports Illustrated published a longform feature story on Knight in January, 1981, detailing everything from Knight's use of hunting to clear his mind to the kind of jokes he told at practices to his ever-growing popularity in the state of Indiana. He settled into the spotlight, both in

---

99 Kravitz, "1975–76 Undefeated Indiana Team Voted Best Ever."

the story and in the real world, the kind of man who state politicians sought approval of, simply because he coached the Indiana University basketball team. A few months after the story was published, Knight and the Hoosiers won the NCAA title, their second in five years.[100]

Knight was just forty years old at the time, and at the start of a road that would be nothing short of legendary, for a variety of reasons. First, however, it's important to talk about the basketball, because the basketball, at its core, was good.

Bloomington, Indiana, was suddenly at the forefront of the college basketball world. Knight brought in some of the game's top players, and the future Hall of Famer continued to gain traction with the hometown crowd and the players who revered him. He yelled, but he yelled at everyone. He shouted and cursed and screamed and, occasionally, threw chairs across the court. It didn't matter, because the teams kept winning. The Hoosiers of the 1980s boasted the likes of Mike Woodson and Isiah Thomas, names that would go on to have dominant NBA careers. Indiana captured its third national title under Knight in 1987, defeating Syracuse on a game-winning jumper from Keith Smart with five seconds left to play.

Once again, the Hoosiers were looking to redeem themselves with a title after a disappointing finish the season before. Indiana was upset by Cleveland State in the first round of the previous NCAA Tournament, and that year's senior class was hoping to avoid becoming the first group in the Knight era to graduate without winning a Big Ten title. It was as good a motivator as any. Indiana shared the conference title with Purdue, but the taste of victory helped spark the team's run in the NCAA Tournament.

Indiana rolled through the postseason, blowing out Fairfield and taking down Auburn 107–90. Knight took on his former player Mike Krzyzewski in the regional, leading Indiana to a victory over Duke and another emotional bullet point in a season that was chock-full of wants and

---

100 Deford, "The Rabbit Hunter: A Penetrating Profile of Bobby Knight."

expectations. The Hoosiers kept winning, defeating Louisiana State University (LSU) and UNLV before capturing a berth in the championship game against Syracuse.

The Orange, despite Indiana's success and perennial dominance, came in as the favorite, bolstered by a roster with three future NBA players in its starting lineup: power forward Derrick Coleman, center Rony Seikaly, and point guard Sherman Douglas. Indiana didn't seem to get that memo—not like Knight would let his players read it. They were there to win, so that's what they were going to do. The game itself was a back-and-forth affair, but in the first NCAA Tournament with a three-point line, the Hoosiers seized the opportunity to dominate from a distance and took a 52–44 lead into halftime.

That's when Smart went to work. He scored twelve of his twenty-three points in the final five minutes of the game, but Indiana struggled to hold its lead down the stretch and found itself trailing 72–68 late in the title tilt. Smart drove the lane, looking to spark another rally, but missed the layup. The ball was rebounded by Syracuse forward Howard Triche, who was immediately fouled. He only hit his first free throw, and Indiana rebounded the miss, getting down the court and cutting into the lead.

Syracuse missed its free throws late in the game, and Indiana kept hitting shots. The Hoosiers took back the ball in the final seconds of play, when Daryl Thomas saw Smart just out of the corner of his eye. He passed it, and Smart took the shot. It went in. Indiana topped Syracuse 74–73, another championship and another magical run that was simply part of Knight's aura in Indiana now. People expected him to win.[101]

Knight was a hero in Indiana. He took teams, any team, with any player, and made them champions, but as he continued to cement himself as one of the best coaches in the sport, his emotions continued to get the best of him. His reaction to a perceived bad call in the LSU game had become a joke and a cautionary tale, with photos of him slamming the

101 "1987 Indiana Basketball: A Real-Life Hoosiers Ending," *The Sports Notebook*, accessed November 2018, http://thesportsnotebook.com/1987-indiana-basketball-sports-history-articles.

phone at the officials table circulating in the daily papers as much as stories about the Hoosiers' latest victory. Knight continued to yell, and as he did, some started to question whether or not he should. There were off-court incidents and reports of vocal beatdowns during practice. Knight won his last conference championship at Indiana in 1993.

He won games, but there were some who started to wonder if he went too far to do just that, and it didn't take long until his time at Indiana was cast in a shadow of doubt.

GETTING EMOTIONAL

Knight was always vocal. He always cared, loudly and often with a variety of curse words that would make even the most roguish sailors on port leave flushed. Knight never pretended to be anything except exactly what he was, a perfectionist who expected his players to dominate and the referees to agree with him. He was more than willing to yell if either didn't follow those rules. That emotional reaction, however, may be the defining characteristic of Knight's legacy. The yelling was loud, and, eventually, it grew strong enough to distract from the victories and the championships, a spiral that began with a chair and ended with a relationship that will likely never recover.

The chair incident happened in 1985, but Knight's fiery temper on the sidelines, and even off it, had been documented for years. There were reports of scuffles, some of them even physical, through Knight's first decade at Indiana and, in 1979, while coaching Team USA at the Pan American Games in San Juan, Puerto Rico, Knight was accused of assaulting a local police officer. He was charged with striking the officer before a practice session and was convicted in absentia. Knight was sentenced to six months in jail but never served his time and, in 1987, the Puerto Rican government dropped the charges.[102]

---

102 Mike Puma, "Knight Known for Titles, Temper," ESPN Classic, accessed November 2018, http://www.espn.com/classic/biography/s/Knight_Bob.html.

Despite the incident, Knight retained his coaching position at Indiana and was even named Team USA coach for the 1984 Olympics. He kept on yelling. The chair incident happened, the phone incident happened, and Knight was fined $10,000 by the NCAA. It didn't stop him. In November 1987, Knight was once again the center of controversy when he was ejected from a game against the Soviet national team. Knight went on to pull his players off the court, resulting in an Indiana forfeit. Neither Knight nor his players spoke to the media after the game.[103]

It continued from there. In 1988, when asked by Connie Chung how he dealt with the stresses of coaching, Knight responded, "I think that if rape is inevitable, relax and enjoy it." The comment prompted a march on the Indiana campus and protests across the school, but Knight's stature on the sideline was just as big as ever. He became the winningest coach in Big Ten history in the 1988–89 season, won his 500th game, and two years later, in 1991, was inducted into the Naismith Memorial Basketball Hall of Fame. The Hoosiers went on to reach their fourth Final Four under Knight the next season.

The wins kept coming, but Knight kept talking and acting out, a balancing act that left some in the basketball world wondering how Indiana continued to support him. The Hoosiers fans, however, didn't have much trouble. The team continued to dominate, setting the standard in the Big Ten and racking up victories. On January 6, 1993, Knight, at the age of fifty-two, became the youngest coach to reach 600 wins, defeating Iowa 75–67.

The late '90s, however, were a different story. From 1995 to 2000, Indiana didn't advance past the second round of the NCAA Tournament, and during the 1995 postseason Knight was fined $30,000 by the NCAA for an outburst during a postgame press conference. The questions started, the murmurings about Knight being too much and too loud, rumors about a coach who had possibly overstayed his welcome and never grown with the times. Even the biggest Indiana fans couldn't

---

103 Associated Press, "Knight Pulls Players from Soviet Game," *Los Angeles Times* (November 1987), http://articles.latimes.com/1987-11-22/sports/sp-23722_1_bob-knight.

justify Knight. There were mutterings about mistreated players and a sudden increase in transfers out of Indiana. The Hoosiers weren't winning and Knight wasn't bringing in the names anymore; something had to give. It was him.

In March 2000, the CNN Sports Illustrated network ran an investigative piece into the darker corners of Knight's program at Indiana. Neil Reed, a former player, spoke about his experience with the coach, claiming he had been choked by Knight during practice. Knight denied the allegations, but less than a month later, the network aired the video, and it suddenly became all but impossible for anyone at Indiana to defend the legendary coach. It got worse. Only a few months later, in September, then-freshman Kent Harvey reportedly spotted Knight in Assembly Hall and called out "Hey, what's up Knight?" The coach grabbed the kid, pulled him aside and, according to reports, said "Show me some f***ing respect. I'm older than you."[104]

It was the last straw, but Knight, ever certain his way was the only way, refused to leave Indiana without a fight. When given the choice of resigning or being fired, he accepted the second option and university president Myles Brand officially relieved the general of his duties after nearly three decades in Bloomington.

Knight's split with Indiana was not a good one. Insults were slung, grudges were kept and, nearly twenty years later, the Hall of Fame coach has been nothing but vocal regarding his resentment toward the entire basketball program. In the immediate aftermath of his firing, Knight continued to talk, loudly. He criticized his successor, Mike Davis; questioned the decisions of the athletic department; and drew a line in the sand that some at Indiana still refuse to cross. You were either with Knight, or you were against him. There was no other option.

Knight returned to the sidelines eventually, taking a job at Texas Tech in 2001. He didn't stop talking or demanding, and it was made clear to

---

104 Wertheim, "Throwing in the Chair: The Increasingly Bizarre and Sad Legacy of Bob Knight and Indiana."

anyone in his new program that Knight expected loyalty. Once again, however, winning helped distract from the noise. Knight led Texas Tech to postseason appearances in his first four years there, going as far as the Sweet Sixteen in 2005. There was no championship though, and Knight announced his retirement from coaching on February 4, 2008. He still refused to go back to Indiana.

Knight was noticeably absent from the fortieth anniversary celebration of the '76 undefeated squad, although many players said they reached out to their former coach. It wasn't the first time that had happened. In 2014, A. J. Guyton, a former star at Indiana near the end of Knight's time, was set to be inducted into the school's Athletic Hall of Fame and took to social media to plead for his coach's return.

He wrote: "Time's ticking and we all deserve a homecoming. I'm asking you Coach Bob Knight, you said you'd do anything for me once I graduated, can you please attend my induction ceremony, which is coming back home to Indiana University?"[105]

Knight didn't show. He kept talking. He started yelling on ESPN as well, serving as an analyst and occasional color commentator for the network's college basketball coverage. Knight finally crossed paths with the Hoosiers again in November 2012, calling an Indiana vs. Georgia game, but once again, the coach's larger and louder-than-life personality hurt him in the long run.

Knight's time in front of the TV cameras was as interesting as it was controversial, a trend that has defined him as much as any game he ever won. He refused to utter the word "Kentucky" on air in 2012, instead referring to the Wildcats as the "team from the SEC"; was rumored to have fallen asleep on set; and, during a 2015 broadcast, yelled at a fan to sit down in front of him.

---

105 "A. J. Guyton to Bob Knight: Come Back to Indiana," *Sports Illustrated* (September 2014), https://www.si.com/college-basketball/2014/09/13/aj-guyton-bob-knight-indiana -open-letter.

It was another less-than-perfect performance, another controversy, and another shrug from Knight. The man who expected dedication from his players wasn't always all that concerned with showing it himself. He wanted what he wanted, and he was going to be damned if he didn't get it. His contract with ESPN wasn't renewed in April 2015, just over seven years after he became one of the "damn people from television" he'd criticized during his coaching days.

CHASING THE NOISE

The questions surrounding Knight have been as loud as he has been since he first started coaching. Is he doing it right? Has he gone too far? How much is enough? There might not ever be answers to those questions. Some Indiana fans still revere Knight and his time in Bloomington, while others are more than happy to never see him don a red sweater again. The only thing that's clear, however, is that Knight's legacy is the opposite. He's a bit of a cliché, an old man who yells at kids when they dare to step on his lawn. Knight wanted it perfect. He wanted it his way. There was no other option, and he was never shy about making sure he got his way.

Knight left coaching with 902 career wins, second only to his former player Mike Krzyzewski. He was a National Coach of the Year four times during his career and was named the first inductee in The Vince Lombardi Titletown Legends in August 2003. He's still part of the college hoops conversation, a name that draws respect as much as ire. And he's never once made excuses for his behavior. Knight is what he is; let the chips fall where they may.

"I have never been, from day one; I'm not the coach for this administration," Knight told the *Indiana Daily Student* in 2000. "But I'm the coach for our program and what we tried to do."[106]

106 Heather Dinich, "Power, Control, and Legacy: Bob Knight's Last Days at IU," ESPN, accessed November 2018, http://www.espn.com/mens-college-basketball/story/_/id/23017830/bob-knight-indiana-hoosiers-firing-lesson-college-coaches.

Knight might not have grown with the times, and while there are plenty, including the coach himself, who'd blame the softness of the next generation, his connection to the game is unquestioned. He built a program at Indiana that's still regarded as one of the top in the nation, a powerhouse that, in his time, was never the subject of NCAA sanctions. There's history there, success and defeat and a motion offense that other coaches still try to emulate. Knight's an enigma, still and probably always, and while his tactics might not have been right, the victories are as impressive as ever.[107]

And if people don't agree, Knight won't be bothered. When asked how he'd write his own obituary, Knight's answer was simple. He told the *New York Times*, "Well, seeing as I won't be able to, I would simply quote Clark Gable. Quite frankly, I just don't give a damn."[108]

● ● ● ● ●

MAKING THE GRADE

Knight prided himself on the academic success of his basketball programs, whether he was at Army, Indiana, or Texas Tech. He didn't just expect wins on the court, he wanted good grades in the classroom, and his players' victories in front of a blackboard were even more meaningful than what they accomplished athletically.

While coaching the Hoosiers at Indiana, Knight graduated nearly eighty percent of his players. The national average, at that time among Division I schools, was an alarmingly low forty-two percent. Knight also set up two chairs, one in history and one in law, and raised millions of dollars for the Indiana library. The fund was eventually named in his honor. Knight's Hoosier teams regularly topped the NCAA graduation rates, and throughout his time in Indiana, Knight was in constant contact with his player's professors. He

---

107 Wertheim, "Throwing in The Chair: The Increasingly Bizarre and Sad Legacy of Bob Knight and Indiana."

108 Andrew Goldman, "Coach Bobby Knight on Why He's So Unpleasant," *New York Times* (March 2013), https://www.nytimes.com/2013/03/03/magazine/coach-bobby-knight-on-why-hes-so-unpleasant.html.

wanted to know how they were doing, what they were doing, or, more importantly, what they could be doing better.

"I was able to keep track on a daily basis who cut class or who was dropping a grade average," Knight told the *New York Times* in 2013.[109]

If a player was slacking off in the classroom, Knight had a simple solution: they'd run. He brought players in at five in the morning and made them run the gym stairs from top to bottom until he told them to stop. He never had to do that more than once with any player.

Knight's opinion on academics didn't change even after his unceremonious dismissal from Indiana. He donated $10,000 to an academic fund as soon as he joined Texas Tech and, less than a year later, saw that fund raise nearly $100,000. He worked closely with the school and his eponymous charity, the Coach Bob Knight Library Fund, an organization that Knight said was frequently ignored by media. Instead, his sideline escapades were reported on, including a physical exchange between Knight and Texas Tech sophomore Michael Prince during a November 2006 game against Gardner-Webb. Knight still continued to focus on academics and charity.[110] In November 2007, Texas Tech honored Knight's charitable work with "A Legacy of Giving: The Bob Knight Exhibit" at the campus library.

Knight spoke, as loudly as ever, about graduation rates, determined to remind fans that there was a college in college basketball. He suggested the NCAA revoke a team scholarship for every player that didn't graduate in five years.

It was a standard that many still see as unreasonable, but that's never been Knight's concern. He cut players for skipping class and, according to a *Slate* article in 2002, even went so far as to put tampons in a player's locker, solely to embarrass him enough that he'd go to class. Knight never saw any of his actions as detrimental to

---

109 Goldman, "Coach Bobby Knight on Why He's So Unpleasant."

110 Thayer Evans, "Knight Raises Chin and Holds Head His High," *New York Times* (November 2006), https://www.nytimes.com/2006/11/15/sports/ncaabasketball/knight-raises-chin-and-holds-his-head-high.html.

his cause of getting his players a degree. An Indiana professor told *Slate*, "Bobby is the greatest teacher I have ever seen."

Knight's dedication to academic excellence may surprise hoops fans. This is, after all, a college world where one-and-done athletes are the norm, but that wasn't the sport Knight wanted. His methods were sometimes mad, the expectations were sometimes seemingly unreachable, and Knight's contributions to the sport didn't always churn out NBA stars. In fact, Knight's career saw few stars graduate to the next level, the biggest names coming out of Indiana including the likes of Mike Woodson and Isiah Thomas in the early '80s. Knight's players, however, did graduate, full stop, and, for the man who wanted nothing more than victories, that may have been the most important one of them all.[111]

● ● ● ● ●

Knight's Best Games

The 1976 NCAA Championship Game

It's almost too obvious, but Indiana's perfect season has never been topped, and Knight's coaching efforts in 1975–76 are still the stuff of college hoops lore. The season itself wasn't easy. It couldn't be. There were new challenges every game, obstacles to overcome, and injuries to deal with. The pressure and expectations only grew as the Hoosiers continued to win. But, in that final game, when it mattered the most, Indiana didn't miss a beat. The Hoosiers defeated Michigan 86–68, outscoring the Wolverines 57–33 in the second half alone to capture the program's first title in over two decades.

Topping UCLA in 1992

There are victories and then there are statements. Indiana's 106–79 showing against UCLA in the 1992 NCAA Tournament was a statement. It was the worst-ever NCAA Tournament loss for the Bruins and a well-rounded effort from Indiana that still inspires awe in college basketball

---

111 Chris Suellentrop, "Bob Knight," *Slate* (March 2002), https://slate.com/news-and-politics/2002/03/bob-knight-college-basketball-s-wicked-stepfather.html.

fans and historians. The Hoosiers took a fifteen-point lead into halftime, shot seventy-two percent for the game, and scored sixty-two points in the second half alone. Calbert Cheaney led the offensive explosion with a team-high twenty-three points, while Damon Bailey chipped in twenty-two, and both Matt Nover and Eric Anderson added seventeen.

CHAPTER SEVEN

JERRY TARKANIAN
Tark the Shark

"He recruited anyone who could shoot a basketball. He was loyal to everybody. He violated about every rule you could violate. But he wasn't the only one. I thought he was a great coach. He got the best out of everybody."

—FORMER *LOS ANGELES TIMES* COLUMNIST JOHN HALL

The image is iconic. Jerry Tarkanian, crouched on the sidelines of a University of Nevada, Las Vegas basketball game with a towel clenched between his teeth. The former Runnin' Rebels coach was a lot of things—a game-changer and an innovator and, on more than one occasion, an accused rule breaker—but he was, first, a dedicated fan of the game and, just like any true fan, Tarkanian put his heart and soul on the line every single time his team stepped onto the hardwood.

Tarkanian, known as "Tark the Shark" throughout his career, was a yeller. He shouted and screamed and paced the sidelines. He demanded answers out of referees, felt every call as if he were the one picking up the foul and, sometimes, had a difficult time staying cool, literally or figuratively. That's where the towel came in.

Tarkanian's habit of chewing on a soaked towel during games began in 1956 when he was coaching high school basketball. It was hot in the gym, and Tarkanian was yelling. He grabbed a towel, got it wet, and held onto it for the rest of the game, occasionally bringing it to his lips so his mouth wouldn't get dry. The habit stuck for the rest of Tarkanian's career.

Gilberto Alvino "Gil" Castillo first met Tarkanian in 1969, after the Hall of Fame coach took over the top gig at Long Beach State, serving as the team's manager. Castillo had a handful of jobs with the squad, but his most important was making sure Tarkanian had towels to chew on during the basketball games.

Castillo provided Tarkanian one dry towel and one wet towel, which the coach would alternate during games. It was, at first, simply a means of making sure Tarkanian could keep yelling throughout games, but it eventually became a superstition as well. The towels were as much a part of Tarkanian's routine as watching game film or coming up with new defensive schemes for his teams, and when Tarkanian took over at UNLV he asked Castillo to come with him.

The pair worked together in Vegas for three more years before Castillo left the program in 1976 to work in the area gaming industry. Still, the partnership has become as much a part of college basketball lore as anything else. When Tarkanian was inducted in the Naismith Memorial Basketball Hall of Fame in 2013, Castillo was by his side, again, and the coach's statue on the UNLV campus depicts him biting on that iconic towel.[112]

The specifications of the towel were passed on from manager to manager after Castillo left UNLV, and when Tarkanian started coaching at Fresno State, the rules were a hot-button issue before Bulldogs' games.

---

112 Ed Koch, "For Years, He Prepared The Wet Towel for Jerry Tarkanian to Chew," *Las Vegas Sun* (July 2014), https://lasvegassun.com/news/2014/jul/01/years-he-prepared-wet -towel-jerry-tarkanian-chew.

"I actually had to draw a diagram on how the towel was folded and fax it," Larry Chin, who served as UNLV manager for Tarkanian's final sixteen years with the team, told Yahoo! Sports. "That's how crazy Tark was about it."

Chin's pre-game ritual with the towel included measuring the fabric's saturation—the towel had to be wet, but not dripping—ensuring that no edges showed when it was folded, and providing a dry towel as a mat to rest the damp one on top of. It was a fine-tuned system and a requirement for Tarkanian, and hardly his only superstition. Tarkanian also kept the seat on his right empty, calling it "the ghost chair" because he didn't like anyone sitting next to him, and talking during bus rides to pre-game meals and games wasn't allowed. He also regularly threw away sports jackets if he lost while wearing them.

Tarkanian was a college basketball paradox, a coach who didn't always follow the rules on or off the court, who shouted and screamed and cared more than just about anyone else at the time. He was confusing and eclectic, but he won, and if he had to chew on some towels to make sure that happened, then Tarkanian wasn't going to bat an eyelash. And his fans loved him for it.

When Tarkanian passed away in February 2015, that same statue was covered in flowers and, of course, towels.

STARTING SMALL

Jerry Tarkanian was born in Ohio, but his story didn't start in the United States. It began with his parents, who escaped from Turkey during the 1915–22 Armenian genocide in which 1.5 million people were killed by the Ottoman government. The couple fled their home, determined to find safety for their family after coming face to face with the horrors of death and war and the kind of hatred that changed the entire world.

Tarkanian's family was shaped by the genocide. His maternal grandfather, Mickael, was an Ottoman government official who was beheaded by Turkish authorities, while his uncle was also killed. Haighouhie,

Tarkanian's mother, left Turkey with her siblings and settled in Lebanon. It was there that she met Tarkanian's father, George, and the two moved to the United States shortly after, welcoming their son in 1930.[113]

It didn't get any easier for the Tarkanian family, however. George died from complications with tuberculosis when Tarkanian was only ten years old, and the young son of immigrants, a kid who was desperate to find his place in a world that was facing another horrendous war, was drawn to the basketball court. It was there, with a ball in his hand and a competitive drive that he learned from his parents, that Tarkanian truly started to develop into himself. He thrived on competition, on making a statement every time he put on a uniform, but finding success still wasn't easy. The family moved to California when Tarkanian was still young, and it was yet another challenge to try and fit in.

"My upbringing was why I always related so well to kids from tough backgrounds or single-family homes," Tarkanian wrote in his autobiography. "I understood what it was like to be raised by one parent, to grow up poor, and have to move around and scrape to get things."[114]

Tarkanian's childhood wasn't easy, but he found a reprieve on the court, continuing to play despite plenty of obstacles that threatened to keep him away from the game he loved. He first played for Pasadena City College in California for the 1950–51 season before eventually earning a scholarship to Fresno State as the team's backup guard. Tarkanian didn't play much with the Bulldogs, but he became the team's leader and the squad actually voted him captain. There was no one else on that roster who loved basketball more than Tarkanian.

He wasn't the basketball star he hoped to be at Fresno State, but Tarkanian's time with the program helped define his entire career. In addition to basketball, Tarkanian worked as a personal aide to football

---

113 Carmen George, "Coach Jerry Tarkanian's Armenian Heritage Remembered in Fresno," *The Fresno Bee* (February 2015,) https://www.fresnobee.com/news/local/article19534953.html.

114 Marek Warszawski, "Legendary Coach and Fresno State Bulldog Jerry Tarkanian Dies at Age 84," *The Fresno Bee* (February 2015), https://www.fresnobee.com/sports/college/mountain-west/fresno-state/bulldogs-basketball/article19534608.html.

coach Carl van Galder, a man who served as a mentor for most of Tarkanian's life and who also introduced him to his future wife Lois Huter. The pair became inseparable during Tarkanian's time at Fresno State, and he regularly credited Huter with helping him graduate.

Tarkanian did, eventually, get his degree and almost immediately used it to get back in the gymnasium. He began his coaching career at Edison High, a short-term job that saw him lead the Tigers to the section finals, and then spent two years at San Joaquin Memorial High. It was there that Tarkanian first started chewing on towels, posting a 26–12 record. It still wasn't enough, though, and Tarkanian, whose parents left chaos to find something better for their family, was desperate for his own next step.

It took some time, and there were two more high school pit stops, but Tarkanian eventually worked his way to the college level. He took over at Riverside City College in 1961, leading the team to three consecutive California Junior College State Championships from 1964–66 before moving to Pasadena City College and winning another title. Tarkanian's success and willingness to play anyone who wanted to be there was enough to make other programs sit up and notice, including Long Beach State.[115]

Tarkanian's legacy may have been defined at UNLV, but it began at Long Beach State in a gym that was nothing short of sweltering, decidedly small, and consistently packed to capacity with fans who wanted to see what this upstart team could do. Fans still talk about waiting for hours to get into Gold Mine Gymnasium, practically standing on top of each other for a few inches of space.

"It was like a mini thunderdome. You couldn't find a seat, you were sitting in the aisles..." Long Beach State alum Angel Perea told Fox

---

115 Warszawski, "Legendary Coach and Fresno State Bulldog Jerry Tarkanian Dies at Age 84."

Sports in 2015. "I don't know how many people they let in there but it was amazing."[116]

Tarkanian took over at Long Beach State in 1968, a small school with even less resources. He didn't care. It was a Division I opportunity and the chance Tarkanian had been waiting for since he learned how basketball was played. He wanted to change the culture at Long Beach, lift the program to heights it had never previously aspired to, and he was going to win. Tarkanian did—for five straight years.

Long Beach State didn't lose a home game under Tarkanian, a streak that became such a norm that, at the time, his son Danny figured "this was how it always was, winning so much." The team was so dominant at the time that, as the story goes, UCLA coach John Wooden refused to schedule an out-of-conference game. The NCAA, however, had other ideas.

Tarkanian's Long Beach State teams faced Wooden's Bruins three straight years in the NCAA Tournament, including a heartbreaker in the 1971 West Regional Final. UCLA topped Long Beach 57–55 after Sidney Wicks's free throw seemed to bounce on the rim forever before, finally, falling through the hoop. The loss still stings in the memories of former players and fans, and while neither were looking for a moral victory, even getting to that point was an accomplishment.

Long Beach State wasn't just an underdog, it was an everydog— the team that accepted anyone who could shoot the ball and play defense, no matter where they came from or what they'd experienced or who their family was. The first time Long Beach reached the NCAA Tournament, in 1970, Tarkanian was quick to point out that his team was made up almost entirely of junior college transfers. These weren't five-star recruits. These were kids who had battled for every minute, and Tarkanian recognized that.

---

116 "Long Beach State Remembers the Jerry Tarkanian Era," FOX Sports (February 2015), https://www.foxsports.com/west/story/long-beach-state-remembers-the-tarkanian -era-022015.

It was a mindset that Tarkanian prided himself on, a belief that grew from a childhood filled with perpetual challenges and obstacles. The one thing that was always there, however, was basketball, and if Tarkanian was going to do anything, he was going to pass that opportunity on to the next generation. Long Beach made four straight NCAA Tournaments under Tarkanian, and despite critics chastising his less-than-usual approach, the program became a regional power. Tarkanian's unorthodox coaching style didn't immediately endear him to the college basketball world, but his success couldn't be ignored, nor could his constant desire to improve.

Tarkanian knew there was more to come, another challenge to meet, and he was willing to bet on himself again—in Las Vegas.

BET ON IT

Tarkanian arrived in Las Vegas in 1973 when basketball was even less popular than spending a losing night at the blackjack table. UNLV wasn't a successful program. It was a bad program, dubbed "Tumbleweed Tech" by locals who hadn't witnessed the Runnin' Rebels notch a single winning season. Tarkanian, however, saw that as a challenge, and his revolutionary style of coaching fit in perfectly with the whirlwind kind of life that Las Vegas is famous for.

Tarkanian changed things in Vegas immediately. He sped up the game, brought in recruits from across the country, and didn't shy away from finding talent at the junior college level. He wanted players who could play and, more importantly, players who were willing to run—as much as possible. The pace of college basketball had been steadily growing for decades before Tarkanian took to the sidelines at UNLV, but the coach shifted it into another gear, sparking a trend of run-and-gun defensive schemes that altered the tempo of the game forever. The Runnin' Rebels were going to do just that, from the first whistle to the final buzzer. Tarkanian's teams won games by simply wearing out everyone else.

"There had been up-tempo teams before," Reggie Theus, who played for UNLV in the 1970s, told ESPN. "But Tark was the one who really started fast-paced basketball. Well, maybe he didn't start it, but he took it to another level."

Tarkanian's ability to change the game wasn't a surprise to any of the athletes who suited up for him. He grew as his teams grew, and his play calls changed every season because his players did. Tarkanian thrived with a zone defense at Long Beach State, but knew that wouldn't work when he got to UNLV, so he changed it. There was no fight, no question, and no attempt to force his new players into his old schemes. Tarkanian worked with what he had, and his players didn't just respect him for it, they thrived because of it.

UNLV immediately started winning under Tarkanian. He posted a 20–6 record in his first season and led the Runnin' Rebels to the second round of the NCAA Tournament the following year. Tarkanian posted 20-win performances in eight of his first nine seasons with the team, and the squad notched a Final Four appearance in 1979. It was an abrupt change of pace for the Vegas program that had never done much of anything, but that was how Tarkanian operated. His practices were quick. There weren't many set plays, and even pre-game stretching was seen as a waste of time.

Tarkanian wanted his team on the court. He wanted them moving, swarming to the ball, and making every player in an opposing jersey as uncomfortable as possible. That was the goal, every single game, to get under the skin of the team on the other side of the court and, more often than not, it worked perfectly. Tarkanian's teams were built on the success of their defense, a full-court attack that the college basketball world was woefully underprepared for. UNLV pushed the ball in transition, keeping teams from ever setting up or settling into plays, and that quick-thinking approach led to decades-long success.

"The offense came out of the defense," Dave Rice, who played for UNLV in the '90s, told ESPN. "A lot of teams didn't commit to defense the way his teams did. He changed the style of play."[117]

The Runnin' Rebels were changing the game of basketball, upping the tempo and the score. Tarkanian encouraged his players to get emotional about the game, to care as much as he did, and while some detractors saw it as "a show," he saw it as an opportunity to give the team the spotlight. Tarkanian brought in players other programs wouldn't look at, transfers and kids who grew up without much of anything. It would be unfair to suggest that Tarkanian saw something of himself in the players he coached, but it may still be true. The son of immigrants, who only ever wanted to make his mom proud when he was on the court, grew up with the intention of giving other kids a chance and making them basketball stars in their own right.

Tarkanian's teams revered him, trusted him, and believed in every single play he drew up. He was superstitious and different, but he smiled during practices and embraced change like an old friend. He built the kind of program that even the locals were interested in, a fan base that had been previously nonexistent turning out in droves to see if the Runnin' Rebels could keep on winning. They could, quite often.

UNLV made it to four Final Fours during Tarkanian's tenure, and the 1977 team averaged a whopping 109 points per game. It was the teams in the early '90s, however, that truly cemented Tarkanian's legacy on the Vegas strip.

US AGAINST THE WORLD

Tarkanian had coached successful teams before the 1989–90 season, but that year everything changed. That season's Runnin' Rebels squad is still considered one of the most dominant rosters ever assembled in college basketball, including eventual NBA stars Larry Johnson, Greg

---

117 Andy Katz, "Tarkanian Changed College Hoops," ESPN (February 2015), https://abcnews.go.com/Sports/tarkanian-changed-college-hoops/story?id=28891820.

Anthony, and Stacey Augmon. The story of the 1990 championship team is as dramatic, emotional, and convoluted as anything that's ever happened in Las Vegas, only this story didn't stay within the city limits.

The program had been dogged by NCAA investigations throughout Tarkanian's career. He was accused of twenty-three rules violations during his time at Long Beach State, and six days after he was hired by UNLV, the NCAA announced it was investigating the program's former coach John Bayer. UNLV was then found guilty of recruiting violations in 1977, and the school served a two-year probation while Tarkanian was suspended for two years. He blocked the suspension, thanks in part to a suit against the NCAA, but the rumors continued to swirl. There were mutterings and discussion of more rule breaking, and six months ahead of the 1990 NCAA Tournament, investigators met with UNLV officials eleven times.

Throughout the course of the season, ten different players were suspended for academic and rules infractions, usually unbilled phone calls and hotel incidents on road trips. It was an exhausting and grueling time, as Tarkanian and his coaching staff tried to ignore anything outside of the gym while still putting together a roster that could compete game in and game out. It also brought the team closer together.

This was a group that hadn't gotten much attention from other big-name college programs, former high school stars who found a home in Vegas under Tarkanian and, when that was challenged, rose up together to fight back the only way they knew how—winning basketball games.

"We stuck together," former guard Anderson Hunt told ESPN. "Like being at a party at the rival's basketball team gym and everybody put their backs together just in case a fight broke out. We were going out there together."[118]

---

118 Greg Garber and Kory Kozak, "Twenty Years Later, UNLV Still Indignant," ESPN (April 2010), http://www.espn.com/mens-college-basketball/tournament/2010/columns/story?id=5045144.

UNLV won thirty-five games that season. Its five losses occurred against powerhouse teams with most of the Runnin' Rebels star power sitting on the bench. The defense was smothering, the game as quick as it had ever been, but the determination of this team was at a whole other level. When asked about the defining moment of that season, most players don't take too long to answer: the victory over Fresno State on January 15. Anthony suffered a broken jaw in the win, hitting a defender while driving to the basket, and the injury was expected to keep him sidelined for at least a few weeks. Anthony showed up at practice the next day with a hockey helmet on. He didn't miss a game.

The team continued to win and continued to ignore the rumors that followed them wherever they went, earning a No. 1 seed in the West heading into the NCAA Tournament. UNLV ran past the early competition, notching a slim 69–67 victory over Ball State in the Sweet Sixteen before decimating Loyola Marymount 131–101 in the regional final and topping Georgia Tech 90–81 in the semis. The team few believed in, a group that prided itself on its us-against-the-world mentality and underdog reputation, had just notched an NCAA championship berth, taking on Goliath in the form of the Duke men's basketball team.

"They was good," Hunt said. "We was the evil."[119]

UNLV stepped onto the court at McNichols Sports Arena in Denver, Colorado, and knew, collectively, a win was imminent. It was a night where everything went right. The Runnin' Rebels hit shot after shot, connecting on 61.2 percent of their attempts from the floor, and brought defensive pressure every time a Duke player even considered touching the ball.[120] Hunt led the charge with twenty-nine points, on twelve of sixteen shooting, but the key, as it always was with UNLV, was defense. The team forced twenty-three Duke turnovers that led to fast break points, slam dunks and, eventually, a 103–73 UNLV victory. It's still the largest margin of victory in an NCAA championship game.

119 Garber and Kozak, "Twenty Years Later, UNLV Still Indignant."

120 "Nevada-Las Vegas vs. Duke Box Score," Sports Reference, accessed November 2018, https://www.sports-reference.com/cbb/boxscores/1991-03-30-duke.html.

The championship celebration in Vegas was epic. It was a dominant showing by UNLV, the kind of basketball that made careers and turned normal players into giants of the sport. Tarkanian was even quoted as calling it "the greatest moment maybe ever in this town," but the thrill of victory didn't last long.

The NCAA infractions committee barred the Runnin' Rebels from post-season play in July 1990 as a result of prior investigations. It was only the second time in its history the NCAA had levied such a punishment.[121]

Tarkanian declined comment at the time of the announcement, while UNLV President Robert Maxson told the *Los Angeles Times,* "This punishment does not fit the offense," and added that the program had done everything the NCAA asked of it thirteen years earlier. Although Maxson publicly supported the basketball program, there were some who questioned his loyalty to Tarkanian and even went so far as to suggest he helped bring the metaphorical spotlight on the coach and team's off-court practices.

UNLV was eventually able to compete in the NCAA Tournament during the 1990–91 season, but the team wasn't able to defend its championship. After staging one of the most dominant performances in a title game the sport had ever seen, the Runnin' Rebels came up short in the rematch against Duke, falling 79–77 in the national semifinal. Hunt's twenty-two-foot shot missed at the buzzer, and the team that came into the game with a 34–0 record walked away with one loss that would define its entire season.

It was a difficult pill for UNLV to swallow, particularly with the NCAA still looming just out of sight no matter what the team did. The blemish is one the players from the early '90s squads still resent, accompanied by questions they do their best to ignore and a legacy that's not quite as perfect as they would hope.

---

121 "NCAA Bars UNLV From Defense of Title," *Los Angeles Times* (July 1990), http://articles .latimes.com/1990-07-20/sports/sp-437_1_unlv-coach-jerry-tarkanian.

"That's the sad thing about it," Hunt told ESPN. "How something can be out there and perceived as something different. My career at UNLV was tarnished a little bit by that."[122]

Tarkanian's success at UNLV was nothing short of dominant, but his battle with the NCAA is what most people remember when they think of the Hall of Famer. It's a fight that defined his career as much as anything, a game within the game that lasted long after the players left the court.

BLOOD IN THE WATER

Tarkanian was never one to do anything the traditional way. He sped up the game, recruited players no one thought deserved a Division I scholarship, and joked with reporters as often as he answered their questions. He also fought back when the NCAA remained a prominent thorn in his side throughout his career. Tarkanian didn't pull punches when going up against the college basketball powers, didn't mince words or shy away from taking legal action, because he didn't just believe the NCAA was affecting his teams—he believed the organization was affecting his livelihood.

Tarkanian's battles with the NCAA have become the stuff of college hoops legend—an "us against them" narrative that made it as far as the United States Supreme Court—but there's much more to the story than slightly confusing legal jargon. According to Tarkanian, the issue began while he was coaching at Long Beach State. He occasionally wrote a guest column for the Long Beach Telegram and, in one issue, claimed the NCAA ignored problems at larger schools, instead going after small programs that were easier to convict. Long Beach State was put on probation after Tarkanian left the program, and the spotlight followed him to UNLV.[123]

---

122 Garber and Kozak, "Twenty Years Later, UNLV Still Indignant."

123 Warszawski, "Legendary Coach and Fresno State Bulldog Jerry Tarkanian Dies at Age 84."

Tarkanian arrived in Vegas under a cloud of accusations, and the NCAA placed UNLV on a two-year probation for "questionable practices," including recruiting violations, only a few months after the Runnin' Rebels made their first-ever Final Four appearance in 1977. Although some of the ten infractions UNLV was charged with occurred before Tarkanian's tenure, the NCAA was adamant the then-coach should also be suspended. So, Tarkanian sued.

District Court Judge James Brennan granted a permanent injunction prohibiting Tarkanian's suspension in October 1977, but the fight between coach and authority was only just beginning. It seemed every season brought a new crop of allegations, and while some were far-fetched, others were alarmingly real. Lloyd Daniels is still a name whispered when UNLV fans discuss the history of their program. A would-be star who grew up on the Brooklyn blacktop, Daniels reportedly failed to get his high school degree, despite attending five different ones. He still would end up at UNLV, however, after Mark Warkentien, a team assistant, became his legal guardian and enrolled him in Mt. San Antonio junior college to improve his academic standing. Daniels was going to help change the game at UNLV, but in 1987 he was caught buying cocaine from an undercover police officer. Many saw the arrest as another Tarkanian misstep.

In May 1991, just fourteen months after UNLV captured its first national championship, Tarkanian's reputation took another hit. The *Las Vegas Review-Journal* published a photo on the front page: a man named Richard Perry sitting in a hot tub with three UNLV players, David Butler, Anderson Hunt, and Moses Scurry. The group were shown drinking and smiling, and those same rumors that had swirled around UNLV for years got even sharper because Perry wasn't just anyone; he had been convicted seven years earlier in the Boston College point-shaving scandal.[124]

Tarkanian said he originally only knew Perry as a summer league coach who helped find less-known talent, including Daniels, but eventually

---

124 Garber and Kozak, "Twenty Years Later, UNLV Still Indignant."

admitted he told his players to keep away from Perry. The FBI and NCAA both investigated the connection, but never found enough evidence to suggest any UNLV player had been involved in point-shaving. That didn't, however, stop the rumors. Tarkanian announced his resignation on June 7, 1991, but coached one final year at UNLV, winning twenty-six games in the 1991–92 season.[125]

Tarkanian went on to briefly coach the San Antonio Spurs before returning to the college game with Fresno State in the waning years of his career. He never dropped his battle with the NCAA. Or, as he liked to call them, the NC-two-A. He accused the organization of unfairly trying to drive him out of coaching, but the Supreme Court threw out Tarkanian's case and, in 1988, ruled that the NCAA had acted as a private organization. The pair was back on the Supreme Court docket again in 1994, when justices shut down Tarkanian's efforts to reinstate a Nevada law that protected him and other UNLV coaches accused of rules violations. Lower courts had previously ruled the law interfered too much with interstate commerce.

In 1997, however, the NCAA lost its own Supreme Court bid to move the case against Tarkanian out of Las Vegas to another Nevada court. And, in 1998, Tarkanian settled for $2.5 million, an out-of-court agreement that wrapped up a twenty-five-year battle. It wasn't a perfect ending, but it was vindication for Tarkanian, proof positive that he'd been on the receiving end of wrongdoing by the NCAA throughout his career.

"I just hope people will now realize that the accusations against me, twenty-five years' worth of them, were unfounded and without evidence," Tarkanian told the *Los Angeles Times* after the settlement.[126]

---

125 A.D. Hopkins, "Jerry Tarkanian," *Las Vegas Review-Journal* (September 1999), https://www.reviewjournal.com/news/jerry-tarkanian.

126 Larry Stewart, "Tarkanian, NCAA Settle for $2.5 Million," *Los Angeles Times* (April 1998), http://articles.latimes.com/1998/apr/02/sports/sp-35333.

WHAT HAPPENS IN VEGAS

Tarkanian loved the fight. He didn't care what it was; if he believed it, he was going to fight for it, whether that was his players or his defensive schemes or his own coaching reputation. He didn't take no for an answer, refused to conform to the normal standards of coaching, and trusted his gut when those same instincts would have been shunned by anyone else. Tarkanian changed college basketball in a city that, even now, most people don't view as an athletic hotbed.

Las Vegas was the perfect place for Tarkanian. It's chaotic and hectic and it never really stops, a constant stream of people and bets and lights and sounds. That was Tarkanian—a whirlwind of coaching energy and belief in what he was doing. He may have been a little stubborn at times, but he also made a determined effort to make sure he got the most out of his players and, more often than not, it worked. Tarkanian's teams weren't full of all-stars, at least not before they got onto the court with the coach. They were ragtag groups of athletes who needed someone to give them a second glance. Tarkanian was only too happy to provide that because once upon a time, he'd been a kid who needed a few extra chances.

Tarkanian's career was far from perfect. Despite the victories and the 1990 championship team, the shadow of controversy and suspension and the entire NCAA will always linger over his legacy. He tried his hand at coaching in the NBA after leaving UNLV, but spent just twenty games with the San Antonio Spurs before he was unceremoniously fired. His final years on the sideline at Fresno State were marred by more accusations of rules violations, including a point-shaving incident in 1997, as well as several player suspensions and a *60 Minutes* interview that painted the program in a less-than-flattering light. Forty-nine of Tarkanian's victories with Fresno State were also later vacated by the NCAA.[127]

---

127 Warszawski, "Legendary Coach and Fresno State Bulldog Jerry Tarkanian Dies at Age 84."

Still, Tarkanian's impact on the college game and the way he helped change how the game was played cannot be overstated. Tarkanian sped up college hoops and brought pressure and an attitude that has come to define the sport in the last two and a half decades. His teams had an edge to them, an underdog mentality that other programs have adopted, and a pressure-filled defensive approach that made the sport as exciting as it had ever been. It made Las Vegas, a city built on luck and in-the-moment feelings, sit up and take notice.

Tarkanian coached for thirty-eight years and never posted a losing record. He was inducted into the Naismith Memorial Basketball Hall of Fame in 2013, an honor that many assumed would never come after his battles with the NCAA. He passed away in February 2015, after years of struggling with his health, and the outpouring of support for Tarkanian was as loud as it had ever been, like a night on the Las Vegas strip.

"To me, he's the greatest man I've ever met," Tarkanian's son Danny told *USA Today* in 2015. "I mean that not only about what he did in his profession but also what kind of family man he was. He was great with the media, was great with the players and, other than one or two other coaches, he was great with the coaches."[128]

Tarkanian was far from a perfect coach. He was a jumble of nerves during games, chewing on towels and patrolling the sidelines with a schedule of superstitions his players never dared object to. He also cared, deeply and completely, and his players knew that too. The entire city of Las Vegas knew it, and Tarkanian never tried to be anything except what he was—brash and different and determined to win. When he passed away, the city of Las Vegas ordered flags to be flown at half-staff at City Hall, a tribute to the man who changed basketball. Tarkanian embodied the city, its ideals and less-than-ideals, and his legacy, no matter what, will have a lasting impact on the sport.

---

128 Eric Prisbell, "UNLV's Jerry Tarkanian, Rebel with a Cause vs. NCAA, Has Died," *IndyStar* via *USA Today* (February 2015), https://www.indystar.com/story/sports/college/2015/02/11/unlvs-jerry-tarkanian-rebel-with-a-cause-vs-ncaa-has-died/23237167.

• • • • •
FAMILY FIRST

Jerry Tarkanian never forgot where he or his parents came from. The son of immigrants, Tarkanian's parents fled Turkey during the Armenian genocide before settling in America, and the future Hall of Fame coach was an outspoken advocate for immigrants, particularly later in his life. He grew up in Ohio, spent years patrolling sidelines on the West Coast, and is still best known for his time at UNLV. Tarkanian eventually returned to Armenia, and his 2006 trip to the country was undeniably emotional. It also explained quite a lot about Tarkanian's personality.

His parents battled, literally and figuratively. They watched their family members killed and were forced out of their homes and away from everything they'd ever known, fleeing on the simple hope that, maybe, things would get better. Tarkanian was constantly trying to live up to that same mindset. He knew his parents were lucky, knew he was even luckier, and never wanted to waste an opportunity when it was handed to him. He made sure his players didn't either, holding them to the highest standards every time they stepped onto the court, no matter what program he was coaching for.

Tarkanian's roots were always part of his personality. He refused to accept anything at face value, always strived for that next step and that next chance to prove himself, and it led to a career that was worthy of the Hall of Fame. It also led to international fame. Rev. Ara Guekguezian of Fresno's Pilgrim Armenian Congregational Church told the *Fresno Bee* in 2015 that traveling with Tarkanian was like watching the prodigal son return home. He posed for pictures throughout their trip to Armenia, signed autographs, and talked basketball with strangers on the sidewalk. And he did it all with a smile on his face.

Tarkanian also met with the coach of the national Armenian basketball team, and while Guekguezian was forced to translate some things, the genuine love of the sport between all of the men there bypassed any sort of language barrier. They talked about the game because they'd both lived the game, drawing on scraps of paper to dissect plays and players, and Guekguezian said both coaches emphasized the importance of defense.[129]

The trip itself didn't define Tarkanian's life or cement his success, but it proved just how far the coach had come. Tarkanian never shied away from how important his family was to him. He and his wife Lois had four children together, including Danny, who played three seasons for his father at UNLV. Tarkanian's story wasn't easy; there was drama and death and college basketball sanctions, but it was his and he owned it until the very end, even when revisiting the places his parents fled. Now, the Tarkanian family hopes to see that story on the big screen, as rumors have started to swirl regarding a potential film adaption of Tarkanian's life.[130]

Tarkanian was a first-generation American who encapsulated every trait of the American dream. He wanted to be better, wanted to be the best, and he never ignored what it took to get there. It was a Hollywood ending in Las Vegas.

● ● ● ● ●

Tarkanian's Best Games

Perfect at the Beach

Before he was the iconic figure chewing on a towel at UNLV games, Tarkanian was the head coach at Long Beach State, a small school in California that hadn't done much before he got there. Then, of course, Tarkanian got there. He posted a perfect record at home while he was at Long Beach, including what he called his best game with the squad, a 76–66 victory over Marquette on March 3, 1973. The size of the crowd has been debated over the years; it was originally listed as 12,987, but the number was probably closer to 11,000. It didn't really matter. The crowd was so large and the demand to see the game so loud that it was broadcast on national TV, the first time Tarkanian and his team were

---

129 George, "Coach Jerry Tarkanian's Armenian Heritage Remembered in Fresno."

130 Mark Anderson, "Hollywood Movie in the Works About Jerry Tarkanian, Las Vegas," *Las Vegas Review-Journal* (April 2018), https://www.reviewjournal.com/sports/unlv/unlv-basketball/hollywood-movie-in-the-works-about-jerry-tarkanian-las-vegas.

featured in the regular season. It also marked the first time Tarkanian stole the national spotlight, with a victory that put him in headlines and in college hoops discussion from coast to coast in his last season with the program.

The 1990 NCAA Championship Game

This was the game that cemented Tarkanian's status. UNLV had been moving up the college basketball ladder for years, but the Runnin' Rebels reached championship status with a 103–73 victory over Duke in the 1990 championship game. It was the largest margin of victory in the title game in NCAA Tournament history, a defensive showing that proved Tarkanian's full-court attack wasn't just potent, it was title-worthy. UNLV swarmed the ball, shutting down Duke's jam-packed roster and forcing turnovers with ease. It was as strong a performance as any of Tarkanian's teams had recorded and, as of 2017, was the last team from a non-power conference to capture a championship.

CHAPTER EIGHT

JIM BOEHEIM
Hometown Hero

"The reason I continued to coach the game of basketball is because I love the game and love to see players work hard and learn from the game to become better players and people... In coaching basketball, I feel like I have never worked a day in my life."

—JIM BOEHEIM ON STICKING WITH COACHING

Jim Boeheim is not much of a talker. He doesn't like speaking during press conferences, has never been all that interested in answering questions in any great detail. In fact, Boeheim's succinctness at the podium has become a bit of a calling card throughout his coaching career.

Boeheim is gruff, reticent and, more often than not, looks close to exhausted by the entire world of college basketball coverage, particularly in the postseason. Of course, that hasn't made much of a difference. Boeheim is a subject of interest, whether he wants to be or not, and part of that is his own doing.

Boeheim has been part of the fabric of Syracuse athletics since his playing days, a constant presence that's become as synonymous with the school as loud crowds in the Carrier Dome and snowstorms in the winter.

Boeheim is Syracuse. And Syracuse is Boeheim. They've gone hand in hand for nearly fifty years now, and there's no reason to imagine that will change any time soon.

There have been plenty of instances when college coaches seem synonymous with the programs they run, but Boeheim has always been a bit different. He's influenced the Syracuse men's basketball team in a way that few other coaches could begin to imagine. Boeheim's personality—those short answers at press conferences and searing looks directed at referees who absolutely got the call wrong—has permeated the Syracuse roster for decades. This is a program that is as steady as any in the country. It's a program that has won consistently and played the same exact defense nearly every game since Boeheim took over.

Syracuse isn't fooling anyone. Teams come into the Carrier Dome knowing exactly what to expect and, for the most part, the same holds true for Boeheim. The Hall of Fame coach isn't going to change for anyone, no matter what people say about his responses to questions or the scandals that have dogged the program in recent years. It doesn't matter. Boeheim is a creature of habit, and the Orange are going to keep playing that 2-3 zone. It's part of their collective personality.

Boeheim and his family are as visible in Syracuse as any celebrity is in Hollywood. They may actually be more famous, because Boeheim has done as much for the area, only a few miles away from where he grew up, as any Hollywood star has done for the biggest blockbuster. Boeheim and his wife, Juli, support area charities, including their own, are seen at local restaurants and on campus, and their kids played basketball at the nearby high school.

It's difficult to imagine a Syracuse men's basketball team without Boeheim. He considered retirement—originally announcing his intent to leave the team in March 2018—but Boeheim never walked away. This is his team, at the deepest most fundamental level, and while it's been far from perfect, the success Boeheim has built at Syracuse is unprecedented, even if he doesn't like to ever talk about it or the legacy he will, eventually, leave behind.

"The only way you stay in coaching is to win games," Boeheim told Syracuse.com in 2017. "It's an accomplishment to stay in this business, and the only way you can do that is by winning games."[131]

STAYING LOCAL

Lyons, New York, is a small town in the western part of the state, established in 1811. According to the 2010 census, there were 5,682 people living there. It's old-school Americana, a town that existed to help move goods and people through the Erie Canal in the nineteenth century. The town website boasts its history, touting itself as the home of Erie Canal Lock 28A, which is located just west of the bridge on Dry Dock Road. Lyons is not the kind of place where much happens anymore, but in the early 1960s, it was the kind of place where basketball was played—and played well.

Boeheim grew up in the small town, a fan of basketball as soon as he realized that basketball was a sport, and he started playing on the varsity team for Lyons High School in 1960. A three-year varsity player, Boeheim was a bona fide star for Lyons, shining a spotlight on the small town that hadn't seen many headlines since the Erie Canal stopped moving freight to Canada.

Lyons went 15–1 in Boeheim's junior year, but it was his senior season that made the difference. The team posted a 14–0 record in the regular season and came into the Class AA championship game 20–0, taking on another undefeated team, East Rochester High School. The game was good, back and forth, and competitive, and Boeheim still

---

131 Bud Poliquin, "What Is Jim Boeheim's Legacy as He Closes In On '1000' Wins?" Syracuse.com (March 2017), https://www.syracuse.com/poliquin/index.ssf/2017/02/jim_boeheim_sitting_on_999_victories_all_of_the_wins_are_nice_im_proud_of_them_a.html.

has positive memories of the matchup—except the ending. Lyons lost by one point in double-overtime.[132]

It was a loss that ended Boeheim's high school career and, while it didn't spark his initial distaste of losing, it certainly helped foster it. Boeheim's time in Lyons—where, it's been speculated, he first learned the concept of a 2-3 zone—was the building block of everything else. He learned the game by playing it, fine-tuning plays on both sides of the ball. He also didn't garner much interest from big-time Division I programs. This was, after all, Lyons, and Lyons, New York, is a very small town.

That didn't stop Boeheim. This was a kid who loved basketball, and he was going to play basketball—at the college just down the road from his hometown. Boeheim enrolled in Syracuse in 1962 and walked onto the basketball team in 1963, an unexpected athlete on an Orange team that was in desperate need of a change. The 1961–62 Syracuse men's basketball team went 2–22, what would eventually go down as the worst season in program history, with three probable starters declared ineligible to play before the year even began. The Orange opened 0–16, with its only victories coming on a last-second score against Boston College and a surprising road win against UConn.[133]

Boeheim saw his first action with Syracuse during his sophomore year. He played in twenty-five games during the 1963–64 season, starting one, and averaging 5.2 points every time he stepped onto the court. It wasn't a record-breaking performance, but Boeheim's determination was obvious every time he put that jersey on. He was named a team captain his senior season and helped lead the Orange to a 22–6 record and the program's second NCAA Tournament berth.

---

132 Mike Waters, "Syracuse's Jim Boeheim Looks Back at His Playing Days at Lyons Central High School," Syracuse.com (October 2013), https://www.syracuse.com/orangebasketball/index.ssf/2013/10/syracuses_jim_boeheim_looks_ba.html.

133 "1961–1962 Syracuse Orange Schedule and Results," Orange Hoops, accessed November 2018, http://www.orangehoops.org/1961-1962.htm.

Once again, however, the latest chapter of Boeheim's playing career ended with a loss. Syracuse fell to Duke 91–81 in the Sweet Sixteen of the 1966 NCAA Tournament, a lopsided loss that stung as much as any for Boeheim.

"We just couldn't quite close it out," Boeheim told Syracuse.com in 2018. "It was a disheartening, disappointing game."

Boeheim finished the game with fifteen points against a Duke defense that shut down the Orange with an airtight zone. The loss was, of course, disappointing, another bitter end for Boeheim, but, as per usual, he didn't dwell long on the could-have-beens. He stayed as determined as ever, certain the next opportunity was only a moment away, and knew the Orange's NCAA Tournament run was the spark the program had been waiting for when he first tried out.[134]

Boeheim didn't have many professional playing offers after graduating from Syracuse. It still didn't stop him from finding a professional team. He played with the Scranton Miners and Scranton Apollos in the Eastern Professional Basketball League for six years after he left college. These weren't cream-of-the-crop players, but neither was Boeheim, and despite the lack of star-power, the drive to win was still there.

"There were great players," Boeheim told Syracuse.com in 2016. "The NBA didn't have the room for all the quality players that you have today. So they played in the Eastern pro league. The talent was unbelievable."

It was not a Hall of Fame career—that would come later, without the ball in his hand—but it was another chance for Boeheim to dissect the game he'd loved for as long as he could remember. The league only played on the weekends, so Boeheim still had time to take graduate classes at Syracuse and, most importantly, work with the team. The schedule wasn't easy and, more often than not, Boeheim found himself alone in his car on I-81, but he thrived on the grind of it all.

---

134 Mike Waters, "Jim Boeheim's Final Syracuse Basketball Game as a Player Was Loss to Duke in 1966," Syracuse.com (January 2014), https://www.syracuse.com/orangebasketball/index.ssf/2014/01/jim_boeheims_history_with_duke.html.

That all changed, however, ahead of the 1970–71 Syracuse season. Boeheim had been working as an unpaid assistant for the Orange for years, enjoying a relatively flexible schedule that let him occasionally miss weekend games so he could play in his own league. But then Ray Danforth, the Syracuse head coach, offered Boeheim a promotion: a coaching job with a salary and a schedule that resulted in far less playing.[135]

Eventually, Boeheim knew he couldn't keep living two lives at once and, well aware his playing days weren't going past the Eastern league, opted to stay in Syracuse instead. He remained an assistant for several years before Danforth retired in 1976, and the hometown kid, the one who'd always done whatever he could to stay as close to the Orange as possible, landed his dream job; Boeheim was named head coach of the Syracuse basketball team and the college hoops world would never be the same.

GETTING IN THE ZONE

Boeheim's approach to coaching has not been without criticism. He's been part of the fabric of Syracuse basketball for as long as many college basketball fans can remember, but those same fans are also quick to point out Boeheim's faults and they're usually more than happy to go down the rather detailed list. Boeheim didn't come from an impressive coaching tree; there was no famous coach to learn from, just his own intuition and tendencies and, sometimes, that grated on people's nerves.

Boeheim's naysayers will proclaim him a whiner, a coach who patrols the sidelines shouting at referees and demanding calls to go his way. He never threw a chair, but he grumbled during press conferences and scowled at cameras. He didn't come from basketball royalty. Syracuse,

135 Mike Waters, "Story Time with Jim Boeheim: Riding Down I-18, Playing Pro Basketball for $100 a Night," Syracuse.com (November 2016), https://www.syracuse.com/orange basketball/index.ssf/2016/11/story_time_with_jim_boeheim_riding_down_i-81_playing _pro_basketball_for_100_a_ni.html.

for the most part, had flown under the radar before Boeheim took over, and for the kid who grew up a few miles away, the job was a chance to prove himself. That had been Boeheim's goal from the very first time he started playing basketball—particularly in the shadow of his father, who demanded perfection from his son in every aspect of his life.

Boeheim's promotion at Syracuse was the opportunity he had waited, literally, his entire life for. He was thirty-one years old at the time. So, what did Boeheim do? The man who had been known for his jump shot during his college days turned his attention to the defensive side of the ball and came up with a scheme that has defined his career and his program more than anything else. Syracuse started playing a 2-3 zone, which consists of two players at the front of the defense and three players behind.

The Orange first experimented with zone as their base defense in 1975, when Boeheim was still an assistant with the team. They went to the Final Four that year, a team that former Louisville coach Rick Pitino told ESPN was "one of the most mediocre Final Four teams of all time."

Boeheim kept the defense when he took the head job, and he never wavered from that course. As the Big East became the Big East in the 1980s, teams across the league started to turn toward man-to-man, tough full-court defensive looks that did their best to stifle opposing offenses. The game picked up speed and, in 1986, when the college game adapted the three-point line, even more teams switched to man-to-man. Boeheim didn't. No one really expected him to.

The zone was still the calling card of the Syracuse defense. There were, of course, moments when the Orange were forced out of the scheme, but as the years went on, Boeheim stayed as committed to his personal brand of defense than ever. It was, simply, common sense: If Syracuse focused on one type of defensive approach, it could be better at that than anybody else. And Boeheim enjoys few things more than being better than everyone else.

Boeheim may have his faults, but there's something to be said for a bit of well-placed stubbornness, and Syracuse's success in its 2-3 zone is unprecedented. As other teams have evolved and maybe even given into some defensive fads, the Orange have stayed true to what's worked.

"The more people played man-to-man, the better our zone got because people didn't see it," Boeheim told ESPN in 2016. "That's just common sense."[136]

The question remains, however, how has the 2-3 zone worked so consistently? That's the most impressive part—and one of the few things that offers fans a bit of insight into Boeheim's personality.

Boeheim doesn't talk much, doesn't speak too often about himself or the things he cares about, but even those fans that hate him have to admit that it's obvious he thrives on control. So does a 2–3 zone. The matchup defense rotates against an opposing offense and, if done right, controls tempo completely. It forces offenses into specific spots on the floor, and while it doesn't offer the full-court pressure of a man-to-man defense, it limits other teams' options. Teams that can shoot well from a distance often find a way to break a zone, but that's the rub—teams have to shoot well from a distance, and that's easier said than done when the options aren't there.

Take, for example, Middle Tennessee, a team that faced Syracuse in the 2016 NCAA Tournament. The team had one day of prep before facing off against the Orange and came into the game averaging 72.7 points. Middle Tennessee scored 50 points against Syracuse, shooting twenty-nine percent from the floor.

There are, of course, exceptions to the rule. Basketball has always been a streaky kind of sport, and if a team gets rolling from a distance, it seems easy to assume they've beaten the Syracuse defense. That's

---

136 Dana O'Neil, "Understanding the Zen of the Syracuse Zone," ESPN (March 2016), http://www.espn.com/mens-college-basketball/story/_/id/15043164/jim-boeheim-stays-true-famous-syracuse-orange-zone-defense.

when the defense changes. It rotates again, it brings pressure from a different spot, and responds to what the other team is doing.

Boeheim's practices have become legendary for their intricacies in teaching those changes. He won't be able to provide in-depth instructions during the game, but he can go into detail at practice. Boeheim spends time with every player, making sure every person on the court knows what to do when faced with a handful of different situations. Then, when faced with those situations, Syracuse reacts and maintains its control.

Duke coach Mike Krzyzewski put it simply, "People say it's a 2-3 zone. No, it's Syracuse's defense."[137]

That, the possessive nature of the Syracuse zone, is what sets it apart from any other team's attempt at a 2-3 defense. Because the Syracuse zone isn't just about Boeheim's approach, it's about the players he has running it. As soon as the Orange started playing exclusively zone, Boeheim's recruiting approach had to change as well. He needed a specific type of coaching staff and a specific type of player, both physically and mentally. This was the system, and if a kid wasn't ready to buy in, then he wasn't going to come to Syracuse.

Take a look at any recent Orange roster. The players have been strong, guys who could battle to spots and challenge screens, but they've also been intuitive and perceptive, aware of minuscule changes on opposing offenses and what they have to do in the zone to combat that. And, just like Boeheim, a lot of those players stayed in Syracuse after the games ended. Mike Hopkins was a four-year player for the Orange turned lead assistant. Adrian Autry was another four-year starter who joined Boeheim's staff, while Gerry McNamara, an assistant coach, played on the 2003 national championship team.

The players in the zone know it backward and forward, as do the coaches. It's entirely possible Boeheim spends most of his waking hours thinking about the next evolution of his zone. Teams know what

---

137 O'Neil, "Understanding the Zen of the Syracuse Zone."

they're facing when they take on Syracuse, but that hasn't made it any easier. The Orange wings fly from corner to corner, the big men down low shift with ease, and the shooting percentages of other teams has continued to sit in the metaphorical basement.

Boeheim's naysayers have claimed he's ignorant of the changes to the game. They say his obsession with the 2-3 is a refusal to evolve or grow, and that may be some of it, but at its core Boeheim's defensive approach has been all about control. The zone has changed, it's had to, but the base is still there, and as soon as Syracuse settles into that defensive look, crouched low with arms outstretched and Boeheim-esque scowls on every player's face, opposing teams know they're in for a fight.

"You do what you do," Boeheim told ESPN of his reason for sticking with zone. "It's like in baseball. If you're a home run hitter, you're not going to go out and try to hit only singles, are you?"[138]

REACHING THE TOP

Boeheim didn't find immediate success at Syracuse, but it was awfully close. He started winning games, fine-tuning the system with the Orange and, of course, implementing that 2-3 zone as soon as he was named head coach in 1976. It drew interest from other, bigger names—including Ohio State in 1986—but Boeheim never felt any inclination to leave Syracuse. This was his home, his team, his entire life and, eventually, he knew that was going to lead to the biggest victory of all: an NCAA championship. It just took him some time to get there.

As a head coach, Boeheim has led Syracuse to a postseason berth in every season the team has been eligible. The team appeared in the national title game in 1987 and 1996, but came up short in heartbreaking fashion in both matchups. Indiana's Keith Smart hit a jumper from the corner in the final seconds to capture the victory for the Hoosiers in 1987, and Kentucky's roster of future NBA stars rallied late to hold

---

138 O'Neil, "Understanding the Zen of the Syracuse Zone."

off the Orange in 1996. It was an almost-there mentality that grated on every single one of Boeheim's nerves. This was, after all, a coach who was in constant competition with himself, always trying to prove his team was the best, and without that championship and the chance to cut down nets, he felt he was coming up short.

Then came 2003 and a recruit that helped lift Syracuse to the top of college basketball: Carmelo Anthony.

Anthony was born in New York City and spent the first eight years of his life in Red Hook, a small Brooklyn neighborhood, before moving to Baltimore. It wasn't an easy shift for Anthony, who spent most of his childhood fine-tuning his basketball skills and doing his best to avoid trouble. He attended Towson Catholic High School for three years, becoming one of the area's top shooters, and racked up the accolades, drawing attention from some of the top college hoops programs in the country.[139] That trouble, however, dogged Anthony, and he was suspended on several occasions for skipping classes.

Anthony once again found himself in a brand-new school ahead of his senior year, transferring to Oak Hill Academy in Virginia. It was a move that would alter the course of his entire career. Anthony thrived that season, playing in a handful of marquee all-star events and watching his on-court star rise.[140] There was talk that he would bypass college completely, partially because of issues with his ACT score, but Anthony opted to take his talents to Syracuse anyway, certain that working with Boeheim and the Orange was simply the next change and challenge, something he was ready to embrace with both hands.

To say that Anthony was a force to be reckoned with on the college hardwood would be a disservice to him and any other player who has had a dominant freshman season. Anthony was more than dominant. He was the spark that made Syracuse go, the catalyst for seemingly

139 "2001 All-Baltimore City/County Basketball," *The Baltimore Sun* (March 2001), http://articles.baltimoresun.com/2001-03-15/sports/0103150119_1_dunbar-walbrook-anthony.

140 "All USA Boys Basketball Team," *USA Today* (May 2002), https://usatoday30.usatoday.com/sports/preps/basketba/2002-05-08-all-usa.htm.

everything the Orange did on either side of the ball, and the unquestioned leader of the 2002–03 team.

Syracuse, before Anthony got there, was not a bad team. Preston Shumpert averaged 20.7 points per game as a senior the year before, but the Orange fell to South Carolina in the NIT semifinals and were clearly frustrated at missing out on the NCAA Tournament. Syracuse lost four of its last six and eight of its last twelve regular-season games, a meltdown that still stresses out Orange fans. The expectations had been high, and while there was obviously talent on that roster, the 2001–02 squad left a slightly bitter taste in its wake. Anthony was there to fix that; and he did.

Anthony set a Syracuse freshman-debut record with twenty-seven points in his first game. The Orange also lost that game. Fans were worried about another meltdown, certain simply putting a big-name recruit on a team of players who were still feeling the aftereffects of last season's disappointments was just a Band-Aid for something much bigger. But Boeheim had seen something from Anthony, knew what he was capable of at the high school level and was positive he could do that in Syracuse. So he kept making sure Anthony got the ball, and Anthony made sure the ball kept going through the net.

Anthony averaged twenty-two points and ten rebounds per game, shooting just over forty-five percent from the floor. Only four other players have ever averaged better in the history of Syracuse basketball. He started every game he played.[141] He was a matchup nightmare for opposing defenders, too strong to guard up close, but with a jumper that required just that. Anthony led Syracuse to a first-place finish in the Big East that year, and if his performance in the regular season was dominant, then his game during the postseason was other level. He posted double-doubles in Syracuse's last three NCAA Tournament games, including thirty-three points and fourteen rebounds against

---

141 "Carmelo Anthony," Sports Reference, accessed November 2018, https://www.sports-reference.com/cbb/players/carmelo-anthony-1/gamelog/9999/.

Texas in the Final Four. And then came the championship game against Kansas.

Syracuse had, of course, been there before and, for one panic-filled moment, it looked as if the Orange were destined for a repeat of "almost." Boeheim stood on the sideline and watched as senior captain Kueth Duany and sophomore Hakim Warrick went a combined one-for-four at the free throw line with only a few seconds left. It, once again, came down to the final play. Kansas star Michael Lee took the three-point attempt with 1.5 seconds on the clock, but the ball never made it to the net. Warrick blocked the shot and the Orange were, finally, champions.

"Our kids had great heart," Boeheim told the *New York Times* after the victory. "We played the best first half we could play, then we just hung on."[142]

Although he didn't have a hand in those final few seconds of emotion-filled basketball, Anthony's performance that season has become the stuff of college hoops legend. He was named Most Outstanding Player at the Final Four, the first freshman since Louisville's Pervis Ellison in 1986. Anthony's off-court efforts—he posted a 1.8 GPA his first semester—kept him from winning the Wooden Award, but his ability to lead the Orange made him a hero in Syracuse. He was the leader of that team, the kind of recruit a coach waits his entire career to find and, for Boeheim, exactly what his team needed to take that next step.

"No college basketball player in America was better than freshman Carmelo Anthony over the course of the 2002–03 season," Boeheim wrote in his autobiography, *Bleeding Orange*. "It's that simple."[143]

Anthony left Syracuse after his freshman season, one of the first one-and-done stars in the new era of college sports, but his relationship

142 Joe Drape, "Freshmen Give Boeheim a Finish to Savor," *New York Times* (April 2003), https://www.nytimes.com/2003/04/07/sports/ncaabasketball/freshmen-give-boeheim-a-finish-to-savor.html.

143 Jim Boeheim and Jack McCallum, *Bleeding Orange: Fifty Years of Blind Referees, Screaming Fans, Beasts of the East, and Syracuse Basketball,* (New York: Harper, 2014).

with Boeheim was never affected by his decision. Boeheim has regularly commented on Anthony's NBA career and the pair have teamed up for Team USA basketball in the past. In fact, it was Boeheim who persuaded Anthony to suit up for the Rio Olympic Games in 2016. They won a gold medal. Winning, it seems, is just how it works when Boeheim and Anthony get together.

THE GOOD, THE BAD, AND THE VACATED GAMES

Boeheim has won games at Syracuse. He's coached good teams and average teams and teams that were nothing short of fantastic. He's also faced his fair share of controversy and, in March 2017, that controversy reached a boiling point when the NCAA laid down sanctions on the Syracuse program that left the world of college athletics reeling.

The report itself was ninety-four pages, focusing mostly on the conduct within the men's basketball program. The investigations, which began in 2007, found discrepancies in the program, particularly regarding academic violations. Syracuse also self-reported ten violations in the case, which included the football team as well, that dated back to 2001. Those violations ranged from academic misconduct, extra benefits, failure to follow the drug-testing policy, and impermissible booster activity. The investigation also referred to Boeheim specifically, detailing, in a statement released by the NCAA the effects of, "the head basketball coach's failure to promote an atmosphere of compliance and monitor his staff."[144]

The NCAA suspended Boeheim for nine games, required a reduction in scholarships for Syracuse basketball, and vacated all wins in which an ineligible player competed from 2004 to 2012. Syracuse was also required to return all funds received from revenue sharing while it was part of the Big East, for its appearances in the 2011, 2012, and 2013 NCAA Tournaments. The football and men's basketball teams were also

---

144 Emily James, "Syracuse Did Not Control Athletics; Basketball Coach Failed to Monitor," NCAA (March 2015), www.ncaa.com.

placed on probation. It was a hammer-type approach by the NCAA that echoed across the sport and put a bit of a dent in Boeheim's legacy.

He released a statement after the rulings were made public, writing that he was "disappointed" and that the NCAA committee "chose to ignore the efforts which I have undertaken over the past thirty-seven years..." The Syracuse athletic community also rallied around Boeheim, with school chancellor Kent Syverud vehemently disagreeing that the college had failed to control its basketball coach.[145]

That, however, was not the consensus across the sports world. The headlines started as soon as the NCAA released its findings. The word "cheater" was thrown around with ease. Boeheim was called every name in the book, his critics certain this was the moment they'd been waiting for, a chance to prove the Syracuse head coach was nothing more than a man who knew how to work the system and had, finally, been caught in the act. And they haven't stopped. A Fox Sports headline on March 20, 2017, just over two years after the NCAA report went public, read, "How a manipulative Jim Boeheim got Syracuse to cave and give him back his job."[146]

Boeheim has become as contentious a figure in college athletics as anyone. The Syracuse faithful love him, and why wouldn't they? He's been at Syracuse as long as some of them have been alive, makes the postseason every year, and seems to embody the western New York mindset every single time he opens his mouth. Boeheim sounds a bit like a nor'easter—sometimes cold, sometimes a little overwhelming, but also undeniably impressive. And then there are those other opinions. The ones who come from fans who hate Syracuse simply because they believe Boeheim has long overstayed his welcome.

145 Eric Prisbell, "NCAA Punishes Syracuse, Jim Boeheim for Violations," *USA Today* (March 2015), https://www.usatoday.com/story/sports/ncaab/acc/2015/03/06/syracuse-college -basketball-ncaa-investigaton/24497089.

146 Chris Chase, "How a Manipulative Jim Boeheim Got Syracuse to Cave and Give Him Back His Job," Fox Sports (March 2017), https://www.foxsports.com/college-basketball/story/ jim-boeheim-syracuse-extension-retire-ncaa-sanctions-tournament-wins-032017.

That 2017 Fox Sports story highlighted Boeheim's contract extension after his heir apparent, longtime assistant Mike Hopkins, left the program for the head coaching job at Washington. Boeheim, quite clearly, wasn't going anywhere, and there were those who found the idea entirely impossible to digest.

So, what's the middle of those two rather diametrically opposed reactions to Boeheim? The truth of the matter is, there might not be one. Boeheim inspires one group and makes the other recoil in disgust. He draws ire from the NCAA but remains the head coach of one of the most impressive programs in the history of the game. He doesn't entirely make sense, and that's part of the problem with Boeheim's legacy as a whole.

After the NCAA sanctions came down on Syracuse, the question started popping up more and more: what to do with those vacated games? They were played, the Orange won or lost, and they happened. There's video evidence. The NCAA didn't care. And, so, the debate began. Boeheim had been closing in on 1,000 career victories prior to the sanctions, and, much like the general opinion regarding him, the discussion about the mark was split right down the middle. Boeheim never seemed to get that memo. He led Syracuse to a 66–62 upset victory of then No. 9 Virginia in February 2017; winning what would have been his 1,000th game. Or was, depending on whom you asked.

"I've been part of 1,000 wins," Boeheim told ESPN after the game. "Whether they're all there or not doesn't matter to me. I've been part of a lot of wins, and I'm really proud of that."[147]

Boeheim's tendency to walk that line—toeing between endearingly cantankerous and a full-blown joke—has been one of the most successful parts of his career. He doesn't fit the mold of Hall of Fame coach. He grew up outside of Syracuse, went to school at Syracuse, and has become so embedded in the town and the program that even

147 Dana O'Neil, "Syracuse Coach Jim Boeheim: 'I've Been a Part of 1,000 Wins...and I'm Proud of That'," ESPN (February 2017), http://www.espn.com/mens-college-basketball/story/_/id/18619901/syracuse-orange-coach-jim-boeheim-part-1000-wins-ncaa-sanctions.

NCAA sanctions couldn't do much to him. Instead, Boeheim led an upstart Orange team to the Final Four in 2016. That team competed in a play-in game. They were never supposed to make it to the Final Four, but that's a bit like Boeheim. He was never supposed to do much, and he always believed he could.

The key to Boeheim over the past five decades has been a deep-rooted desire to prove himself. He's spoken about his father, a man who constantly challenged him and appeared to thrive on defeating his son at anything and everything, but that fire never really went out. Boeheim wants to win and is a little scared of what happens if he doesn't. He wrote about it on the second page of his autobiography, calling it a "fear of failing every day."[148] The opinions are still there, good and bad and filled with references to an NCAA investigation, but Boeheim has only ever wanted to win, and as long as he's doing that, he's less worried about what people think.

ORANGE YOU GLAD

Boeheim may never leave Syracuse. He turned seventy-four earlier in the 2018–19 season, the oldest active Division I coach, and said he has every intention of remaining with the program as long as his son plays. His son, Buddy, joined the team as a freshman in 2018. That means Boeheim, reasonably, could still be patrolling sidelines through 2022–23. If that math holds out, Boeheim will have been head coach at Syracuse for nearly fifty years.

It's not unheard of for a coach to spend his entire career with one program, but Boeheim has turned longevity into an art form. He's already been inducted into the Naismith Memorial Basketball Hall of Fame, the College Basketball Hall of Fame, and won more coaching honors than some others will ever accumulate in his career. So, why stick around? Easy. Boeheim couldn't imagine doing anything else.

---

148 Boeheim and McCallum, *Bleeding Orange: Fifty Years of Blind Referees, Screaming Fans, Beasts of the East, and Syracuse Basketball*.

"I never really thought that I was going to get out of coaching ever," he told Syracuse.com in 2017. "Go as long as you can do a good job. It shouldn't be an age thing."[149]

Boeheim's eventual retirement has been the subject of speculation and debate for years, and that's unlikely to change any time soon, but it hasn't seemed to bother him yet. Let the people talk. Boeheim wants to keep coaching, so that's what he's going to do. It would be impossible to discuss legacy now, not without an ending date, but Boeheim's impact on the game can't be overlooked. His commitment to zone defense is legendary, his personality even more so. Of course, there are others who would say the zone is simply a product of stubbornness and that same personality no longer has a place in modern sports.

That split, the differing opinions between fans and foes, has become Boeheim's trademark as much as anything, but at his very core, the Syracuse coach is just that. He's part of the city, part of the community, and, perhaps, bigger than the school itself. Boeheim's legacy can't be documented yet, but his influence on the Orange is far greater than just about any other college coach at any program. They go hand in hand, and through the good and the bad and the postseason berths, it's been a partnership that has shaped both of them in equal measure.

● ● ● ● ● ●

GIVING BACK

Boeheim didn't often walk away from basketball. He stayed at practices longer than everyone else, watched more game film than was probably necessary, and spent time with players to fine-tune the zone everyone knew was coming at Syracuse. That changed in 2001. Boeheim took a leave of absence from the team mid-season when he was diagnosed with prostate cancer, a fight he

---

149 Mike Waters, "Jim Boeheim Set to Be the Oldest Coach in D-I History: 'Go As Long As You Can Do a Good Job,'" Syracuse.com (November 2017), https://www.syracuse.com/orangebasketball/index.ssf/2017/11/syracuse_basketball_coach_jim_boeheim_will_keep_on_coaching.html.

never expected but was just as determined to win as any basketball game he'd ever coached.

The leave lasted ten days—as long as the surgery to remove his prostate and a short recovery could be. Boeheim didn't want to stay away longer and, really, thrived on the competitive nature of basketball to keep himself focused. He told *Men's Journal*: "The best thing is to keep moving and get right back into the game. I'm competitive, so I'd rather be coaching my team instead of watching them play on television."[150]

Boeheim is the first to admit that he's one of the lucky ones. Cancer, in any form, is a terrifying word to hear, and in the time since his diagnosis, Boeheim has done his best to make sure that it's one others won't be forced to contend with. He and his wife, Juli, started their eponymous foundation in 2009 to do just that, supporting local kids in the Central New York area as well as providing funding for research and advocacy in eliminating cancer.

The Jim and Juli Boeheim Foundation hosts several annual events and, since its inception, has raised millions for organizations like the Make-A-Wish Foundation and the American Cancer Society. It's an off-court endeavor that has become almost as important as basketball itself, a chance to give back to the community that has given so much to Boeheim and his family.

"We get a lot of support from the community," Boeheim told *The Daily Orange* in 2018. "So for us to give back is a powerful thing."

Boeheim's cancer diagnosis was an eye-opening experience, particularly after he saw his mother suffer from the disease as well. She passed away from leukemia in 1977, just a year after he took over at Syracuse. Boeheim had been mulling over the possibility of starting a charity before his diagnosis and had given money to Coaches vs. Cancer, and he's never regretted the decision. It's only grown in the last few years.

The foundation has focused on cancer research quite a bit, but the Boeheims have yet to find a cause they'll walk away from. They've

---

150 Holly C. Corbett, "Hall of Fame Coach Beats Cancer," *Men's Journal*, accessed November 2018, https://www.mensjournal.com/sports/hall-fame-coach-beats-cancer.

donated regularly to the area Boys & Girls Clubs and the Y as well, becoming a fixture in the lives of local kids and their families. Just as Boeheim has no plans of leaving the Syracuse sidelines any time soon, his family has no plans of walking away from the community that's supported them for nearly five decades. This is their home and they're going to help it because, when Boeheim needed those ten days to help himself, Syracuse waited and supported and cheered his return.

"This is something we never want to let go of," Juli Boeheim told the *Daily Orange*.[151]

● ● ● ● ●

Boeheim's Best Games

The 2003 NCAA Championship Game

It finally happened. Syracuse had been in the title game before and each one had ended in bitter disappointment. There were final-second misses and final-second makes and Boeheim was still a fantastic coach who had, simply, never won the big one. Then the 2002–03 season and Carmelo Anthony happened and "almost" became "finally." There were plenty of incredible games for the Orange that season: defeating No. 2 Pittsburgh, topping Georgetown in OT, any time Anthony scored double-digit points. The championship, game, however, was different because it was a championship, and because it wasn't perfect. Anthony didn't have his best game, Syracuse missed field throws down the stretch and, for a moment, it looked like Boeheim's legacy would be one of nearly-there titles. It wasn't until Hakim Warrick blocked Kansas's Michael Lee with seconds on the clock that Syracuse fans, and Boeheim, breathed a sigh of relief. The Orange held on for the 81–78 victory, still the only NCAA title in program history.

---

151 Matthew Gutierrez, "Jim and Juli Boeheim have raised millions for their philanthropy foundation," *Daily Orange* (April 2018), http://dailyorange.com/2018/04/jim-juli-boeheim-raised-millions-philanthropy-foundation.

The Six-OT Game

Ask any college hoops fan about the six-overtime game and they'll probably let out a sigh. Because the six-overtime game was exhausting. It was exhausting to watch and exhausting to play and exhausting to coach. It was a battle of two Big East powers: Syracuse and UConn squaring off in the conference tournament at Madison Square Garden in 2009. It was big names and bigger players and the game that, simply, would not end. The game lasted 226 minutes. Two hundred and forty-four total points were scored. Eight players fouled out. The score was tied twenty-two times. The most impressive part in a game that was chock-full of historic moments? Syracuse held on in the first OT despite never actually leading. The Orange outscored UConn 17-7 in the final overtime, though, holding on for the victory as exhaustion settled in on both sides in a game that still stands out as one of the best.

CHAPTER NINE

LOU CARNESECCA
Looie

"My way of trying to motivate my players is
to tell them how good they can be; to build
them up instead of tearing them down."

–LOU CARNESECCA ON HIS APPROACH TO COACHING

The sweater was ugly. There's no other word for it. It was a patchwork of mismatched colors, red and blue and for reasons that would have any fashionista scratching their head, brown as well. It didn't even look all that comfortable, the fabric appearing scratchy and well-worn, reportedly made of wool. Lou Carnesecca didn't care. He was chilly. He needed a sweater, so he put that one on and became a legend.

Carnesecca didn't stop wearing the sweaters. They continued to get increasingly bright, patterns that drew as much attention as the plays on the court. There were more stripes and more mismatched color schemes, even a tan snowflake-patterned sweater that made hoops fans across the country widen their eyes.

Carnesecca didn't care. If St. John's continued to win, he'd put on anything and wear it with pride. When asked about the red and blue and brown monstrosity after a victory against Pittsburgh during the 1984–85 season, Carnesecca smiled and responded, "It's ugly, isn't it?"[152]

It was. It was ugly and only slightly ridiculous, but Carnesecca and St. John's were stealing the national spotlight, and as far as the coach was concerned, there was something to be said for consistency. His team continued to play well when he wore the ugly sweater and he'd never really been much for fashion anyway. If he kept wearing the sweater, he didn't have to think about a suit before the game. That left more time for practices, more time for working one-on-one with players and, most importantly, more time to come up with schemes against some of the top teams in the country. This was the '80s, after all, a time when the Big East was the Big East in all the ways that mattered. These weren't easy games, they were battles, staged on hardwood and underneath the basket. They were matchups that required teams to go jumpshot for jumpshot, metaphorical pressure cookers that saw fans shout and media speculate. And Carnesecca's sweater choices were as much a distraction as they were superstition.

His players could simply play the game, while he wore ugly sweaters and answered questions about them. Carnesecca's less-than-fashion-forward sideline stylings became as much a part of his reputation as his team's victories, but while the sweater itself was ugly, it was also a microcosm of everything Carnesecca meant to the program. And to New York City basketball itself. At the height of its basketball dominance, New York was much like Carnesecca's patchwork sweaters, a mix of players and talent that, at first glance, didn't really go together, but when nudged in the right direction, could play the game at a level previously never even imagined. New York was the center of the basketball universe, and when Carnesecca was patrolling the sidelines for St. John's sporting that absolutely ugly sweater, his team was at the center of basketball in the city.

---

152 Fred Lief, "Lou Carnesecca, Who Made Winning Basketball and Pullover Sweaters," UPI (March 1985), https://www.upi.com/Archives/1985/03/20/Lou-Carnesecca-who-made-winning -basketball-and-pullover-sweaters/1993480142800.

Carnesecca was a New York kid, born and bred in the city that went on to revere him as a basketball savant. He knew the streets, knew the neighborhoods, knew every kid who became a star on the playgrounds and the open-air courts. Carnesecca watched and waited, recruiting from his own backyard to fill the St. John's roster with local talent that didn't back down from anything—even the best teams in the Big East. These were city kids, and there was more than just winning on the line. It was about pride. It was about defending your home turf and your home court and living up to a set of expectations the city itself set. Playgrounds weren't an easy place to grow up. The crowds on those blacktops weren't silent. They yelled and jeered and demanded excellence. Carnesecca was part of that crowd as well, and his was a mindset that helped shape the St. John's basketball program for over two decades. These kids grew up with a ball in their hand and the knowledge that Carnesecca could bring them to the next level.

The sweater was ugly, but the basketball IQ was a thing of beauty, and Carnesecca's teams respected that. It was that respect, that genuine trust between coach and players, that led St. John's to the top of the country in the mid-'80s and helped cement Carnesecca as one of the best coaches in the history of the game.

"The coach's office is always open and you don't necessarily go in there to discuss X's and O's," Chris Mullin told UPI in 1985. "I can't say enough about him."[153]

STARTING UPTOWN

Carnesecca grew up in Manhattan, the son of a grocery store owner. He was, actually, not all that great at playing basketball. That's not to say he didn't try. Carnesecca played, took his turns on the courts dotting the city, and sat in stands while other kids his age showed off their skills in front of raucous crowds. Carnesecca, however, was never the big name when it came to basketball. It was baseball that was his first athletic love.

---

153 Lief, "Lou Carnesecca, Who Made Winning Basketball and Pullover Sweaters."

Carnesecca played half a dozen pick-up games a week, dashing to the sandlot with a bat and a glove and the hope that he and his friends could get in a few makeshift innings before it got dark. There weren't many rules to those games, but they were where Carnesecca developed his competitive spirit and his love of a team. Carnesecca wasn't a perfect athlete, but he knew that he could help other athletes win, and that was almost better.

Carnesecca took his athletic talents, even as minimal as they were, to Archbishop Molloy High School, then known as St. Ann's, in Queens. The commute wasn't easy, but it was worth it, another chance for Carnesecca to prove himself and foster relationships that would go on to define the rest of his life. Plus, he got to keep playing baseball.

"[He was] a good little player," former teammate Jack Curran, who would go on to coach basketball and baseball at Archbishop Molloy, told the *New York Daily News* in 2006. "Good little infielder, good hitter."[154]

Carnesecca thrived in Queens, but the world was at war and he answered the call, serving three years in the US Coast Guard during World War II. When he returned to the city, Carnesecca did his best to live up to his family's expectations. His father wanted him to be a doctor and he enrolled at Fordham University in the Bronx. Carnesecca only lasted a few weeks before returning to Queens and enrolling at St. John's University. His friends were there, and he started playing basketball again. There were no records set, no national championships won, barely more than a bench to be warmed on the St. John's junior varsity squad. Carnesecca saw action in three games with the team in the 1946–47 season, but it was enough to keep his interest in the sport. He knew he was never going to become a star athlete, and while baseball might have been his first love, basketball was his truest love.

---

154 Ebenezer Samuel, "Daily News Sports Hall of Fame Candidates," *New York Daily News* (June 2006), https://www.nydailynews.com/archives/nydn-features/ daily-news-sports-hall-fame-candidates-introducing-candidates-bill-bradley-article-1.560042.

Carnesecca began coaching nearly a decade after graduating college, taking the reins at Archbishop Molloy. He wasn't ever a dominant athlete, but Carnesecca knew how to get dominance out of his players. His practices were creative, out of the box and, sometimes, unexpected. He regularly devised brand-new drills to challenge his squad. A favorite of his at Molloy required players to shoot over a raised broom to get a perfect arc on their shot. The ball would never get blocked with Carnesecca as coach.

Those early days of coaching weren't easy for Carnesecca. The broom he used to help fine-tune technique was also, occasionally, used to swat at players who dared to step out of line. When he wasn't coaching, Carnesecca was still in the gym, picking up a few extra dollars officiating basketball games. The hard work, however, paid off, and Carnesecca's star began to rise in his hometown.

He spent two years at the high school level, including an undefeated record in his second season, before returning to St. John's as an assistant for the Redmen under legendary coach Joe Lapchick. Carnesecca was a basketball sponge in those early days at St. John's. He listened intently to everything Lapchick said, absorbed every trick and every play scheme, and kept a watchful eye on everything that was happening across the city. Carnesecca had always built relationships. He was an affable guy, quick with a smile and a "how are you?" and "how's the family?", and that kind of genuine interest proved critical on the recruiting trail.

Carnesecca spent his time as an assistant flitting from one court to the next, one parish hall to another, building friendships and ties with the priests and nuns at local Catholic schools, introducing himself to parents of star athletes, and making sure when those athletes considered colleges, their first thought would immediately be of St. John's.

Lapchick left St. John's after the 1964–65 season, a year that ended with an NIT title and a future that stretched out in front of Carnesecca. He didn't hesitate taking the next step, assuming head coaching duties when Lapchick retired. There was one final lesson to absorb, though, standing next to Lapchick while the coach addressed the team.

"Today you walked with kings," he told them. It was a string of words Carnesecca never forgot, and one he took to heart, determined to make sure the players he would go on to coach felt the same way. Carnesecca was never a great athlete, knew his name was never destined to be splashed across stat lines, but that never stopped him from caring. And throughout the rest of his career, no one wanted more for his players.[155]

THERE AND BACK AGAIN

Carnesecca settled into head coaching with the same ease he did everything else. He smiled and talked, held quiet conversations with players and loud exclamations during games, and was a fiery personality on the sideline that was as New York as bagels and crowded sidewalks. Carnesecca was a whirlwind when his teams took the hardwood, waving his arms and jumping and feeling, everything and anything, as much as his players did. He wanted to win, because he knew what winning could do to a team. It could make them, and for five years it did.

St. John's continued to win under Carnesecca. The Redmen returned to the NIT in his first season, falling in the first round, but Carnesecca was named "Coach of the Year" by the Metropolitan Basketball Writers Association in his second year. He'd always known players were the heart and soul of a team, but running his own program threw the fact into sharp focus for Carnesecca. He wanted to be more than just a coach to these kids. He wanted to be an advisor and a mentor and, occasionally, when the situation called for it, a friend. Carnesecca wanted his players to trust him, but he also thrived on competition, and when the opportunity to coach at the professional level presented itself, he couldn't say no.

---

155 George Vecsey, "A Vintage Year for Looie," *New York Times* (1983), https://www.nytimes.com/1983/03/14/sports/a-vintage-year-for-looie.html.

His players at St. John's understood, and Carnesecca's players at the next level excelled under his coaching. He served as the coach and general manager of the New York Nets, a charter franchise of the American Basketball Association (ABA), leading the team to the finals and a game seven matchup against the Indiana Pacers in his first season. The squad came up short, but Carnesecca once again learned the valuable lesson of players. The Nets were nothing short of dominant that year, sparked by the talented Rick Barry, but as soon as Barry left, the team lost fifty games. It was a give and take that Carnesecca would spend his entire career trying to fine-tune. He could coach all he wanted, but he needed the players to implement his vision.

"[Coaches] are fifteen percent [of the team]," Carnesecca told the St. John's student newspaper in 2013. "Sometimes five [percent]."[156]

Carnesecca spent three seasons with the Nets, playing at the Island Garden in West Hempstead, New York, an arena the coach referred to as "the closest thing to the North Pole" and the "only place where you practice with coats on."[157] He posted a 114–138 record with the Nets, and while the initial appeal of the pros was something he couldn't deny, it didn't take Carnesecca long to miss his home court. The New York City native returned to St. John's for the second time in 1973, a head coaching stint that would last for the rest of his career.

Carnesecca was never tempted to leave Queens again, settling back into the position at St. John's like he was simply taking his next deep breath. It didn't take long until his name and St. John's were synonymous and he became the face of not just the basketball program, but the school itself, and as Carnesecca and the Redmen started picking up victories again, the coach's star only continued to rise. He didn't entertain any other job offers, never considered walking away from the court at Alumni Hall on campus, and, with Carnesecca at the helm, St. John's

---

156 Jon Perez, "Hanging with 'Looie': Carnesecca Sits Down with the Torch, Reflects on Past," *The Torch* (October 2013), https://www.torchonline.com/news/2013/10/02/2226902.

157 Moke Hamilton, "Lou Carnesecca Reminisces Over ABA Days," SNY (September 2012), https://www.sny.tv/nets/news/lou-carnesecca-reminisces-over-aba-days/149443096.

quickly became a consistent and national force. He was home again, and Carnesecca was going to make sure everyone knew it.

HITTING THE TRAIL

Carnesecca always prided himself on his hometown connections. He knew New York like the back of his hand, could list the best delis and the best pizza slices with ease and, most importantly, knew what local kids could do the most for his basketball program. When he'd served as an assistant under Lapchick, Carnesecca worked for hours fostering relationships with area schools and AAU teams, building links that proved invaluable once he took over at St. John's. Those relationships were still there, even after the ABA stint, and Carnesecca's ability to bring in some of the area's top talent was, perhaps, his greatest accomplishment as a basketball coach.

Carnesecca's personable attitude appealed to everyone in the New York City basketball world in the late '70s. He was close to the public school coaches because he was a local guy, and having a conversation with him was much like having a conversation with the regulars at the bodega down the block. The Catholic school coaches saw one of their own in Carnesecca, particularly when his former baseball teammate Jack Curran took over the basketball team at their alma mater Archbishop Molloy. And the AAU coaches trusted him, bolstered by Carnesecca's easy presence and certainty that the players in that league were just as talented as anyone else.

Carnesecca could talk to anyone and did, and, more often than not, it ended with athletes coming to St. John's.

"The beauty of Lou Carnesecca was that he dealt with all the factions and got kids," former Big East commissioner Mike Tranghese told the *New York Post* in 2008.[158]

---

158 Lenn Robbins, "Rise and Fall of St. John's," https://nypost.com/2008/02/03/ rise-and-fall-of-st-johns.

Carnesecca also had a bit of a trick up his recruiting sleeve. St. John's, in those early days of his second stint with the team, was a commuter school. The student population was large, and it was all New York based, because there were no dorms on campus. That meant, by NCAA rules, the school could award a room-and-board stipend to a scholarship athlete who chose to live off campus, and in those days, St. John's athletes didn't have much of a choice. According to the *New York Post*, athletes at St. John's received about $700 a month to pay for housing. Two players could share an apartment just off campus for about $600 a month, split evenly, and pocket the rest of the money, while still playing sports at the highest level.

Carnesecca wasn't drawing athletes in with promises of immediate riches, but the stipend certainly didn't hurt, particularly when big-name recruits were considering suiting up for St. John's. Either way, St. John's started bringing in some of the area's best basketball talent, and the country had no choice but take notice, particularly during the 1979 NCAA Tournament.

On a day that would go on to be known as "Black Sunday," St. John's defeated Duke 80–78 in the second-round of the tournament, an upset that few in the college basketball world ever expected to see. The Redmen went on to top Rutgers with another two-point victory, advancing to the Regional Finals before falling to fellow underdog Penn. The run was an impressive one, sparked by leading scorer Reggie Carter, a local kid who averaged double digits every time he stepped on the court.[159]

Although St. John's came up short of a national title run that year, the unexpected postseason performance gave Carnesecca even more to work with on the recruiting trail. He was building something in Queens, bolstered by a foundation of area talent and a Big East that was as competitive as any league in the country. Basketball was in the soul of New York City at that time, with playgrounds filled with kids doing their best impression of Walt Frazier and the Knicks and dreams of hearing

---

159 Perez, "Hanging with 'Looie.'"

their own name announced at Madison Square Garden. And one of those kids, with a jumpshot that would go down as one of the best the college basketball game would ever see, had found his way onto Carnesecca's recruiting radar.

Chris Mullin wasn't the most imposing figure on the basketball court, all limbs and far too lanky to be very intimidating, but Carnesecca knew his name—and his jumper. The pair moved in the same circles for years, aware of the other and what they were each trying to accomplish and, finally, in 1981, Mullin made a decision that would shape the St. John's basketball program for decades to come. He took his talents to Queens and changed everything.

THE STAR

Chris Mullin grew up in Brooklyn, a playground hero who'd regularly take the subway with friends around the city looking for the best game. They were trips that sometimes felt more intimidating than simple pick-up games. Mullin often found himself taking the train into some of the city's toughest neighborhoods, and it was almost too obvious that he stuck out amongst the crowd, and not because of his talent, at least not at first.

Mullin kept going, though, determined to play and even more determined to prove himself, particularly against the talent that stalked New York City playgrounds. He hit shot after shot, picking up confidence with every bucket. If he didn't keep scoring, he knew he wouldn't be welcomed back, and the last thing Mullin wanted was to be kept away from the game he loved so much.

It didn't take long for the playground crowd to respect him. He'd proven his worth and, with two years left in his high school hoops career, transferred to Xaverian High School and a new set of critics. There were some who labeled him "unathletic," concerned by his lack of muscle or slim build, certain he wouldn't be able to succeed at the college level. Mullin, as per usual, just kept sinking jumpers. He led Xaverian to a state title in 1981 and was named "Mr. Basketball" in New York State that season, suddenly drawing interest from some of the top basketball teams in the country.

Carnesecca, however, had been watching for a while. He first saw Mullin when he was a ten-year-old kid, attending the coach's summer camps at St. John's. The jumper wasn't quite as good then as it would be a decade later, but Carnesecca never forgot about the kid with the Brooklyn accent, and he kept his ear open for any news about his game—or his college decision. Carnesecca patrolled the city playgrounds as much as anyone, listening to the rumors and details of the exploits on the blacktop, and he knew what Mullin could bring to St. John's. The problem, however, was getting him to Queens.

Mullin had silenced his doubters time and time again, and with a jumpshot that was smoother than actual silk, the city kid was considering leaving the blacktop behind. He had offers from a handful of college programs, including Virginia and Villanova, and was seriously considering Duke, but something stopped him. Duke hadn't always been there. Duke didn't know about the subway trips or the pick-up games without foul calls, matchups that were closer to battles, littered with elbows and body checks. Carnesecca did. He'd been there since the start, and that made all the difference for Mullin.

"When I went on those visits, whether it be Virginia, Duke, Villanova, [couldn't] compare to what I thought I had in St. John's and being home and being able to play for Coach Carnesecca," Mullin told the New York Post in 2015. "I felt it was the best place for me."[160]

St. John's had been successful under Carnesecca. The Redmen's run in the 1979 NCAA Tournament had been the jumping-off point, but the addition of Mullin was like an electrical current through the entire program, and the entire city of New York. St. John's advanced to the Sweet Sixteen with Mullin on the court in the 1982–83 season, but it was the

---

160 Howie Kussoy, "Chris Mullin's NYC Rise, Struggle with Demons and Triumphant Return Home," New York Post (April 2015), https://nypost.com/2015/04/01/mullins-30-years-away -from-st-johns-full-of-twists-and-turns.

1984–85 season that became the marker that all other squads will be measured against. It was also the season of the sweater.

St. John's opened up the 1984–85 season with five straight victories and had lost just one game heading into a February 27 matchup against Georgetown at Madison Square Garden. The Redmen were ranked No. 1 in the country at the time, the Hoyas No. 2, and in a game that would pit Mullin against Patrick Ewing, the world's most famous arena was all but shaking on 34th street in Midtown Manhattan. Carnesecca wore his sweater, the same ugly pattern that he'd tugged on for the last thirteen games, a superstition and a trend that seemed to go hand in hand with St. John's continued success. The Redmen had already topped Georgetown once that season, and the hype surrounding the rematch was unprecedented. Hoyas coach John Thompson even went so far as to get his own sweater, an almost identical imitation of Carnesecca's now-iconic look, holding open his sports jacket to show off the argyle. The game lived up to the expectations, the kind of fervent crowd Mullin had dreamed of when considering his college options, shouting and screaming and reacting to every foul as if it were being called against them.

St. John's fell 85–69 on its home court, but the game, and the performances in that game, were the highlight of a Big East era that hoops fans still speak of in hushed tones. It was Mullin vs. Ewing, Carnesecca vs. Thompson, sweater vs. sweater. It was college basketball in its purest form, a battle for supremacy in the middle of New York City when New York City was still the middle of the basketball world.[161]

The loss was disappointing, but Carnesecca never stopped smiling. He had a habit of that. When asked about the status of the sweater after the game, he cracked a joke, telling reporters, "She took very good

---

161 Scott Allen, "Georgetown Tifo of John Thompson Celebrates 30th Anniversary of 'The Sweater Game,'" The *Washington Post* (February 2015), https://www.washingtonpost.com/news/dc-sports-bog/wp/2015/02/18/georgetown-tifo-of-john-thompson-celebrates-30th-anniversary-of-the-sweater-game/?noredirect=on&utm_term=.bf50a73322a2.

care of me for a long time. But she has received notice from me: One more game like that and she's gone!"[162]

St. John's bounced back in its final game of the regular season, but Georgetown remained a constant thorn in the Redmen's collective side. The Hoyas notched another victory in the Big East championship game, sending St. John's to the NCAA Tournament with hopes of rediscovering its early-season dominance. It worked.

St. John's rolled through the opening rounds of the NCAA Tournament, led by Mullin's jumper and a New York attitude that was equal parts confident and hopeful. Carnesecca was a character on the sidelines throughout his career, but perhaps no more than that season. He ran and jumped and screamed, voice going hoarse by the end of every game. He never focused that emotion on his players, however. Carnesecca was as supportive of his team as any coach at any point in hoops history, priding himself on encouraging his players when the going got tough. And, despite another dominant run in the NCAA Tournament, the going got tough for St. John's in the Final Four.

The Redmen, once again, fell to Georgetown, a lopsided 77–59 loss that saw Mullin score fewer than ten points for the first time in nearly 100 games. It was an abrupt end to a season that included everything from *Sports Illustrated* covers to discussions of sideline fashion, but Carnesecca still couldn't wipe the smile off his face. This was a brand-new mark for St. John's basketball, a record-breaking season highlighted by Mullin's ascension to the top of the program's all-time scoring list, and Carnesecca knew they'd accomplished something important that year.

He brought Mullin into the program for that reason, to shine a spotlight on New York City basketball and what a program without any dorm rooms could do. Carnesecca was proud, no matter what.

---

162 "The Sweater Is Warned," *New York Times* (March 1985), https://www.nytimes.com /1985/03/01/sports/the-sweater-is-warned-although-st-john-s-was.html.

"I think [winning a championship] would've been a wonderful thing for the team, for the players, for the alumni, faculty," Carnesecca told the St. John's student newspaper in 2013. "But you know, the world as it is, is wonderful."[163]

STICKING AROUND

Carnesecca left the St. John's basketball program for good in 1992, wrapping up a career that included 526 victories at the college level, five Big East regular season titles, two Big East conference titles, and more than a handful of Coach of the Year honors. He was inducted into the Naismith Memorial Basketball Hall of Fame the same year, and while his coaching career is far behind him, Carnesecca's influence on the team and the entire St. John's community can still be seen in just about everything. And so can he. Carnesecca has an office on campus, in the gym that now bears his name—the old Alumni Hall was renamed as Carnesecca Arena on November 23, 2004. He's been spotted in the hallways below the arena, nodding at students heading to the gym and basketball stars hoping to bring St. John's back to the Final Four and that elusive national championship.

Carnesecca is in the fabric of St. John's. He is the face of the basketball team and the school itself, even nearly thirty years after he stopped suiting up in questionably bright sweaters. The program itself, however, has been through its own trials and tribulations since Carnesecca.

Brian Mahoney took over the reins after Carnesecca stepped down, but the longtime assistant struggled to find his footing as head coach. The relationships between area schools and St. John's were strained, and Mahoney was fired after three straight losing seasons. Then came Fran Fraschilla, who got St. John's back to the NCAA Tournament, but was gone by 1998. Mike Jarvis took over the program on June 11, 1998, but the cracks were starting to grow in a program that was floundering without Carnesecca.

---

163 Perez, "Hanging with 'Looie.'"

Erick Barkley, a Fraschilla recruit from local high school powerhouse Christ the King, was being investigated by the NCAA regarding payment for his prep-school tuition, while Grady Reynolds, a Jarvis recruit, was charged in 2002 for assaulting and harassing a St. John's swimmer. The microscope continued to get closer and closer, and when Jarvis wanted a large extension in 2003, the administration cut him loose.[164]

It all continued to dissolve from there and, in February 2004, after a loss at Pittsburgh, six St. John's players reportedly visited Club Erotica before bringing an area woman back to the team hotel. There were accusations and lies and an NCAA investigation that ended with a self-imposed probation by St. John's, a loss of scholarships, and no Big East tournament that season.[165]

St. John's, which eventually changed its nickname from Redmen to Red Storm, has done its best to pull itself out of the shadows of the NCAA and the downward slide the program has been on since Carnesecca's retirement. There have been a few NCAA Tournament trips since then, but neither head coaches Norm Roberts nor Steve Lavin were able to live up to Carnesecca's legend. Once again, that's where Mullin came in.

The former St. John's star was named head coach of the Red Storm in 2015, stepping into the same shoes his mentor once filled, and Carnesecca, as always, was right nearby. He's over ninety years old, closer to frail than anything else, but Carnesecca regularly sits in the stands at as many St. John's games as he's able, nodding to the cameras and supporting the program he's always believed in. He's never lost hope in the school or the players it can bring in, certain the Red Storm can still be a beacon of basketball hope in New York.

Carnesecca knew he could never stay "Coach" forever—he even dabbled in TV for some time after walking away from the sidelines, where

---

164 Robbins, "Rise and Fall of St. John's."

165 "St. John's University Announces Findings of Self-Inquiry into Alleged NCAA Violations," St. John's Athletics (November 2004), https://redstormsports.com/news/2004/11/26/ st_john_s_university_announces_findings_of_self_inquiry_into_alleged_ncaa_violations. aspx?path=general.

his fashion choices were still as colorful as ever—but there was always a draw to the city, and home, a place that defined him as much as he defined it. New York City basketball may not be the center of the hoops universe anymore, and most big-name high school players leave local for prep programs and AAU teams that crisscross the country as much as any Division I college team does, but there's still an aura on the playgrounds and the concrete, an echo of the history and accolades. Carnesecca, even decades after he hung up his sneakers and folded up his sweater, can still hear it perfectly.

After everything, it'd be easy for Carnesecca to look back longingly, but that's not his game. He's part of the now, a recognizable face on campus and at Madison Square Garden, and he's excited for whatever comes next.

"I'm not looking back, just ahead," Carnesecca told *Newsday* in 2015. "But it's wonderful to still be able to come and enjoy the games."[166]

● ● ● ● ●

THE ONE THAT GOT AWAY

Lou Carnesecca prided himself on being able to recruit anyone. He knew everyone, after all, and it was a matter of pride that he could turn those relationships into basketball scholarships and, he hoped, victories for the St. John's men's basketball team. Most of the time it worked. Carnesecca was a hero and a legend in Queens while he was coaching the Redmen, the epitome of Big East success when the standard of success was measured by winning in the Big East. He always got his players, and their numbers are now hanging in the rafters of the arena named for Carnesecca.

It wasn't just Mullin, although the Brooklyn star may have been Carnesecca's best and most notable recruit. Mark Jackson, who graduated from Bishop Loughlin in Brooklyn, was a dominant point

166 Neil Best, "Lou Carnesecca, 90, Enjoys the Atmosphere at MSG but Wishes St. John's Had Won," *Newsday* (January 2015), https://www.newsday.com/sports/columnists/neil-best/louie-carnesecca-90-enjoys-the-atmosphere-at-msg-but-wishes-st-john-s-had-won-1.9844720.

guard for St. John's before being selected with the first overall pick by the New York Knicks in the 1987 NBA Draft. Walter Berry, who graduated from Benjamin Franklin High School in Manhattan and was known as "The Truth," also had a solid NBA career before taking his talents to Europe, competing across the continent until 2002.

Carnesecca's ability to keep New York City kids in New York City was unparalleled, but even the Hall of Fame coach came up short once. It just so happened that the one that got away turned out to be one of the best to ever play the game: Julius Erving.

Erving was another homegrown talent, a playground hero who played his high school ball at Roosevelt High School on Long Island. He was one of the most fundamentally sound players in the area—the complete package. And while he didn't wow anyone with his trick shots at that point in his career, Erving was still one of the most dominant scorers in miles. It was also at that point that, as the story goes, he picked up his moniker of "Dr. J." According to former teammates, one of Erving's friends started calling him "Doctor," and the name stuck, going on to highlight the way Erving operated on the hardwood. Despite his offensive prowess, Erving wasn't picking up many recruiting looks. He had interest from three schools: Hofstra, UMass, and St. John's. [167]

Carnesecca had every intention of trying to keep Erving in the area, but the UMass staff got there first. Erving and his family visited the campus, and his college fate was officially sealed. Erving took his talents to New England in 1968, averaging 26.3 points and 20.2 rebounds per game in two seasons at the varsity level. Again, however, Erving's star refused to rise completely, and his name was relatively unknown ahead of graduating. He signed as an undergraduate free agent with the ABA's Virginia Squires in 1971, another missed opportunity for Carnesecca while he was coaching in the league.

The Squires suffered financial problems after Erving's first season with the team and, in an attempt to balance the books, offered the

---

167 "Julius Erving," NBA, accessed November 2018, http://www.nba.com/history/players/erving_bio.html.

future star to the New York Nets in exchange for cash. Carnesecca declined. It's a decision that still doesn't make complete sense to him today.

"I felt that wasn't the right thing to do at that time," Carnesecca told the St. John's student newspaper in 2013. "I was wrong, because what I was doing was stopping a young man from making a living. Can you imagine Rick Barry and him together? I'd still be in the NBA." [168]

Erving did, eventually, play for the Nets, joining the squad ahead of the 1973–74 season, after Carnesecca had already returned to St. John's. He went on to lead the Nets to two titles in three seasons and, in the 1976 postseason, averaged a whopping 34.7 points per game en route to an MVP honor. After the ABA folded, Erving continued his dominance in the NBA, competing for the Philadelphia 76ers and immediately making a name for himself. Erving racked up points, rebounds, steals, and even more MVP trophies. He was a doctor of the game, fine-tuning his approach every time he stepped on the court.

When he retired at the age of thirty-seven, Erving had scored over 30,000 points in his pro career, shooting just over fifty percent from the field. He was elected to the Naismith Memorial Basketball Hall of Fame in 1993, just one year after Carnesecca. It was a career that was nothing short of incredible, and while Carnesecca couldn't ever fault Erving for any of his accomplishments, there were always a few questions about the city kid who got out of the city and what could have been if he stayed home.

● ● ● ● ●

_____

168 Perez, "Hanging with 'Looie."

Carnesecca's Best Games

At the Top

Carnesecca became the all-time winningest coach in St. John's history on February 11, 1984, with a 68–62 victory over Connecticut. The win was his 335th career victory, surpassing his mentor Joe Lapchick in the process. It wasn't a particularly dominant showing by St. John's, which didn't win any titles, nor did it lead to much more than a few smiles on players' faces as they walked off the court. But it did something bigger; it put Carnesecca at the very top of the basketball world in New York City. He added onto the all-time total for several seasons after, but that initial mark was more than enough to set Carnesecca apart from the rest.

Beast of the East

Is it an upset if it's No. 3 topping No. 1? It is if those two teams are both in the Big East and both boasting some of the biggest names in college hoops at the time. St. John's defeated then-No. 1 Georgetown on January 26, 1985, as Chris Mullin notched one of the most dominant offensive performances of his career. Mullin scored a game-high twenty points and Walter Berry added fourteen, but St. John's victory came from its smothering and relatively simple man-to-man defense. Carnesecca kept his team moving, pursuing every Georgetown dribble and, in the end, it led to a St. John's upset victory and lifted the team to No. 1 in the nation.

CHAPTER TEN

JIM CALHOUN
New England Grit

"I'll do everything in my power to make UConn
the best basketball program it can be. I can't do
any more than that. I don't work miracles."

**JIM CALHOUN AT HIS FIRST UCONN PRESS
CONFERENCE ON MAY 15, 1986**

Jim Calhoun had a picture on one of the walls in his office when he was
at UConn. It was a nondescript kid, certainly not anyone Calhoun knew,
staring up at a basketball hoop. It was, for all intents and purposes,
a stock photo. But it was a picture that the former Huskies coach felt
resonated with him and with the kind of basketball culture he hoped to
create in Storrs.

As long as there was a kid, any kid, from any background and any
circumstance who could look up at a basketball hoop and feel something, then Calhoun wanted to coach him. He wanted to help him win.
Because, once upon a time, Calhoun had looked up at a hoop with a
ball at his feet and hoped, eventually, he could win something.

To understand Jim Calhoun is to understand the drive that pushes him every single day—even now. This is not a man who simply wants to do well. This is a man who thrives on victory and shuns defeat, who has cemented himself as one of the most successful program-builders in all of college basketball.

Calhoun's dominance at the NCAA level was built out of a distinct set of challenges as a child. He was born in May, 1942, in Braintree, Massachusetts, a small town less than fifteen miles south of Boston.[169] Braintree is the kind of place that thrived on its history. It was incorporated in 1640 and still touts itself as the birthplace of John Adams and John Quincy Adams, not to mention John Hancock and General Sylvanus Thayer, the founder of West Point. Braintree is quintessential New England. It's church steeples and brightly colored leaves in the fall. It's the proud heritage that Calhoun still regards as the building block of his personality. He's still got that bit of Boston accent when he talks.

Calhoun grew up around sports, anxious to prove himself among the relatively small masses in Braintree. He suited up for his high school baseball and football teams and was talented at both, but basketball was different. Basketball, Calhoun knew, was the sport that was going to get him out of Braintree.

"I was a big baseball fan and I loved the contact in football, but I was tall, so basketball was appealing," Calhoun said. "It's an active sport and I fell in love with it. That's the bottom line. I loved all sports, still do. Basketball became the thing I loved because I thought there was so much you could do with it. If you had some ability, you could do something."

Calhoun had every intention of getting out of Braintree with a basketball in his hand and a focus that no one in the entire continental United States, let alone the surrounding New England area, was going to be able to dent. He earned a basketball scholarship to Lowell State, but

---

169 "Jim Calhoun," UConn Athletics, accessed November 2018, https://uconnhuskies.com/staff.aspx?staff=182.

spent just three months at the school, barely enough time to lace up his sneakers and get on the court, before he knew he needed to come home.[170] The world, it seemed, had other plans for Calhoun.

His father passed away when he was just fifteen years old, and despite grand plans to leave Braintree and take on the basketball world, Calhoun knew he couldn't walk away from his family. So, he came back, picking up odd jobs that included stone cutter, headstone engraver, scrap yard worker, shampoo-factory worker, and grave digger, supporting his mother and five brothers and sisters while watching his friends live out the dream he'd always thought was his.

It was a bitter pill to swallow for Calhoun, the kid who looked up at a hoop and saw it as a ticket to everything he ever wanted. He couldn't give it up. He kept playing. He worked and worked and then, for good measure, worked some more, and when came home after work, he grabbed his basketball and went back to the court. There was something about standing on the blacktop with a ball in his hand and a game plan forming in his head that was calming.

Basketball, as far as Calhoun was concerned, was therapeutic. It was a moment away from everything else, the expectations and the disappointments and the frustration that ran through every inch of him from the time he woke up until the time he put his head on the pillow. Basketball was his and only his. He didn't owe anyone anything while he was on the court, and he didn't need anyone else on the court to learn the game.

"After the football practices would end by the basketball courts, I'd stop by and play for an hour or so," Calhoun said. "So, I guess, in the solitude of playing, as I was going through everything else, I kind of just resolved and learned how to play my game. I played it all out in my head."

---

170 Dick Weiss, "UConn Basketball Coach Jim Calhoun to Retire after Legendary College Career: source," *New York Daily News* (September 2012), https://www.nydailynews.com/sports/college/uconn-basketball-coach-jim-calhoun-retires-legendary-college-career-article-1.1158031.

GOING ONE ON ONE

Calhoun perfected his game by himself, taking jumpshot after jump-shot and running his own layup lines as if he were playing at Boston Garden. He came back every night as soon as the Braintree football team had finished practice, shooting under the dim lights and shadows that worked their way onto the court from the field. It wasn't perfect. It wasn't what he wanted, but it didn't deter his drive or, more importantly, his determination.

He kept shooting. He kept game planning for matchups and teams he wasn't sure he would ever face. He kept working. He never once looked up at that basketball hoop and thought, for even a moment, that he couldn't put the ball through it.

Basketball was still going to get Calhoun out of Braintree. It did. Twenty months after he took an indefinite leave of absence from Lowell State, Calhoun went back to school, completing his education at American International College in Springfield, Massachusetts, the same city that boasts the Naismith Memorial Basketball Hall of Fame.

"You could get lost in the game by yourself," Calhoun said. "I love the game and the game eventually became something incredibly important in my life in the sense that it was the way for me to get to school. After my dad passed away, I wouldn't have been able to make it through without a basketball scholarship."

Calhoun found his footing at American International. He was named an All-New England player, lettered all three years he competed with the program, and led the Yellow Jackets in scoring as a junior and senior. He wrapped up his collegiate career as the fourth all-time leading scorer in program history and led American International to its first-ever NCAA Division II playoff berth in 1968. Calhoun was named to the inaugural American International Hall of Fame in 2005.[171]

---

171 "Jim Calhoun, Class of 1968," American International College, accessed November 2018, https://aicyellowjackets.com/hof.aspx?hof=2&path=&kiosk=.

Calhoun has never forgotten his roots. He wasn't a Division I prospect. He wasn't picking up headlines or front-page photos, even in the local papers, and he wasn't drawing much interest from professional squads. None of that mattered. Calhoun still loved the game and if he couldn't play it himself at the next level, then he was going to help whoever he could.

Calhoun's coaching career began at Old Lyme High School, after he accepted a sixth-grade teaching position at the school, taking on a junior-varsity team that hadn't won a game in two years. His squad finished 3–17 in his first season on the sidelines. Calhoun still wasn't deterred. He wanted to win and he knew there were kids out there who wanted the same. He found them at Dedham High School in Massachusetts.[172]

"The varsity won three games before I got there," Calhoun said. "But by that second year we were winning games and were 21–1. I've had to do a lot of different things, but I've always wanted to win."

In 1972, Calhoun and the Dedham High boys' basketball team made it as far as the state semifinal tournament, falling just short of their ultimate goal at Boston Garden. It was disappointing at the time, another obstacle in what felt like a long line of insurmountable challenges, but Calhoun's players never forgot what he did for them that season. He sparked something in that program, jumpstarting the group and leaving each one of his players wanting a little bit more, even after he left following the end of the season.

"He was fiery and passionate," Norm Jones, who was a junior during the '72 run, told the *Hartford Courant* in 2011. "And remember, he was only twenty-eight years old. He could still play. So take that fire and

---

172 Chip Malafronte, "Through the years with Jim Calhoun," *New Haven Register* (March 2005), https://www.nhregister.com/news/article/Through-the-years-with-Jim-Calhoun-11651744.php.

passion and throw in the fact that he could get out on the court and hammer us on the backboards."[173]

Calhoun graduated up the coaching ladder to the college game in 1972, taking the head job at Northeastern University, which was a Division II program at the time. He didn't balk at the level of competition. He never did. He simply wanted to keep winning, so that's exactly what Calhoun did.

The Huskies went 19–7 in Calhoun's first season and, in 1981, made the program's first-ever NCAA Tournament appearance, notching a victory over Fresno State in the first round before falling to Utah. Northeastern went on to make Tournament appearances in 1982, 1984, 1985, and 1986, the last of which was, arguably, Calhoun's best team with the program. That year's Huskies squad, led by the late, great Boston Celtics star Reggie Lewis, posted a 26–5 record and put Northeastern hoops on the college basketball map.

Northeastern fell to eventual NCAA runner-up Oklahoma in the first round of the Tournament that year, but Calhoun's legacy was already starting to grow. He was developing a reputation, taking unknown programs and building them up from scratch, finding talent and honing talent and, as per usual, looking up at that hoop with one very specific goal: getting the ball through it.

Calhoun posted a 248–137 career record at Northeastern in fourteen seasons with the program, but in May 1986 got an opportunity he simply couldn't ignore. He was hired as the seventeenth men's basketball coach at the University of Connecticut, a program that had reached the NCAA Tournament just twice in the last twenty years.[174]

---

173 Mike Anthony, "Jim Calhoun Welcomed Back By High School He Coached," *Hartford Courant* (June 2011), https://www.courant.com/sports/uconn-mens-basketball/hc-xpm-2011-06-02-hc-uconn-calhoun-dedham-graduation-0620110601-story.html.

174 "Jim Calhoun Coaching Record," Sports-Reference, accessed November 2018, https://www.sports-reference.com/cbb/coaches/jim-calhoun-1.html.

WRITING THE STORY IN STORRS

This was another challenge, another obstacle, and Calhoun's determination was just as pointed as ever. He'd heard of UConn, of course, knew of the program and its potential, but he knew that no one had been able to take the team from the bottom of the basketball barrel. This was not the UConn of now, the storied program with banners hanging in the rafters and memories of monumental games that are still talked about in hushed tones in the hallways at Storrs. This was a UConn that didn't know what winning felt like, that had forgotten the rush and the adrenaline that came with final-second victories and unexpected upsets. This was a UConn that was entrenched right in the middle, not quite without hope, but certainly lingering in the shadows.

That was, of course, until Calhoun signed on the dotted line, stood in front of the podium at his introductory press conference, and decided, without much fanfare, that he was going to bring another group of Huskies back into the athletic spotlight. Calhoun knew he had an uphill battle ahead of him, but that had become the subheadline of his entire life, and it didn't take long for him to start implementing his own system into the very fabric of UConn basketball. This team was going to look up at the hoop, score, win, and change an entire basketball culture, and the players were going to work for it.

"It was special at UConn. People support it there. They want to win," Calhoun said. "Even many, many years ago. We had five straight losing seasons and then I came in and contributed one more to it. But in doing so, I was able to get our own culture, the kids we needed, and the kind of things we needed to get that program going."

UConn won just nine games in Calhoun's first year with the team, but went 15–14 in his second season, good enough to earn a berth to the National Invitation Tournament. It wasn't the NCAA Tournament, but it was the postseason and, for Calhoun, an opportunity to challenge both his players and himself. The team went on to win five straight games in the NIT, defeating Ohio State 72-67 to win the championship and capture UConn's first basketball title in decades.

The victory catapulted UConn into the national discussion, earning more than a few headlines and, most importantly, gave Calhoun a foundation on which to build the rest of his program, particularly against the challenging competition the Huskies faced in the Big East.

He reminisced about the turning point, telling the *New Haven Register* in 2006, "I knew the difficulty of the job. When the Big East exploded on the scene, it was almost like a few years ago with the Southeastern Conference and football. It became 'the thing.' The Big East was a nightly show, with Pearl Washington, Patrick Ewing, Chris Mullin on TV. It was as special as you're gonna find... I thought, 'OK, we've got some work to do here.'"[175]

Calhoun went back to work. He was named the National Coach of the Year in 1990 after leading UConn to Elite Eight and, despite failing to Duke on a buzzer-beater shot to end the season, the Huskies were an undeniable force across the country. This was no longer a team that hoped to, maybe, make a postseason tournament. This was a team that expected to make the Big Dance every season and, with every season that went on, expected to get closer and closer to another championship.

That, however, took some time. UConn recorded back-to-back NCAA Tournament appearances in 1991 and 1992, but the Huskies seemed snake-bitten by the Madness in March, never able to take that last, big step. The squad kept winning, capturing its first No. 1 ranking in the pools in February 1995 and recording a Big East-record twenty-three consecutive games from November 25, 1995 to February 17, 1996. But the Huskies failed to reach the Final Four until 1999. That's when everything changed.

---

175 "Jim Calhoun, UConn Pairing Reaches 30-year Anniversary," *New Haven Register* (May 2016), https://www.nhregister.com/uconn/article/Jim-Calhoun-UConn-pairing-reaches-30-year-11333746.php.

EMBRACING THE CHALLENGE

UConn finally made it over the Final Four hump, defeating Ohio State, the same program it beat in its NIT-winning season, in the national semifinals. The Huskies went on to top Duke 77–74, a program that had ended UConn's season more than once in the previous decade, winning the school's first-ever national title.

It went on from there. UConn made it back to the NCAA Tournament the very next season, but fell to Tennessee in the second round of play, and Calhoun continued to pick up personal coaching records. He became the twenty-sixth coach and, at the time, the eleventh active coach to reach the 600-win plateau in December 2001. The Huskies made their fifteenth straight postseason in March 2002, another Elite Eight showing and, in July of that year, Calhoun became one of the inaugural inductees into the New England Basketball Hall of Fame. UConn kept winning. Calhoun kept winning. And then came yet another obstacle.

Calhoun announced he had been diagnosed with prostate cancer on February 3, 2003. It was a setback that would have rattled anyone, and there would have been plenty who understood if Calhoun had chosen to step away from the game for the remainder of the season. He didn't. He missed five games, underwent surgery to remove his prostate, and returned to the Huskies bench to watch his team record a victory over St. John's on February 22.

UConn captured another Big East regular-season title that year, advancing to the Sweet Sixteen and, in November 2003, Calhoun recorded his 400th win at UConn and his 650th career victory within weeks of each other. That was only the start of a historic season for Calhoun. The Huskies defeated Vermont, DePaul, Vanderbilt, and Alabama in the NCAA Tournament, earning the school's second Final Four berth before taking down Duke and Georgia Tech to win UConn's second national championship in March 2004.

It was the second time Calhoun found himself looking up at the hoop so he could cut down the net, and the feeling didn't diminish upon repeat. If anything, it got better.

Calhoun didn't slow down, even after the second title run. He couldn't bring himself to, not when he loved the game as much as he had when he was a teenager. He paced the sidelines, followed the recruiting trail, and continued to build something in Storrs, because two national championships were nice, but they weren't enough. There were still more hills to climb, more obstacles to overcome, and more records to be broken.

Calhoun cemented his name in basketball history on September 9, 2005, when he was inducted into the Naismith Memorial Basketball Hall of Fame, just a few miles down the road from where he played his college ball. The honor, however, didn't make much of a difference to Calhoun's coaching style. He still held his teams to the highest standard, still expected that extra bit of work and looked for the kind of player he was, the one who'd spend hours on a blacktop with only a few pinpricks of light so he could fine-tune his jumper.

Calhoun was constantly looking for the worker, the hard-nosed kid who wanted to prove himself by winning. He found plenty of players like that over his career, ones who, from the national title in 2004 until his second medical-induced leave of absence in 2010, helped him secure his 700th and 800th career victories and a third Final Four appearance. Calhoun coached talented kids, hard-working kids, and kids with the kind of natural-born talent mere mortals could only dream of. Calhoun still talks about some of his players like they were his own sons, beams every time he thinks about Ray Allen being inducted in the Naismith Basketball Hall of Fame. Allen played for the Huskies from 1993 to 1996, fine-tuning his jumper in Storrs. Calhoun recounted one of his more memorable moments with the future NBA champ, telling the *Hartford Courant* he stopped Allen once when he was leaving practice in 1993. He asked him if he was leaving and then asked if he'd shot 100 percent that night. He hadn't.

"Oh, I thought you wanted to be great," Calhoun told Allen. "And he kind of just looked at me. I remember it so vividly."[176]

Allen stayed at practice a little longer, going on to become one of the most potent 3-point shooters the NBA has ever seen. Calhoun always demanded the best of his players, but he also cared deeply about his players. He's spoken at length about how the passing of Lewis affected both him and his family. Calhoun cared about every single kid who suited up for him at any level. It was part of his coaching DNA. He respected them all and wanted them all to succeed. He believed they all could.

And then there was Kemba Walker.

WALKING INTO HISTORY

Kemba Walker was the blueprint of the player Calhoun dreamed up in Braintree: a New York City talent who grew up on playgrounds, with a jumpshot so sweet it could have rotted the teeth of everyone in the entire state of Connecticut. Walker was the kind of talent that other talent looks to, the player everyone on the UConn roster flocked to before, during, and after practice. When the game was on the line, they wanted him to have the ball. Walker was the difference-maker and, in his junior season, which saw lingering rumors over NCAA sanctions and a preseason rankings snub, he was the guy who helped Calhoun keep the Huskies on track.

"Kemba was special," Calhoun said. "The guys turned to him. They trusted him and they believed in him. I've had plenty of talented guys, guys who went onto the NBA and first-round picks, but Kemba was different."

UConn was a college basketball powerhouse in 2010, but it was also a program facing plenty of questions, and Walker did his best to answer

---

176 Mike Anthony, "Mike Anthony: Ray Allen's Greatness The Product of An Obsession," *Hartford Courant* (September 2018), https://www.courant.com/sports/uconn-mens-basketball/hc-sp-ray-allen-hall-of-fame-jim-calhoun-column-20180831-story.html.

them. He led the Huskies, a team with seven freshmen on the roster that year, to a victory at the Maui Invitational in November and a No. 4 ranking, but UConn struggled in the final stretch of the regular season, dropping four of its last five and falling to the nine seed in the upcoming Big East Tournament.

There were more questions. Could this team win in the conference tournament? If it didn't win, would it make the NCAA Tournament? Was youth the problem? Or was it the plethora of off-court distractions? Did any of it matter when the Big East was so chock-full of talent?

Calhoun spoke publicly about the tournament seeding, criticizing matchups and schedules, but there wasn't anything he could do. There were plural consecutive games to play. That's when the fun started.

UConn played five games in five days from March 8 to March 12—Tuesday, Wednesday, Thursday, Friday, and Saturday—taking the court at Madison Square Garden and looking up at that hoop and that iconic scoreboard with one thought in its collective mind: to keep winning. The Huskies rolled past DePaul and Georgetown, but then came Pittsburgh and Walker's jump into college basketball immortality.

The moment played out like this: March 10, 2011, a jam-packed Madison Square Garden, screaming fans, painted faces, nerves almost palpable in the air. There were eighteen seconds on the clock. Walker inbounded the ball, got it back, and dribbled around the three-point line. He kept dribbling. The seconds ticked by. He drifted back toward mid-court only to dribble some more, working a switch from the Pitt defenders. Then came the crossover. Walker made his move, a quick stutter step and juke that left his defender on his heels and, with two seconds left, just enough time to look up at the hoop, he took his shot. The ball went through as time expired, lifting UConn to a 76–74 victory and a season that wasn't over yet.

The cameras, naturally, panned to Calhoun on the sidelines, a show of emotion that was as genuine as anything he exhibited throughout his career. There was shouting and yelling and, of course, another game to play, only now, UConn felt like it was competing with a stacked deck, and Calhoun knew Walker was the king—in all four suits.

"The day we beat Pittsburgh, Kemba makes this great move to shake the center down," Calhoun told Boston.com in April 2018. "He falls, and all of a sudden, it was just special. I could tell we were going to overcome almost anything. I said it that night, and little did I know, we won the next two games, and of course, we won six more in the national championship."[177]

Pittsburgh defeated Syracuse and Louisville in the next two days to capture the program's seventh Big East title, securing a No. 3 seed in the upcoming NCAA Tournament. There were, luckily, a few more days in between those games, but the excitement of the conference championship didn't wane. If anything, now that the Huskies were back on the national stage, the team wanted to win even more. This was a group that had embraced its underdog role from the very beginning, and with Walker leading the charge, Calhoun was confident in what his players could accomplish. So were they, and the Huskies knew that made them dangerous.

"Any game we went into, we always felt like we had a chance to win—even if they were ranked higher or whatever it was," former UConn guard-forward Jeremy Lamb told Boston.com. "We always knew we had the best player in the country in Kemba [Walker]. We had some great role players around him. The way our team was set up, it was just perfect."

UConn won eleven consecutive postseason games, taking down Bucknell, Cincinnati, San Diego State, Arizona, Kentucky, and Butler en route to the program's third and, possibly most improbable, national championship. It was dramatic. It was unexpected. It was a group of nineteen and twenty-year-old kids who simply refused to go home because their coach told them they didn't have any other option.

---

177 Nicole Yang, "Reliving UConn's Incredible 2011 Championship Run with Jim Calhoun, Jeremy Lamb, and Kemba Walker," Boston.com (April 2018), https://www.boston.com/sports/ncaa-tournament/2018/04/02/uconn-2011-championship-jim-calhoun-kemba-walker.

Calhoun likes to tell the story of how, when it seemed his squad might have been feeling the effects of so many games in so few days, he'd ask them if they'd rather "go home and practice." He'd ask, "Or you want to keep playing in front of thousands of people, have everybody love you and see how great you are?"

The answer for the Huskies was easy. They wanted to play. That didn't make things any easier, but the Huskies couldn't stop. They got on the buses and the planes and stepped into new arenas with screaming fans that were rooting for and against them, playing every single game like it was going to be their last. That was the way Calhoun taught them to play and that was the way Calhoun built his program. They believed in themselves, even when common sense told them not to.

"There were so many emotions," Walker told Boston.com "I just remember everybody saying we couldn't do it. Each and every game, they said there's no way we could win another game, there's no way we could win another game. But we did anyway."

Cutting down nets, putting on championship hats, posing for photos with the championship trophy was certainly the goal, but Calhoun is quick to point out that the journey mattered more. This was the title run that, to this day, defines his legacy at UConn, and Walker's penchant for late-game dramatics is still what most people think of when they consider recent Huskies history. But when asked about March 2011, Calhoun doesn't immediately drift back to those memories. He thinks about buses and planes and sometimes sluggish practices. He thinks about a group of guys who became something bigger than themselves, who brought the sports world to its feet and made sure everyone held their breath.

It wasn't just about basketball. It was about the players, culture, and relationships that are just as important now as they were nearly a decade before. Walker and Lamb were teammates in Charlotte in 2018, and the two reminisce about the run even now. That's what Calhoun is most proud of.

"If you look around the world and the idea of having teammates and caring about the game is everywhere. That doesn't ever change," Calhoun said. "It's about getting on the bus and going somewhere with a group of guys and working for it. Together. And we've had great teams at UConn, we've even had dream teams, but that group and those guys, that was the dream season."

DEFYING EXPECTATIONS

UConn's 2011 championship was a picture-perfect ending to a year that had some wondering if Calhoun still had it. At sixty-eight years old, he became the oldest coach to win a national championship, and just the fifth NCAA Division I coach to win a third title, but lingering health issues left his future in Storrs hazy. Calhoun had already battled cancer once and, in June 2009, had completed a fifty-mile bike challenge after falling and breaking several ribs. He also took a leave of absence from UConn in January 2010 due to a "serious" health condition, but returned to the court on February 13.[178] Calhoun announced another leave on February 3, 2012, as a result of spinal stenosis. He returned the next month, less than a week after back surgery, coaching the Huskies to a victory over Pittsburgh in the final game of the regular season.[179]

Calhoun never lost his determination or his drive, despite the issues he faced off the court. Instead, he and his wife Patty turned their attention to helping others, supporting a handful of charities, including Coaches vs. Cancer. He also kept coaching. Calhoun pushed himself to the limit, more than once, constantly searching for that thrill of victory and avoiding the agony of defeat. He'd faced every challenge he could have ever thought of, stumbled, and maybe fallen a few times, but there was something to be said for sheer stubbornness, and even Calhoun will admit to having a stubborn streak a mile wide. If he was ever going to

---

178 Malafronte, "Through The Years With Jim Calhoun."

179 "Jim Calhoun on Indefinite Medical Leave," ESPN (February 2012), http://www.espn.com /mens-college-basketball/story/_/id/7537722/connecticut-huskies-coach-jim-calhoun -takes-indefinite-medical-leave.

leave the game, it was going to be on his terms and his alone. Those terms came on September 13, 2012.

Calhoun announced his retirement from coaching and helped hand-select his successor, Kevin Ollie, leaving a mark on the UConn basketball program and college hoops as a whole that cannot be overstated. Thirty-one of Calhoun's former players went on to professional careers in the NBA, Chinese Basketball Association, or international leagues, and he became the first coach in NCAA history to have won at least 240 games at two different Division I schools.

Calhoun wasn't an easy coach. He wasn't an easy man to play for. He'll admit to that. There was shouting from the sidelines, shouting at the referees, and a standard that, when he first took over a team, might have seemed unreasonable. Calhoun never demanded perfection, but he demanded respect and a work ethic that grew from years of challenges in Braintree, Massachusetts. There were moments where he was too abrasive, too brash, a little too New England, but Calhoun wouldn't change a single moment.

He looks back on his Division I career with pride and remembers every player because he was doing it for the players. It's their legacy he's most proud of, no matter where he goes.

"You know, if I yelled or shouted at a ref or a reporter or something, I was doing it to protect my players," Calhoun said. "I wanted to make sure they were OK. Even now. It's all over the world. I've been to Israel quite a bit because I have quite a few players who compete over there, but I can talk basketball anywhere. I get off the plane in Tel Aviv and can talk about the game."

Calhoun spent a few years in retirement, fielding rumors that he was planning to take over a high school program on Long Island after he and his wife bought a house in the Hamptons, but nothing came of the stories. That was, of course, until Calhoun managed to surprise everyone. Retirement wasn't really for him anyway.

BACK IN THE GAME

Calhoun was named the head men's basketball coach at Saint Joseph in West Hartford, Connecticut, on September 18, 2018, nearly a year after he'd first taken the position of basketball consultant at the school. Rumors had swirled for quite some time that Calhoun would eventually take the head coaching gig, but he was still under contract with UConn at the time, working as special assistant to the director of athletics. That, however, didn't stop him from wanting to help St. Joseph's get its men's basketball program off the ground and, now, he's got his sights set on winning a few games as well.

The school competed at the NCAA Division III level for years, but only on the women's side, and Calhoun's introduction was seen as a "big splash" as the program began its transition to co-ed sports in 2018.

"[Calhoun] comes across so sincere when he talks about what led him to go into basketball," St. Joseph president Rhonda Free told the *Hartford Courant* in 2017. "He was doing this for all the right reasons, he was excited. He has values that are the ones that we share."[180]

These are not the same caliber of athletes that Calhoun was used to at UConn, or even at Northeastern, but they're still athletes and, for him, that's what matters. He wants to give a few kids a chance.

"I've never met an athlete that didn't want to compete," Calhoun said. "The talent may be different, but if there's a drive and a desire, then we can work with that."

Calhoun is excited to get back to basics. He wasn't a Division I talent, didn't start there and has always loved the thrill of building something from the ground up. St. Joseph is a challenge, but it's just another one on a long list that he's certain won't end anytime soon. These kids may not compete for a national title, but they'll practice and they'll

---

180 Dom Amore, "'Always a Huskie,' Calhoun Introduced As St. Joseph Men's Basketball Consultant," *Hartford Courant* (September 2017), https://www.courant.com/sports/uconn-huskies/hc-jim-calhoun-st-josephs-0929-20170928-story.html.

play and they'll look up at that hoop and know they can put the ball through the net.

Calhoun doesn't know where that picture of the anonymous kid that once hung on his UConn office wall has gone. It could be anywhere at this point, but it doesn't really matter. Calhoun talks about the picture and the kids who suited up for him over his fifty-year career, who learned everything they did about the game because of that picture. They learned to love the game as much as anything, and to appreciate what you could do with the kind of determination that Calhoun has always had—the kid who wouldn't get off the blacktop, even after they shut the lights off on him.

"It's been a true love affair," Calhoun said. "After my wife and my family and my God, basketball is the thing I love. I love what the game can do. It just takes the old expression, a boy, a ball, and a dream."

● ● ● ● ●

STATISTICALLY UNIMPRESSIVE, EMOTIONALLY DOMINANT

It was an incredibly bad basketball game. The NCAA Tournament was good, chock-full of competition, drama, and impressive stat lines, but the championship game was historically bad. The University of Connecticut won its third NCAA title with a 53–41 victory over Butler at Reliant Stadium in 2011, the cap to a Cinderella run for the ages. But while the Huskies' climb to the top of the college basketball world is still a journey they talk about with reverence throughout Storrs, the final matchup is something most of the athletic world would like to forget.

UConn and Butler combined to shoot 26.1 percent from the floor, the worst field goal percentage in a national title game since 1948. In that game, Kentucky and Baylor shot 25.9 percent, but those two teams also scored six more points. The stats only got worse from there. The 2011 national championship game boasted the fewest total points in a title game since 1949; UConn made two three-point shots in the semifinal and title game, and Butler connected on just three two-point field goals. Three baskets in the national championship game.

This, however, is not to say that UConn's run at glory should be discredited. In fact, those bad stats are also a testament to how talented the UConn roster was in 2011 and how easily the Huskies separated themselves from Butler once the opening whistle blew. This was a UConn team that did what it had to when it had to in order to ensure a victory, the kind of mindset that Calhoun had done his best to instill in his players from the very first moment he stepped on campus.

UConn played defense and it played defense well. The Huskies might not have shot well, but they made sure Butler didn't either and, for good measure, blocked ten shots, keeping the Bulldogs out of the paint and away from the boards. UConn's defense kept Butler off the scoreboard for six minutes and nineteen seconds straight in the second half. [181]

It wasn't very exciting basketball to watch. It wasn't even very good basketball to watch. Sometimes, the ball simply would not go through the net, but despite all of that, and despite the NCAA violations that loomed over UConn during the NCAA Tournament run, the Huskies championship performance was one for the history books.

Calhoun and the Huskies would have loved one last, perfect game, of course, but a few months removed from missing the cut of several national pre-season polls, the end of UConn's season seemed to mirror the start. It wasn't perfect, but it was another win, and that's all the Huskies were ever trying to accomplish.

The championship put Calhoun in exclusive company, one of just five coaches who have captured three or more national titles. Calhoun wanted better stats. He wanted his team to shoot more consistently, and for Kemba Walker, who was named the MVP, to walk off the court with one more dominant showing to his name, but

---

181 Pat Forde, "UConn's Title Win a Sore Sight," ESPN (April 2011), http://www.espn.com/mens-college-basketball/tournament/2011/columns/story?columnist=forde_pat&id=6294241.

despite the less-than-impressive box score, Calhoun could never find himself to be anything less than overjoyed with what his team accomplished that season. He watched his players make history, made a little himself, and let the country take in one of the most remarkable sports runs any team has ever accomplished.

When asked by reporters after the championship game to look back on his legacy and the names he'd be associated with for the rest of his life, Calhoun flashed a smile. "My father told me years ago, 'you're known by the company you keep,'" he said. "That's awfully sweet company." [182]

● ● ● ● ●

Calhoun's Best Games

The 1999 NCAA Championship Game

The final play came down to a scrum on the ground. It made sense. This was a UConn team that wasn't supposed to be in the title game, an underdog in the truest sense against a Duke team that had been waiting years to get back to the top of the metaphorical mountain. So, when Khalid El-Amin put UConn up by three points with a pair of free throws and seconds left on the clock, it made sense to just about everyone watching that Duke would respond. That, however, is not what happened. Instead, the Blue Devils stumbled on the play and the ball wound up on the floor. There were bodies everywhere, hands grasping and nerves on the sharpest of edges, but as the final buzzer sounded, it was UConn that came up with the ball and the win to defeat Duke 77–74. The victory was a turning point for the Huskies, making their first Final Four appearance and capturing their first championship under Calhoun. The team wasn't supposed to win, but Calhoun never doubted, and he knew, when it mattered, his team could prove just as physical as anyone.

---

182 Kenneth Best, "Huskies Win Third National Championship," *UConn Today* (April 2011), https://today.uconn.edu/2011/04/huskies-win-third-national-championship.

Topping Duke, Again

Emeka Okafor was the guy for UConn during the 2003–04 season. He made the Huskies go, sparked the offense, and helped lock in on defense. For most of the NCAA semifinal against Duke, he mostly sat on the bench with foul trouble. That changed with nine minutes left in regulation. Okafor returned to the floor, leading UConn on a 12–0 run to lift the Huskies to a 79–78 victory and a berth to the national title game. Unlike their 1999 meeting in the championship game, UConn came into this matchup as the favorite. It wasn't particularly smooth sailing for the Huskies, but as with most Calhoun teams coming out of Storrs, this one figured out a way to make it work. Okafor made his presence known, and while UConn went on to capture another title, defeating Georgia Tech on April 5, the resilience the Huskies showed getting there was the difference-maker.

CONCLUSION

College basketball has changed quite a bit in the last hundred or so years. The peach baskets are gone. The scores are considerably higher. The players rarely stick around for all four years of college. That, however, isn't entirely bad—and it probably won't stop any time soon. College basketball, much like the world itself, has evolved and grown, changing with the times and the people who have been part of it, including the coaches who have left their mark on the sport.

The ten coaches featured in this anthology were, and in some cases still are, some of the best the sport has had to offer. Their names are still whispered in hushed tones, reverent recollections of the start of something great, a string of successes and winning that shaped their respective programs and the players who suited up for them. They're honored with eponymous arenas and courts, regarded as some of the greatest minds in all sports, and quoted long after some of them have gone. They've set records only to watch those records be broken, won games, captured championships, mentored players who went on to dominant professional careers, and helped Team USA become the dominant basketball powerhouse across the globe. And, eventually, they will be surpassed.

Basketball is a game of runs, of finding your stride and settling into a shooting rhythm. Basketball has changed since Dr. James Naismith first invented it and then taught it to Phog Allen—and since Phog Allen taught it to Adolph Rupp and Dean Smith. The rules that were nothing short of certain have been broken—sometimes drawing the ire of the NCAA—and the game has grown. It's been sped up and then slowed down, and it's settled into a 2-3 zone that shouldn't surprise anyone when they play in Syracuse, which still manages to do the defensive trick.

Basketball has faced its fair share of criticism—legacies slightly dented under accusations of racism and tempers that were absolutely legendary. It hasn't always been perfect, but that's half the fun, watching the sport change, growing with the times and the coaches that brought their own ideas to the hardwood. This has made basketball as exciting, and occasionally maddening, as anything else in the world.

The sport won't stay stagnant—it can't, there's a shot clock—but it can continue to change, and the coaches who were so dominant, so tied up in college hoops and their teams, may not be the best to ever pace the sidelines. That, however, doesn't mean they'll be forgotten. We still remember Naismith, still talk about those first games and the beginnings of basketball, because those beginnings helped alter the course of the athletic world. The coaches featured in this anthology did the same, in their own way, and while their accomplishments may be passed and their records broken, the things they accomplished and the lives they affected won't change.

They'll be remembered, stories passed down and repeated by fans because, at one point, these were the best of the best, the ones who altered the course of basketball evolution. And while the sport won't stay the same forever, its history will.

BIBLIOGRAPHY

Introduction

Martinez, Courtney. "The First Intercollegiate Basketball Game Was Played on Feb. 8, 1895." NCAA. February 9, 2017. https://www.ncaa.com/news/basketball-men/article/2016-02-09/possible-first-intercollegiate-basketball-game-was-played-feb.

Chapter 1: John Wooden

Amadeo, Kimberly. "Great Depression Timeline." The Balance. April 30, 2018. https://www.thebalance.com/great-depression-timeline-1929-1941-4048064.

"Coach John Wooden–Biography." UCLA Bruins. Accessed November 2018. https://uclabruins.com/sports/2013/4/17/208274589.aspx.

"John Wooden." Basketball Hall of Fame. Accessed November 2018. http://www.hoophall.com/hall-of-famers/john-wooden1.

Office of Media Relations. "John Wooden's Former Players React to the Death of Their Coach." UCLA Athletics Newsroom. June 5, 2010. http://newsroom.ucla.edu/stories/john-wooden-s-former-players-react-159695

"Pyramid of Success." John Wooden. Accessed November 2018. http://www.coachwooden.com/pyramid-of-success.

"The Journey." John Wooden. Accessed November 2018. http://www.coachwooden.com/the-journey.

"The Wooden Effect." SUCCESS Magazine. Accessed November 2018. http://www.thewoodeneffect.com.

Farmer, Sam. "It's No Surprise Where the Legendary UCLA Coach Picked up His Wholesome Values." Los Angeles Times. June 18, 2006. http://articles.latimes.com/2006/jun/18/sports/sp-wooden18.

Gilberto, Gerard. "#Flashback Friday: March 29, 1975–March 31, 1975." NCAA. February 13, 2015. https://www.ncaa.com/news/basketball-men/flashback-friday/2015-02-13/going-out-style.

Harper, Zach. "Warriors' Bob Myers Patiently Built the Next Influential Team Model." CBS Sports. June 17, 2015. https://www.cbssports.com/nba/news/warriors-bob-myers-patiently-built-the-next-influential-team-model.

Putz, Paul. "John Wooden's Homespun Creed Was Not So Homespun." *Slate*. May 17, 2017. https://slate.com/culture/2017/05/john-woodens-seven-point-creed-came-from-a-1931-magazine-article.html.

Wiedeman, Reeves. "Catching Up with the Players from the 1964 NCAA Championship Game." *New York Magazine*. March 25, 2014. http://nymag.com/intelligencer/2014/03/march-madness-memories-1964-championship.html.

Wooden, John, and Steve Jamison. *My Personal Best: Life Lessons from an All-American Journey*. New York: McGraw-Hill Education, 2004.

Chapter 2: Phog Allen

"Games of the XVth Olympiad—1952." USA Basketball. June 10, 2010. https://www.usab.com/history/national-team-mens/games-of-the-xvth-olympiad-1952.aspx.

"Phog Allen, Basketball Coach of Kansas Jayhawks Dies at 88." *New York Times*. September 17, 1974. https://www.nytimes.com/1974/09/17/archives/phog-allen-basketball-coach-of-kansas-jayhawks-dies-at-88.html.

"The John W. Bunn Lifetime Achievement Award." Naismith Basketball Hall of Fame. Updated 2018. Accessed November 2018. http://www.hoophall.com/awards/john-w-bunn-lifetime-achievement-award.

Belt, Mike. "Kansas Basketball Family Mourns Allen's Death." KU Sports. April 6, 2003. http://www2.kusports.com/news/2003/apr/06/kansas_basketball_family.

Chiusano, Anthony. "KU-WVU Breaks Record for Loudest Crowd Roar." NCAA. February 14, 2017. https://www.ncaa.com/news/basketball-men/article/2017-02-13/kansas-west-virginia-allen-fieldhouse-breaks-record-loudest.

Hersey, Mark D. "Phog's First Farewell." KU History. March 3, 2018. http://kuhistory.com/articles/phogs-first-farewell.

Herzog, Brad. "The Dream Team of 1936 in the First Olympic Basketball Competition, the U.S. Won the Gold Medal Easily." *Sports Illustrated*. July 22, 1996. https://www.si.com/vault/2016/08/17/dream-team-1936-first-olympic-basketball-competition-us-won-gold-medal-easily.

Kerkhoff, Blair. "Phog Allen: Remembered as a Jayhawk but his Greatness Began in Jackson County." Jackson County Historical Society Journal. Summer 2014. http://www.jchs.org.

Mayer, Bill. "Phog Allen Protege List Goes On." KU Sports. February 5, 2010. http://www2.kusports.com/news/2010/feb/05/phog-allen-protege-list-goes.

Newell, Jesse. "Jayhawk Flashback: Video of 1952 NCAA championship game." KU Sports. May 28, 2010. http://www2.kusports.com/news/2010/may/28/jayhawk-flashback-video-1952-ncaa-championship-gam.

Newell, Jesse. "The story behind KU's 'Beware of the Phog' Banner...From the Men Who Created It." *Kansas City Star*. January 13, 2018. https://www.kansascity.com/sports/college/big-12/university-of-kansas/article194617979.html.

Sandomir, Richard. "Naismith's Papers Fetch Record $4.3 Million." *New York Times*. December 10, 2010. https://www.nytimes.com/2010/12/11/sports/ncaabasketball/11naismith.html.

Schwartz, Larry. "Basketball Pioneer Phog Allen Dies at 88." ESPN Classic. September 17, 1974. http://www.espn.com/classic/s/moment010916-phog-allen.html.

Shaw, Braden. "1952: Kansas' First NCAA National Championship." *The University Daily Kansan*. February 2018. http://www.kansan.com/special_issues/2018_120_years/kansas-first-ncaa-national-championship/article_4f66bad0-15f1-11e8-a2a3-836c44e4ab96.html.

SportsDayDFW.com. "Larry Brown's Coaching Tree: From Dean Smith to Gregg Popovich, Brown Has Extensive Ties." SportsDay. March 2014. https://sportsday.dallasnews.com/college-sports/smumustangs/2016/07/08/20140318-larry-brown-s-coaching-tree-from-dean-smith-to-gregg-popovich-brown-has-extensive-ties.

Thomas, Clinton. "The Man Behind March Madness." *News Press Now*. March 15, 2009. http://www.newspressnow.com/news/the-man-behind-march-madness/article_eaa2fef0-85ed-530d-b526-9663e9447682.html.

Chapter 3: Adolph Rupp

"Adolph F. Rupp." Naismith Basketball Hall of Fame. Accessed November 2018. http://www.hoophall.com/hall-of-famers/adolph-rupp.

"Adolph Rupp." Kansas Sports Hall of Fame. 2013. http://www.kshof.org/component/content/article/2-kansas-sports-hall-of-fame/inductees/222-rupp-adolph.html.

"The Little-Known Story of the 1948 Kentucky Wildcats That Started It All." Team USA. March 26, 2015. https://www.teamusa.org/News/2015/March/26/From-Madness-to-Medals.

Bird, Darrell. "Adolph Rupp's Legendary Career Was Not Without Its Challenges." 247Sports.com. December 10, 2017. https://247sports.com/college/kentucky/Article/Gambling-scandal-alleged-racism-make-41-year-career-of-UK-coach-Adolph-Rupp-all-the-more-fascinating-112057946.

Carter, Bob. "Rupp: Baron of Bluegrass." ESPN Classic. Accessed November 2018. http://www.espn.com/classic/biography/s/Rupp_Adolph.html.

Goldaper, Sam. "Adolph F. Rupp Dies: Tribute for Renowned Coach Scheduled for Tonight." The New York Times. December 12, 1977. https://www.nytimes.com/1977/12/12/archives/adolph-f-rupp-dies-tribute-for-renowned-coach-scheduled-tonight.html.

Kansas Athletics. "Once a Jayhawk, Always a Jayhawk: Adolph Rupp." University of Kansas. November 13, 2014. https://kuathletics.com/story.aspx?filename=MBB_1112145519&file_date=11/12/2014.

Kentucky Athletics Department. "1948 Men's Basketball National Champions." University of Kentucky. Accessed November 2018. https://ukathletics.com/sports/2016/5/16/_131461809047653077.aspx.

Livingston, Bill. "Re-examining Kentucky's Reputation for Racism as the 2015 NCAA Tournament Starts." Cleveland.com. March 19, 2015. https://www.cleveland.com/livingston/index.ssf/2015/03/long_the_bastion_of_the_basket.html.

Morrissey, Rick. "Past Imperfect; Future Intense." Chicago Tribune. November 30, 1997. https://www.chicagotribune.com/news/ct-xpm-1997-11-30-9712020327-story.html.

Reed, William F. "A Dark Night in Kentucky." Sports Illustrated. February 21, 1994. https://www.si.com/vault/1994/02/21/130514/a-dark-night-in-kentucky-in-1955-georgia-tech-ended-the-wildcats-129-game-home-winning-streak.

Tax, Jeremiah. "Big Week for the Man in Brown." Sports Illustrated. December 16, 1957. https://www.si.com/vault/1957/12/16/605646/big-week-for-the-man-in-brown.

Tucker, Kyle. "Forever linked: Kentucky-Kansas Connection Goes Back to Phog Allen, Adolph Rupp." The Atlanta Journal-Constitution. January 27, 2017. https://www.myajc.com/sports/college/forever-linked-kentucky-kansas-connection-goes-back-phog-allen-adolph-rupp/77m5MjXGFlZkTOFw3kCznM.

Chapter 4: Dean Smith

"1976 United States Men's Olympic Basketball." Basketball Reference. August 2018. https://www.basketball-reference.com/olympics/teams/USA/1976.

"Dean E. Smith." Naismith Basketball Hall of Fame. Accessed November 2018. http://www.hoophall.com/hall-of-famers/dean-smith.

Airman Magazine Staff. "Coaching Giant." *Airman Magazine*. February 18, 2015. http://airman.dodlive.mil/2015/02/18/coaching-giant.

Associated Press. "Charles Scott Joins College Hoops Hall of Fame." UNC Athletics. November 22, 2015. https://goheels.com/news/2015/11/22/210521190.aspx.

Bolick, Jan. "Great Expectations at the Dean Dome." 97.9 The Hill: WCHL. August 22, 2012. https://chapelboro.com/uncategorized/great-expectations-at-the-dean-dome-2.

Bonnell, Rick. "Michael Jordan on Dean Smith: 'He Never Put One Kid Ahead of Another,'" The News & Observer. Updated February 8, 2015. https://www.news observer.com/sports/college/acc/unc/article10285415.html.

Brown, C.L., and the Associated Press. "Dean Smith Dies at Age of 83." ESPN. February 12, 2015. http://www.espn.com/mens-college-basketball/story/_/id/12296176/dean-smith-former-north-carolina-tar-heels-coach-dies-age-83.

Dufresne, Chris. "Growing up to Appreciate Dean Smith's Greatness." *Los Angeles Times*. February 8, 2015. https://www.latimes.com/sports/la-sp-0209-dean-smith-appreciation-20150209-column.html.

Halberstam, David. *Playing for Keeps: Michael Jordan and the World He Made*. New York: Random House, 1999.

Hickey, Pat. "Montreal Olympics: Puerto Ricans Pushed U.S. Hoops Team to the Brink." *Montreal Gazette*. July 24, 2016. https://montrealgazette.com/sports/montreal-olympics-puerto-ricans-pushed-u-s-hoops-team-to-the-brink.

Holliday, Bob. "For Dean Smith, Team Was More Important Than Talent." WRAL Sports Fan. February 22, 2015. https://www.wralsportsfan.com/for-dean-smith-team-was-more-important-than-talent/14462845.

Logan, Greg. "Charles Scott Recalls His Journey with Dean Smith to Desegregate ACC." *Newsday*. February 8, 2015. https://www.newsday.com/sports/columnists/greg-logan/charlie-scott-recalls-his-journey-with-dean-smith-to-desegregate-acc-1.9917991.

McGrath, Dan. "Dean Smith on Jordan: 'He'd Listen Closely to What the Coaches Said and Then Go Do It.'" *Chicago Tribune*. September 10, 2009. https://www.chicagotribune.com/sports/basketball/bulls/michaeljordan/chi-10-jordan-3-chapelhill-deanssep10-story.html.

O'Connor, Ian. "Dean Smith Fought for Integration." ABC News via ESPN. February 8, 2015. https://abcnews.go.com/Sports/dean-smith-fought-integration/story?id=28815822.

Rafferty, Scott. "Flashback: Michael Jordan Begins Legendary Rise with Game-Winning NCAA Championship Shot." *Rolling Stone*. March 19, 2017. https://www.rollingstone.com/culture/culture-sports/flashback-michael-jordan-begins-legendary-rise-with-game-winning-ncaa-championship-shot-111612.

Richmond, Sam. "Dean Smith to MJ." NCAA. August 12, 2015. https://www.ncaa.com/news/basketball-men/article/2015-08-12/35-years-ago-dean-smith-writes-legendary-recruiting-letter

Schwartz, Nick. "Michael Jordan on Dean Smith: 'He Was My Mentor, My Teacher, My Second Father.'" *USA Today*. February 8, 2015. https://ftw.usatoday.com/2015/02/michael-jordan-remembers-dean-smith.

Wolff, Alexander. "Dean Smith: 1997 Sportsman of the Year." *Sports Illustrated*. December 22, 1997. https://www.si.com/vault/1997/12/22/236257/fanfare-for-an-uncommon-man-he-became-the-winningest-college-basketball-coach-of-all-time-and-capped-an-exemplary-career-with-a-graceful-retirement-for-all-of-that-we-honor-north-carolinas-dean-smith.

Chapter 5: Mike Krzyzewski

"Duke Basketball" Coach K. Accessed November 2018. www.coachk.com.

"Duke's Coach K Recalls Coaching 'The Shot' Moment of 1992." *Bloomberg*. March 15, 2017. https://www.bloomberg.com/news/videos/2017-03-15/duke-coach-k-recalls-coaching-the-shot-moment-of-1992-video.

Bella, Timothy. "Mike Krzyzewski's Humble Beginnings as Duke's Basketball Coach." *Atlantic*. November 16, 2011. https://www.theatlantic.com/entertainment/archive/2011/11/mike-krzyzewskis-humble-beginnings-as-dukes-basketball-coach/248572.

Davis, Seth. "Coach K Passes Mentor, Colleague, Friend on Historic Night at MSG." *Sports Illustrated*. November 16, 2011. https://www.si.com/more-sports/2011/11/16/coach-k.

Greene, Dan. "How Duke Transformed Its Defense from a Susceptible Shortcoming to a Special, Stifling Zone." *Sports Illustrated*. March 21, 2018. https://www.si.com/college-basketball/2018/03/21/duke-zone-defense-ncaa-tournament-march-madness.

Hartwell, Darren. "Jayson Tatum's Attempt to Spell 'Krzyzewski' on Live TV Went Horribly Wrong." NESN. May 31, 2018. https://nesn.com/2018/05/jayson-tatums-attempt-to-spell-krzyzewski-on-live-tv-went-horribly-wrong.

Morris, Ron. "Duke's Coach K Teaches 'Next Play' to Keep Teams Looking Forward." *The News & Observer*. December 29, 2016. https://www.newsobserver.com/sports/college/acc/duke/article123638384.html.

O'Neil, Dana. "Do You Know Mike Krzyzewski?" ESPN. January 25, 2015. http://www.espn.com/espn/feature/story/_/id/12161880/duke-blue-devils-coach-mike-krzyzewski-think-is.

Parrish, Gary. "Candid Coaches: Who Is the Most Powerful Person in All of College Basketball?" CBS Sports. September 1, 2017. https://www.cbssports.com/college-basketball/news/candid-coaches-who-is-the-most-powerful-person-in-all-of-college-basketball.

Pierce, Zack. "25 Years Ago Today, Christian Laettner and Duke Broke Kentucky's Heart." FOX Sports. March 28, 2017. https://www.foxsports.com/college-basketball/story/christian-laettner-duke-the-shot-kentucky-25-years-ago-ncaa-tournament-032817.

SI Wire. "Coach K nabs 1000th Wins as Duke Takes Down St. John's." *Sports Illustrated*. January 25, 2015. https://www.si.com/college-basketball/2015/01/25/duke-st-johns-1000-wins-coach-k-madison-square-garden-ncaa-basketball.

Thamel, Pete. "How Three Games Made Duke Mike Krzyzewski Rethink His Defensive Philosophy." Yahoo! Sports. March 21, 2018. https://sports.yahoo.com/three-games-made-dukes-mike-krzyzewski-rethink-defensive-philosophy-205049704.html.

Wojciechowski, Gene. *The Last Great Game: Duke vs. Kentucky and the 2.1 Seconds That Changed College Basketball*. New York: Penguin, 2012.

Chapter 6: Bobby Knight

"1987 Indiana Basketball: A Real-Life Hoosiers Ending." The Sports Notebook. Accessed November 2018. http://thesportsnotebook.com/1987-indiana-basketball-sports-history-articles.

Associated Press. "Knight Pulls Players from Soviet Game." *Los Angeles Times*. November 22, 1987. http://articles.latimes.com/1987-11-22/sports/sp-23722_1_bob-knight.

Deford, Frank. "The Rabbit Hunter: A Penetrating Profile of Bobby Knight." *Sports Illustrated*. January 14, 1981. https://www.si.com/college-basketball/2015/01/14/rabbit-hunter-frank-deford-bobby-kight-si-60.

Delsohn, Steve and Mark Heisler. *Bob Knight: The Unauthorized Biography*. New York: Simon & Schuster, 2006.

Dinich, Heather. "Power, Control, and Legacy: Bob Knight's Last Days at IU." ESPN. Accessed November 2018. http://www.espn.com/mens-college-basketball/story/_/id/23017830/bob-knight-indiana-hoosiers-firing-lesson-college-coaches.

Evans, Thayer. "Knight Raises Chin and Holds Head His High." *New York Times*. November 15, 2006. https://www.nytimes.com/2006/11/15/sports/ncaabasketball/knight-raises-chin-and-holds-his-head-high.html.

Goldman, Andrew. "Coach Bobby Knight on Why He's So Unpleasant." *New York Times*. March 1, 2013. https://www.nytimes.com/2013/03/03/magazine/coach-bobby-knight-on-why-hes-so-unpleasant.html.

Kravitz, Bob. "1975–76 Undefeated Indiana Team Voted Best Ever." *USA Today*. April 6, 2013. https://www.usatoday.com/story/sports/ncaab/2013/04/06/undefeated-indiana-team-voted-best-ever/2058825.

Lopresti, Mike. "40 Years Later, Remembering the Undefeated 1976 Hoosiers." NCAA. January 6, 2016. https://www.ncaa.com/news/basketball-men/article/2016-01-06/indiana-basketball-remembering-undefeated-1976-hoosiers-40.

Puma, Mike. "Knight Known for Titles, Temper." ESPN Classic. Accessed November 2018. http://www.espn.com/classic/biography/s/Knight_Bob.html.

Rock, Brad and Warnick, Lee. *Greatest Moments in BYU Sports*. Salt Lake City: Bookcraft, 1984.

SI Wire. "A.J. Guyton to Bob Knight: Come Back to Indiana." *Sports Illustrated*. September 13, 2014. https://www.si.com/college-basketball/2014/09/13/aj-guyton-bob-knight-indiana-open-letter.

Suellentrop, Chris. "Bob Knight." *Slate*. March 15, 2002. https://slate.com/news-and-politics/2002/03/bob-knight-college-basketball-s-wicked-stepfather.html.

Wertheim, Jon. "Throwing in the Chair: The Increasingly Bizarre and Sad Legacy of Bob Knight and Indiana." *Indianapolis Monthly*. March 2017. https://www.indianapolismonthly.com/longform/throwing-in-the-chair-what-to-make-of-bob-knight/.

Wertheim, L. Jon. "All the Rage: Bobby Knight's Infamous Chair Game 30 Years Later." *Sports Illustrated*. 2015. Accessed November 2018. https://www.si.com/longform/2015/1985/knight/index.html.

Chapter 7: Jerry Tarkanian

"Long Beach State Remembers the Jerry Tarkanian Era." FOX Sports. February 20, 2015. https://www.foxsports.com/west/story/long-beach-state-remembers-the-tarkanian-era-022015.

"Nevada-Las Vegas vs. Duke Box Score." Sports Reference. Accessed November 2018. https://www.sports-reference.com/cbb/boxscores/1991-03-30-duke.html.

Anderson, Mark. "Hollywood Movie in the Works About Jerry Tarkanian, Las Vegas." *Las Vegas Review-Journal*. April 11, 2018. https://www.reviewjournal.com/sports/unlv/unlv-basketball/hollywood-movie-in-the-works-about-jerry-tarkanian-las-vegas.

Associated Press. "NCAA Bars UNLV from Defense of Title." *Los Angeles Times*. July 20, 1990. http://articles.latimes.com/1990-07-20/sports/sp-437_1_unlv-coach-jerry-tarkanian.

Garber, Greg and Kory Kozak. "Twenty Years Later, UNLV Still Indignant." ESPN. April 1, 2010. http://www.espn.com/mens-college-basketball/tournament/2010/columns/story?id=5045144.

George, Carmen. "Coach Jerry Tarkanian's Armenian Heritage Remembered in Fresno." *The Fresno Bee*. February 12, 2015. https://www.fresnobee.com/news/local/article19534953.html.

Hopkins, A.D. "Jerry Tarkanian." *Las Vegas Review-Journal*. Updated September 12, 1999. https://www.reviewjournal.com/news/jerry-tarkanian.

Katz, Andy. "Tarkanian Changed College Hoops." ABC News via ESPN. February 11, 2015. https://abcnews.go.com/Sports/tarkanian-changed-college-hoops/story?id=28891820.

Koch, Ed. "For Years, He Prepared the Wet Towel for Jerry Tarkanian to Chew." *Las Vegas Sun*. July 1, 2014. https://lasvegassun.com/news/2014/jul/01/years-he-prepared-wet-towel-jerry-tarkanian-chew.

Prisbell, Eric. "UNLV's Jerry Tarkanian, Rebel with a Cause vs. NCAA, Has Died." *IndyStar* via *USA Today*. February 11, 2015. https://www.indystar.com/story/sports/college/2015/02/11/unlvs-jerry-tarkanian-rebel-with-a-cause-vs-ncaa-has-died/23237167.

Stewart, Larry. "Tarkanian, NCAA Settle for $2.5 Million." *Los Angeles Times*. April 2, 1998. http://articles.latimes.com/1998/apr/02/sports/sp-35333.

Warszawski, Marek. "Legendary Coach and Fresno State Bulldog Jerry Tarkanian Dies at Age 84." *The Fresno Bee*. February 11, 2015. https://www.fresnobee.com/sports/college/mountain-west/fresno-state/bulldogs-basketball/article19534608.html.

Chapter 8: Jim Boeheim

"1961–1962 Syracuse Orangemen." Orange Hoops. Accessed November 2018. http://www.orangehoops.org/1961-1962.htm.

"2001 All-Baltimore City/County Basketball." *The Baltimore Sun*. March 15, 2001. http://articles.baltimoresun.com/2001-03-15/sports/0103150119_1_dunbar -walbrook-anthony.

"All USA Boys Basketball Team." *USA Today*. May 7, 2002. https://usatoday30 .usatoday.com/sports/preps/basketba/2002-05-08-all-usa.htm.

"Carmelo Anthony." Sports Reference. Accessed November 2018. https://www .sports-reference.com/cbb/players/carmelo-anthony-1/gamelog/9999.

Boeheim, Jim and Jack McCallum. *Bleeding Orange: Fifty Years of Blind Referees, Screaming Fans, Beasts of the East, and Syracuse Basketball*. New York: Harper Collins, 2014.

Chase, Chris. "How a Manipulative Jim Boeheim Got Syracuse to Cave and Give Him Back His Job." Fox Sports. March 20, 2017. https://www.foxsports.com/college-basketball/story/jim-boeheim-syracuse-extension-retire-ncaa-sanctions-tournament -wins-032017.

Corbett, Holly C. "Hall of Fame Coach Beats Cancer." *Men's Journal*. Accessed November 2018. https://www.mensjournal.com/sports/hall-fame-coach-beats-cancer.

Drape, Joe. "Freshmen Give Boeheim a Finish to Savor." *New York Times*. April 7, 2003. https://www.nytimes.com/2003/04/07/sports/ncaabasketball/freshmen-give-boeheim-a-finish-to-savor.html.

Gutierrez, Matthew. "Jim and Juli Boeheim Have Raised Millions for Their Philanthropy Foundation." *The Daily Orange*. April 24, 2018. http://dailyorange.com/2018/04/ jim-juli-boeheim-raised-millions-philanthropy-foundation.

James, Emily. "Syracuse Did Not Control Athletics; Basketball Coach Failed to Monitor." NCAA. March 6, 2015. http://www.ncaa.com.

O'Neil, Dana. "Syracuse Coach Jim Boeheim: 'I've Been a Part of 1,000 Wins...And I'm Proud Of That.'" ESPN. February 4, 2017. http://www.espn.com/mens-college-basketball/story/_/id/18619901/syracuse-orange-coach-jim-boeheim-part-1000 -wins-ncaa-sanctions.

O'Neil, Dana. "Understanding the Zen of the Syracuse Zone." ESPN. March 25, 2016. http://www.espn.com/mens-college-basketball/story/_/id/15043164/ jim-boeheim-stays-true-famous-syracuse-orange-zone-defense.

Poliquin, Bud. "What Is Jim Boeheim's Legacy as He Closes in on '1000' Wins?" Syracuse.com. March 26, 2017. https://www.syracuse.com/poliquin/index.ssf/2017 /02/jim_boeheim_sitting_on_999_victories_all_of_the_wins_are_nice_im_proud_of_ them_a.html.

Prisbell, Eric. "NCAA Punishes Syracuse, Jim Boeheim for Violations." *USA Today*. March 6, 2015. https://www.usatoday.com/story/sports/ncaab/acc/2015/03/06/syracuse-college-basketball-ncaa-investigaton/24497089.

Waters, Mike. "Jim Boeheim Set to Be the Oldest Coach in D-I History: 'Go As Long As You Can Do a Good Job.'" Syracuse.com. November 7, 2017. https://www.syracuse.com/orangebasketball/index.ssf/2017/11/syracuse_basketball_coach_jim_boeheim_will_keep_on_coaching.html.

Waters, Mike. "Jim Boeheim's Final Syracuse Basketball Game as a Player Was Loss to Duke in 1966." Syracuse.com. January 27, 2014. https://www.syracuse.com/orangebasketball/index.ssf/2014/01/jim_boeheims_history_with_duke.html.

Waters, Mike. "Story Time with Jim Boeheim: Riding Down I-18, Playing Pro Basketball for $100 a Night." Syracuse.com. November 14, 2016. https://www.syracuse.com/orangebasketball/index.ssf/2016/11/story_time_with_jim_boeheim_riding_down_i-81_playing_pro_basketball_for_100_a_ni.html.

Waters, Mike. "Syracuse's Jim Boeheim Looks Back at His Playing Days at Lyons Central High School." Syracuse.com. October 10, 2013. https://www.syracuse.com/orangebasketball/index.ssf/2013/10/syracuses_jim_boeheim_looks_ba.html.

Chapter 9: Lou Carnesecca

"Julius Erving." NBA. Accessed November 2018. http://www.nba.com/history/players/erving_bio.html.

"St. John's University Announces Findings of Self-Inquiry into Alleged NCAA Violations." St. John's Athletics. November 26, 2004. https://redstormsports.com/news/2004/11/26/st_john_s_university_announces_findings_of_self_inquiry_into_alleged_ncaa_violations.aspx?path=general.

"The Sweater Is Warned." *New York Times*. March 1, 1985. https://www.nytimes.com/1985/03/01/sports/the-sweater-is-warned-although-st-john-s-was.html.

Allen, Scott. "Georgetown Tifo of John Thompson Celebrates 30th Anniversary of 'The Sweater Game.'" *The Washington Post*. February 18, 2015. https://www.washingtonpost.com/news/dc-sports-bog/wp/2015/02/18/georgetown-tifo-of-john-thompson-celebrates-30th-anniversary-of-the-sweater-game/?noredirect=on&utm_term=.bf50a73322a2.

Best, Neil. "Lou Carnesecca, 90, Enjoys the Atmosphere at MSG but Wishes St. John's Had Won." *Newsday*. January 25, 2015. https://www.newsday.com/sports/columnists/neil-best/louie-carnesecca-90-enjoys-the-atmosphere-at-msg-but-wishes-st-john-s-had-won-1.9844720.

Hamilton, Moke. "Lou Carnesecca Reminisces Over ABA Days." SNY. September 19, 2012. https://www.sny.tv/nets/news/lou-carnesecca-reminisces-over-aba-days /149443096.

Kussoy, Howie. "Chris Mullin's NYC Rise, Struggle With Demons and Triumphant Return Home." *New York Post.* April 1, 2015. https://nypost.com/2015/04/01/mullins-30-years -away-from-st-johns-full-of-twists-and-turns.

Lief, Fred. "Lou Carnesecca, Who Made Winning Basketball and Pullover Sweaters." UPI. March 20, 1985. https://www.upi.com/Archives/1985/03/20/Lou-Carnesecca -who-made-winning-basketball-and-pullover-sweaters/1993480142800.

Perez, Jon. "Hanging with 'Looie': Carnesecca Sits Down with the Torch, Reflects on Past." *The Torch.* October 2, 2013. https://www.torchonline.com/news/2013/10/02 /2226902.

Robbins, Lenn. "Rise and Fall of St. John's." *New York Post.* February 3, 2008. https:// nypost.com/2008/02/03/rise-and-fall-of-st-johns.

Samuel, Ebenezer. "Daily News Sports Hall of Fame Candidates." *New York Daily News.* June 18, 2006. https://www.nydailynews.com/archives/nydn-features/daily-news -sports-hall-fame-candidates-introducing-candidates-bill-bradley-article-1.560042.

Vecsey, George. "A Vintage Year for Looie." *New York Times.* March 14, 1983. https:// www.nytimes.com/1983/03/14/sports/a-vintage-year-for-looie.html.

Chapter 10: Jim Calhoun

"Jim Calhoun Coaching Record." Sports-Reference. Accessed November 2018. https:// www.sports-reference.com/cbb/coaches/jim-calhoun-1.html.

"Jim Calhoun on Indefinite Medical Leave." ESPN. February 3, 2012. http://www.espn .com/mens-college-basketball/story/_/id/7537722/connecticut-huskies-coach-jim -calhoun-takes-indefinite-medical-leave.

"Jim Calhoun, Class of 1968." American International College. Accessed November 2018. https://aicyellowjackets.com/hof.aspx?hof=2&path=&kiosk=.

"Jim Calhoun, UConn Pairing Reaches 30-Year Anniversary." *New Haven Register.* May 13, 2016. https://www.nhregister.com/uconn/article/Jim-Calhoun-UConn-pairing- reaches-30-year-11333746.php.

"Jim Calhoun." UConn Athletics. Accessed November 2018. https://uconnhuskies.com/ staff.aspx?staff=182.

Amore, Dom. "'Always a Huskie,' Calhoun Introduced as St. Joseph Men's Basketball Consultant." *Hartford Courant*. September 28, 2017. https://www.courant.com/sports/uconn-huskies/hc-jim-calhoun-st-josephs-0929-20170928-story.html.

Anthony, Mike, "Mike Anthony: Ray Allen's Greatness the Product of An Obsession." *Hartford Courant*. September 2, 2018. https://www.courant.com/sports/uconn-mens-basketball/hc-sp-ray-allen-hall-of-fame-jim-calhoun-column-20180831-story.html.

Anthony, Mike. "Jim Calhoun Welcomed Back by High School He Coached." *Hartford Courant*. June 2, 2011. https://www.courant.com/sports/uconn-mens-basketball/hc-xpm-2011-06-02-hc-uconn-calhoun-dedham-graduation-0620110601-story.html.

Best, Kenneth. "Huskies Win Third National Championship." *UConn Today*. April 5, 2011. https://today.uconn.edu/2011/04/huskies-win-third-national-championship.

Forde, Pat. "UConn's Title Win a Sore Sight." ESPN. April 5, 2011. http://www.espn.com/mens-college-basketball/tournament/2011/columns/story?columnist=forde_pat&id=6294241.

Malafronte, Chip. "Through the Years with Jim Calhoun." *New Haven Register*. March 3, 2005. https://www.nhregister.com/news/article/Through-the-years-with-Jim-Calhoun-11651744.php.

Weiss, Dick, "UConn basketball coach Jim Calhoun to Retire After Legendary College Career: Source." *New York Daily News*. September 13, 2012. https://www.nydailynews.com/sports/college/uconn-basketball-coach-jim-calhoun-retires-legendary-college-career-article-1.1158031.

Yang, Nicole. "Reliving UConn's Incredible 2011 Championship Run with Jim Calhoun, Jeremy Lamb, and Kemba Walker." Boston.com. April 2, 2018. https://www.boston.com/sports/ncaa-tournament/2018/04/02/uconn-2011-championship-jim-calhoun-kemba-walker.

ACKNOWLEDGMENTS

There are not enough words to express how thankful I am for everyone who helped make this book a reality. Still, an attempt will be made for people who deserve a few more thanks than average:

Justin, who never argued when it was decreed that he was simply going to become a college basketball fan as soon as we started dating. Instead, he looked up ticket prices, learned rosters, and helped assuage every worry I had while writing this book. Missy, my best friend and hero, who was very quick to tell me that I needed to write this book when I first heard about the idea. To all the wonderful people at Ulysses Press for believing in me and helping me along this journey, thank you for all the incredible work you've done to bring this book to life. And, really, thank you to college basketball for existing, eliciting feelings and making me tear up on more than one occasion because the best kind of emotions are sports emotions.

ABOUT THE AUTHOR

Laura Amato is an upstate New York native and a graduate of St. John's University. An award-winning sports journalist and first-time author, she's watched more college basketball games than she's willing to admit and has spent a considerable amount of time in the Madison Square Garden press room. She now lives in New York City with her husband, and while she loves nothing more than March Madness, iced caramel lattes, well-cultivated music playlists, and the New York Rangers are close behind.